DAILY NOTES

FROM

NATHAN CASSIDY

VOL I

Copyright © 2024 Nathan Cassidy
All rights reserved.
ISBN: 9798326893970

DAILY NOTES VOL I

The first three seasons of my
daily podcast 'Daily Notes' ran every day
from January 1st 2021
to September 22nd 2023.

One thousand episodes and one million downloads.

Here is Volume I of extracts from these seasons and
stories inspired by it, from 2023.

I play the piano on the podcast as a backing to the words,
so whilst reading this book I encourage
you to listen to the *suggested tracks*.

Or don't.
Just read the book, listen to the podcast, do what you want.

Do what you want.

DAILY NOTES VOL I

DAILY NOTES VOL I

February 15th 2023
Ed Sheeran – Give Me Love

Valentine's Day yesterday did you send a card? I just want to buy one saying 'I love you' and a picture of a heart. Why do I have to trawl through this avalanche of bullshit built by morons for morons? A picture of Yoda… 'Yoda one for me'. A picture of two turtles - 'I turtley fancy you'. Unless you're a zoophile, a chelenophile and want to fuck a turtle (yeah that's the correct scientific word for it, chelenophile, someone that's sexually attracted to turtles). Anyone thinking the same thing as me - why have they named that? As soon as you name it the perverts are more likely to do it. Take the name away and it dies, it's like Prince. Unless you are sending this to a turtle you particularly want to slip a finger under their cock block of a shell, then have a fucking word with yourself.

Can we actually stop while we're here thinking that there is anything funny about word play. There isn't. Apologies to any comedian you like who does wordplay but comedians that try to hide behind wordplay and one-liners, make sure you heckle them with the following… 'What do you actually think about anything?' If I want wordplay I'd go back to the 1970s when everyone was doing wordplay to hide the fact they were paedophiles. And if you asked them 'what do you actually think about anything?' they'd stumble… 'Oh shit you got me, I like kids. And whenever I see a little guy who can't really talk properly I think… Yoda one for me.'

I bought a card for my son for his birthday of an Andy Warhol painting, and he said 'I love that who is the artist', and I said 'I'll show you, he's my biggest inspiration', and I showed him a picture and he said 'oh yeah, Jeffrey Dahmer'. And I thought, what should I be most concerned about - the fact you think Jeffrey Dahmer painted *Campbell's Soup* or the fact you thought my 'biggest inspiration' is the world's most notorious serial killer? I can't even watch the adaptations of killings, people love watching this shit. If they were watching real footage of murders they'd be sectioned, as long as it's dramatized but still looks exactly like the real thing they feel it's legitimized by Netflix and we can sit around watching heads in their fridge as entertainment like it's a Gordon Ramsay cooking challenge, or *Is it Cake?* Is it cake? No it's the severed head of Jeffrey Dahmer's 17th victim. Is it though, or is it cake? No it's the severed head of Jeffrey Dahmer's victim - I'm taking it to the laboratory. Yeah sure, or are you taking it to the patisserie?

Jeffery Dahmer is now huge on TikTok, the teen market love him, who do I have to kill to get more followers? But success is all about connections of course, nepotism. Looking at Wikipedia, Jeffrey's dad Lionel Dahmer has written books, TV series, he's been on Oprah talking about his serial killers, and what a surprise - his son becomes a serial killer – nepotism – it's who you know in this game.

Privilege. You see some comedians in interviews with famous dads, oh how did you get into comedy? – and they say oh when I was five I was in the queue for the zoo – the zoo file? That's right the zoo file – and I saw a hyena laughing and that inspired me, and I'm there thinking… are you going to mention your grandad is John Logie Baird, inventor of television, you lying cunt?

I've suggested here I think some comedians aren't amazing, can I just make it clear that I love you all, I'm just here to give you all love. But never EVER with witty wordplay. And I don't want to fuck turtles.

DAILY NOTES VOL I

February 16th 2023
Rich Flex – Drake & 21 Savage

Straight after Valentine's, lots of couples will now of course be splitting up. I've said it before and I'll say it again looks and personality both turn to dust, looks you wonder why they don't look like they used to, because you don't notice how bad you look, and personality any tiny thing becomes enormous, like my partner likes making little molehills in the garden it was really cute, pretending we had a mole she made molehills and she's now made so many molehills its now a fucking mountain, … that kind of thing. Anyway looks, personality, the only thing that matters, the only thing that lasts … money.

If you don't have sufficient money between you, then you will inevitably break up because one of you will always have more and eventually tire of your lack of money or you'll both have nothing and your head will be turned by someone that can pay for your dementia care. Have you got 85,000 pounds in the bank? (that's what it is in the UK) Ok cool, I'll flip to you then. Who am I walking away from? I genuinely can't remember.

But of course there is the main reason for couples divorcing, separating… You know recently in the UK they have taken away the need to apportion blame, and give reasons for the divorce. Because they ended up finding it very difficult to put into words pretty much the only reason for divorce which is always… bla bla bla ra ra ra I'm a woman ra ra bla bla bla… they just found that too hard to spell on the form. And I'm only saying 'bla bla bla I'm a woman' because I'm fair and accurate, no of course - joking - it's because I'm a heterosexual man so that's the relationships I'm in, you know in your instance this could me a man. I'll do the man's voice too to even it up… 'Leave me alone, I just want to watch the rugby'.

And of course this is a stereotype, or is it, or is this the one stereotype that's not a stereotype, because I don't know any man that moans, I don't, I just don't. I know men that moan about their lives or the football or work, but I don't know any man that moans that someone hasn't washed up properly, that someone hasn't hung the wet washing properly, hasn't put the right pan on the right hob, 'put the pan on the right size hob Nathan' - no, no man has ever done that, but there is no march for the men is there because then apparently I'm making a mountain out of a molehill, but you see the issue put together enough molehills it becomes a mountain and it blocks out the sun and then everyone dies.

Anyway, hope you're in love today, I'm sure yours will last – as long as you're rich and she's happy to do all the cooking and washing up, yes, like the 1970s, and you may think this whole entry has had a whiff of the 1970s but things were better then – no one , hardly anyone divorced – progress my ass. Happy fucking Valentine's day.

DAILY NOTES VOL I

February 17th 2023
I'm not Here to Make Friends - Sam Smith

I'm not here to make friends - anti-vaxxers, they bang on a bit don't they? Kill yourself, alternatively just hang around - an easily curable condition will get you. And obviously every death during lockdown was a tragedy, but when a fierce anti-vaxxer died as happened a few times, you couldn't help, could you, having a little private... party, socially distanced of course, at Downing Street.

Of course not there's ever anything funny about death. The only thing sometimes death of course is a blessed relief, my grandad spent the last few years of his life wearing nappies. You know, the worst paedophile. Not true, there's always someone worse off than you. Gary Glitter has been released and one of the rules of his release is he's not allowed within 200m of any infant school. Which is fair enough. And this guy's now keeping busy, he's got a job, he's a handyman, he mainly focuses on painting a circle with a 200m radius around every infant school in London, he's built viewing platforms the lot, fairgrounds, big signs saying 'wanna be in my gang?' Very industrious. He's keeping within the letter if not the spirit of the law – and that's one more than the actual police.

Yes it's a worrying statistic isn't it – criminals have now statistically committed less crimes than the police. My biggest worry is how shit crime thrillers are going to be in the future – as every film is now just Poirot displaying devastating intuition by yet again handing himself for his latest sexual assault. 'I've gathered you all here today to say... It was me again.' Ah brilliant Poirot get back in prison you disgusting old pervert. And of course if there are any police reading, obviously it's not all police, as the saying goes, it's just one or two bad orchards.

And there's me making jokes about three quote controversial subjects anti-vaxx, paedophiles and the institutionally awful police. And I thought about putting the orchards thing on twitter yesterday because some police officer had been given a 30-odd year sentence for a catalogue of hideous crimes but of course I didn't, because I'm not here to make friends, but I'll tell you something, I can't be bothered to hear from my enemies. And my goodness twitter is the place you'll hear from your enemies. I do not care. They're jokes about real life. Real life is the problem, close your phone and deal with real life rather than the people making jokes about real life. Because if you don't like the jokes, firstly another joke will be along any second and most importantly, it's not real life. That's what you should be angry about, if you're angry about anything but real life you're an idiot. And I'll tell you that to your face, and never to your twitter.

February 18th 2023
Carly Pearce – What He Didn't Do

There is no religion any more is there. Football is the new religion. In that it's a lot of deluded people singing and they don't like gay people. There was so much furore wasn't there about Qatar's human rights record and David Beckham being an ambassador, how could he, did you see what he did, lets shred some money. Yeah that's what Beckham did, but let's look at what he didn't do, he didn't play football over there. Because look at Qatar's record with LGBT. what about football's record with LGBT – it's not good.

There are so few openly gay male footballers it's front page news when one comes out, now why is that, we're tip toeing around the truth aren't we so I'm going to say it, and it may be unpalatable for some to hear and I am not virtue signalling in any way – a lot of male football fans, and it is male football fans, a lot, not all, of male football fans, and it's not the majority but a minority of billions is still millions, a lot of male football fans are scum. Racist, homophobic, ant-semitic, novelty Valentine card loving scum. And that's why you can easily hold a football tournament in Qatar because the sport itself is a human rights travesty, full of homophobia, racism, antisemitism. Complaining about holding a football tournament in Qatar would be like these people complaining that there's still a McDonalds in Russia - 'We must not allow a regime responsible for the slaughter of thousands… to open another outlet in Moscow'.

Vladimir Putin is sitting on a huge pile of gold, you know this, about 140 billion dollars of gold that's free of sanctions, and it's a bargaining chip with the West, so here's something we can all do, because back me up we cared more about it at the start of the war – particularly comedians – let's do a benefit gig – how can I make this war about me… can I have a medal? And now we're all just watching *Love Island*… This is what we can do - hand in your gold – to me, send it to me right now I'll stick it down the nearest drain, that would actually help. Because gold only has value because we say it has value, sorry that's *Love Island*.

Hand it in, but you won't will you because it's shiny. And that's the thing, it's never about what you do that causes problems – I'm a good person, I go to work, I care for my family and I stay in most of the time – you are the worst person imaginable, because of what don't you do – you go to work so you're probably not helping anyone, you care for your family so you don't have to give a fuck about anyone else and you stay in - what good do you think you'll be doing today from inside your four walls – you're awful, you're worse than Beckham and Putin. I mean Putin's bad, but think about all the things he hasn't done. Thank fuck for the things he hasn't done. When you look at all the awful things he hasn't done, you see him in a whole new light. Vote for Putin. Or don't. Makes absolutely no difference.

DAILY NOTES VOL I

February 19th 2023
Escapism – RAYE Featuring 070 Shake

When I was 12 I missed out by a whisker on being a child star, they took kids from schools and made them TV actors and I just missed out on the audition, 40 kids went through a series of 3 auditions, I got to know them all, they were like family but a family I actually liked and had something about them, and then at the last minute I was culled from the group. And 10% of these 40 kids are still famous today. 90% of them have had their lives totally fucked by taking them out of education and promising them a dream that was never going to happen. But little do they know that they're still kind of famous to me... because every single day I look at their Facebook updates about how shit their lives are, and I applaud and punch the air, I scream yeah, wooh! Go failure!!

I'm not bitter it just blame my teeth, I haven't got fame teeth. You need fame teeth to escape the life that they had planned for you. My son has recently got braces, he's 15 and all kids want braces now, they find them attractive. When I had braces as a kid I got the nickname 'brace face' and was totally humiliated, and that was by the dentist. Now my son is getting so much attention from girls also with braces, he's got them on for two years so strange to imagine his first sexual experience will be him in braces and a girl braces, in the brace position, which some people have said is a strange thing to imagine and I don't mean he's going to have sex in a plane crash - although the lack of oxygen would heighten the orgasm. Now that is a strange thing to imagine.

So, very soon my son will have fame teeth, and he may well have the fame I never had and never will have, he will escape the path that was laid for him just because of his teeth and not because of his talent, and I will not be bitter, I'll just set up a fake Facebook profile for him where he spends all day every day complaining about being sad and how lonely he is and I'll be like wooh! Yeah! That's my son! And despite his good teeth he's still not as famous as me! Wooh! Yeah.

Don't blame me, it's just my escapism.

DAILY NOTES VOL I

February 20th 2023
I Never Liked You – Future

My old music teacher was a paedophile. A music teacher who played violin, literally a kiddy fiddler. Hiding in plain sight. Well in reality hiding in his basement studio behind the piano. We didn't know or call him a paedophile at the time, he was just our music teacher, who we knew was having sex with some of the boys. But we didn't join the dots because me and my friends all wanted to have sex with the teachers so we just thought, and it's crazy to think this looking back, lucky bastards. We want to be doing that. I wanted to have sex with my English teacher at 14 years old so bad that for two years I pretended to really love Animal Farm. I mean maybe she shouldn't have been showing me videos of extreme bestiality. But it was the 80's, things were different then, they used to wheel porn videos into the classroom on the big telly. Simpler times.

Simpler times the past. Everyone loves the past don't we? There's nothing better than the past, for all of us that's all we have. I'm going to blow your mind with this one – the future never happens. And thank goodness, because the future is shit isn't it? The future is full of growing old, and gas bills. The past is full of magic, and simple things made out to be wonderful. I wish I could convince myself that the magic of my childhood was still real.

I never went skiing as a kid. I was too poor. While other kids were on the slopes with apres ski, I was down the shopping centre, The Palisades Shopping Centre in Birmingham, trying to pretend to myself that the escalator was a ski slope. You could go down on the normal slope or sit on the edges, the black run, and sometimes the escalator would stop and it would feel like you were in ski boots. Magical times. If I did that today people would try to have me sectioned. And kids aren't even doing that today, they're staring at their phones until they tell them that they're depressed. I heard a comedian once saying that walking on an escalator when it's broken is the strangest feeling in the world, but I disagree. I feel that the strangest feeling in the world is where you get to about my age and think… soon I'm going to die. I mean if you're on an escalator and it's not moving but you are, imagine being dead, and the planet is moving, but you're not moving, ever again. And that's why the past is beautiful, and the future is hard. I never liked you future.

DAILY NOTES VOL I

February 21st 2023
Nonsense – Sabrina Carpenter

The world is full of things that we just accept that are actually nonsense. Aliens, ghosts – Jesus, the number of ghost stories. No actual evidence anywhere and people are making millions. If this was a ghost podcast it would be doing so much better. Edith was a maths teacher and she died and then every time I used my calculator to write 58008 I saw her boobs in the screen. Nonsense. So much nonsense – astrology – I think you will have a birthday in the next 12 months – psychic mediums, karma, fate and God. And on the flipside there are things that people thought were made up that are actually real – the duck billed platypus, M.E (oh you've got to stay in bed all day you're just a lazy cunt) – the lighter was invented before the match, and the aliveness in you is a spirit that is a non-material reality and being a non-material reality it is indestructible, your spirit will live on, it is infinite and eternal, ghosts are in fact real but nobody believes they are real because the spirit is invisible but the feeling of aliveness is most intimate and unmistakeable. That's what somebody says on Reddit anyway.

It sounds true right, until you look at it again and think no its nonsense. No its not nonsense is it – we're alive right now, and that feeling of being alive cannot be explained through biology. Goats are alive but don't feel the same thing we do, ducked billed platypus are alive but even they don't think they're special but humans are special because our spirit lives on, my grandma's spirit lives on in me and that's not mumbo jumbo, and she's not even dead, my grandma is 100 this year and since she slowed down a few years ago I have truly felt her spirit moving into me, I have been becoming more and more like her - kind, generous, funny, all the good and none of the bad, and in turn my spirit has transferred into her to make room for hers so she is more mardy, insouciant and irritable when the room isn't really fucking warm. I don't believe in ghosts but I do believe in spirit. Her spirit lives on.

And if you don't believe that, that's fair enough…as my grandma would say, I like you but you don't like me. Light another fire Nathan, do you know the lighter was invented before the match? Maybe, just maybe, we don't know everything after all.

DAILY NOTES VOL I

February 22nd 2023
The Kid LAROI – Love Again

I think I'm at peak 'I'm going to die' thoughts at my age. Apparently as you get older those thoughts dissipate and of course you rarely think that when you're young. All you think when you're a kid is – I want to go to go on a sex holiday. We all can remember our first sex holiday – sex at school was so hard as I went to an all-boys school and the only sex available was the illegal sex with the teacher behind the piano. But good news for kids we could all go on sex holidays couldn't we at 17/18 where kids in my case from the UK would fly to Ibiza or Tenerife to have sex with other 17 year olds. It was amazing. Flying around the world to have sex with 17 year olds, I really felt like Royalty.

And parents totally approved of this. In fact, I pulled – and am using the word 'pulled' there in its historical context – that's what we called it at the time – pulling – you can't cancel me for a word that we used at the time – I pulled a 17 year old girl in Tenerife who was walking along the road with her parents. I stopped her and in front of her parents said 'hi, do you want to come with me and my mate' and her parents just let me walk off with her daughter – everyone was complicit – you went to Tenerife at 16/17 to have sex and the parents were completely in on it – if I'd been doing that in the house it would be 'how could you Nathan, you're 16/17,' but they would gladly buy me a ticket to Tenerife for my sex holiday.

And now I know why they did this, because my kids are approaching the age where they will have sex, fine, whatever, a second ago they were babies and now they are potentially going to have babies fine, whatever, nightmare, all good, just not in the house, not so I can hear, please God not so I can hear, so I've got an idea kids, here are two first class tickets to Tenerife – joking there are no first class tickets to Tenerife, it's a cattle truck for fucks, get on that plane to Tenerife and just wander around the streets and pull and that's the only word for it, pull kids away from their parents who because it's sunny will think that's absolutely fine but in the UK they would be horrified and call the police. But there's no police in Tenerife, only batons and handcuffs. Fly, fly away my children, and go be fucked on the sex island. Love, love and love again.

February 23rd 2023
Hotel Ugly – Shut Up Moms Calling

My son never listens to me. I've brought my kids up amazingly, of course I have, and they are amazing, but I was too nice to them when they were very young, I did everything for them, I loved them, I didn't want them to have to do the washing up, they were six, enjoy your years where you don't have to do the washing up I thought, you have years ahead of you as an adult where you have to do the washing up, I love you, you sit there and watch television you cute little cuties. Now they're 15 and 12 – do the fucking washing up.

Particularly my son, take that downstairs, yeah sure but no. He's not even that rude about it and most often he says yes of course I'll do it and then just doesn't do it, he won't do fucking anything. And the worst thing about this is, it's no one's fault but mine. Because when he was a young kid, I did everything for him, put a mask on a cat with vertical lines for the first six months or its life and it will never be able to see horizontal lines, and in the same breath, do everything for your son for the first seven years of his life and he will never be able to see the dirty fucking plates. Clear them away! No! Why not? Because I can't even see them. You've brought me up not to even see those mother fuckers. Damn.

And talking about mother fuckers, you do not fuck with my mom. Shut up, my mom's calling... what do you want mom? Yes mom, anything you say mom, because it's in me, she did the job you need to do when the kid is five years old – clear that shit away, wash up, that is your job not mine. Why have a kid if they don't wash up? It's so fucking obvious now. That's why you have a kid, to do the washing up – it's a free dishwasher. Now I've got two kids who won't do anything because they don't even see it. Shut up, mom's calling, let me ignore what she says for a few seconds too. Fuuuck.

I'm a man shouting at a cat to see horizontal lines after fucking up that same cat in a weird psychology experiment. I'm shouting shut up in a wind tunnel in space in a black hole. When in reality I'm doing none of those things, what am I doing in reality, I'm doing the fucking washing up. And it's all my own fault. Piss take

DAILY NOTES VOL I

February 24th 2023
Everything I Love – Morgan Wallen

How can we connect – if it's not over TikTok – well we're all reading this right? We're all reading the same thing, so maybe I could do something on this podcast today that stays with everyone forever, so we all have a connection that no one else has, we are connected. You know, if you love someone you say I will do anything for you, or a best friend I will do anything for you. Whether that's true or not I'm not sure. How about your fellow man, people you don't know, the people listening to this right now. For so many, strangers lives are totally expendable. When we find out that Prince Harry has killed 25 Taliban we all think one of several things don't we, oh that's a silly thing to say, oh the Taliban are going to retaliate, I wonder what Charles thinks, the only thing that none of us thought was – those poor Taliban, those poor Taliban guys, imagine being killed by a ginger Royal. Which makes us as bad as Harry if not worse. To us they are chess pieces too.

And now the Queen's dead we're all thinking the same thing – Game Over. Has anyone seen the trailer of the new M Night Shyamalan movie 'Knock at the Cabin'? In this film, two parents, after watching the movie *The Sixth Sense* comment to their kids 'That was amazing I assume all of this director's films will be brilliant', and are then forced because of their short sighted stupidity to choose between the death of one of the family or the death of the entire world in a tsunami. Not even a contest. When it comes to a choice between people you know and people you don't know, the people you don't know can all go to their watery hell, free up the roads and the healthcare for people I actually give a fuck about, just don't make me watch the tsunami on television, because I think I'll enjoy it too much.

The only person that wouldn't make this decision of course is Prince Harry, who would gladly sacrifice his entire family, particularly that gas-lighter Meghan, so the entire world could be spared and he'd force us to watch his accompanying Netflix documentary called 'Spared'. The only people he would want killed is the Taliban, not by a tsunami he would want to shoot them himself to satisfy his blood lust. It doesn't have to be this way. I will do anything for you. I've got to the mid-point of my life and what have I done – I've spent it telling jokes. Useless. Here's my plea, I'm channelling my grandma now, I'll do anything for you, within reason. Think – what would a grandma do – that stuff. My grandma would do anything for anyone, the DMs are open, ask anything of me, I'm here for you. I love everything and everyone so I will do everything for you. Fuck, I might regret that. Maybe you can all just die instead.

DAILY NOTES VOL I

February 25th 2023
Ceilings – Lizzie McAlpine

There's always grey areas in the law isn't there, and they are called grey areas because rich powerful men with grey hair can seemingly do what the fuck they like. When Prince Andrew paid off Virginia Giuffre with 16 million dollars everyone was like oh that sweating bullshitting fuck got away with it, and no one seemed to question, what you can just pay to get out of stuff? Who set up that system? Oh there's the whole series of laws, good I think that captures everything, yes one more thing, you can pay to get out of any of them. What? Who passed that rule? Oh don't worry it's all gone through the whole process – parliament and Royal Assent. That's his mom and dad! He's been given a sick note for sexual assault. Sorry Andrew can't come into school today – oh no, that's the only thing he wants to do.

There are ceilings in life aren't there, and they are often called glass ceilings, as in invisible barriers stopping advancements, but am not sure they are glass ceilings, they are just ceilings aren't they, completely visible to most people who cannot break through them. And the thing is, the privileged can't see them as ceilings because for them they aren't ceilings, they are floors, they are above you in a world you can't see, and the best you can hope for in life is their rock bottom. So what can we do? How can we level the playing field? Well it's obvious isn't it, the only way to break through our ceiling is to make holes in their floor, take their floor from under them, and question more, argue more, protest more, when we know what is going on in the upper floor and yet we ignore it – oh they just pay to get out of shit, damn that system – no - protest, argue, write a comedy book that tens read, anything to shine a light, anything to try to make a small hole in their foundations so one day they may come crashing down. Our ceilings will always be ceilings until we do that, and if we don't break through, we will just spend our lives listening to the bang, bang bang bang, as they have sex upstairs. Who's that upstairs? Prince Andrew? Oh that's fine then – he can have sex with who he wants because he'll just pay people off and the actual Queen will help him. Carry on queuing people, that's what they want. They want you down there in the queue and not up there laughing at you through the ceiling that nobody sees.

DAILY NOTES VOL I

February 26th 2023
Heart To Heart – Mac DeMarco

A couple of years ago my dad got TB because in Birmingham it's the year 1789 - anyway he's in hospital and he's very ill and I go to see him, and he's falling asleep. And what you want in that moment is a heart to heart. But of course I couldn't do that because my dad has never said I love you, hence why I'm a comedian, so nothing is ever serious it's always a lie or a joke, hence why I'm a comedian. So he was there on what could have been his death bed, and he was a big fan of British soap Opera Eastenders, and so as he was falling asleep he said the following words… 'Send for Dr Legg'. And he just fell asleep. Now Dr Legg was the doctor in *Eastenders* at the time. And as he fell asleep I got incredibly sad thinking well my dad could be dead now, but I was more sad thinking those could have been his final words. What shit final words. Imagine trying to explain those final words to people that have never seen *EastEnders*. I tried to do this as a routine in Lisbon and no one understood me, probably because I can't speak Portuguese very well – I said perna de medico which apparently means Doctor's Leg.

Anyway have cool final words – George Washington's final words were 'Tis well', which I love, a politician lying to their final breath. And Steve Jobs' final words were 'Oh wow, oh wow, oh wow' – I mean essentially that's the same thing over and over again just slightly smaller but what do you expect from the inventor of the iPhone? So they say tell your parents and your kids that you love them because you may not get the chance again, and my dad has proven to me already that he knows this and still won't tell me he loves me, more recently he went in for a quadruple bypass and he phoned me up and said I'm going for a quadruple bypass and I thought I've got to do this, I've got to say it… so I said oh dad, what can I say I love you, and he paused for a second and he said no don't say that, you're only saying that because you think I might die, take it back, and I say alright I don't love you and I never have, and he said thanks very much and then hung up. And I spent the next two days terrified that those were gonna be his final words. What were your dad's final words? 'Thanks very much'. Why did he say that? Because I said I don't love you and I never have. Harsh. I know right. How is he anyway? Well, after I said I've never loved you, you'll never believe it, he's now a stand-up comedian.

DAILY NOTES VOL I

February 27th 2023
Unstoppable – Sia

It's my grandma's 100th year this year, she's unstoppable, and what I'm so pleased about is she's seeing me get successful in comedy, and she's incredibly supportive - ask her who her favourite comedian is, she won't even hesitate - Phil Wang. 'Become as successful as Phil Wang and you can take me on a tour around America. That's what I want to do when I'm 100, I want to do a tour of America with you like Phil Wang, and then I can die.' I said to her grandma I will never be as popular as Phil Wang – because he has a funny surname. And all his jokes are about his funny surname. And she said, 'What are you talking about? Your surname contains the word ass.' That isn't Wang is it. I can't go on at the O2 and open with 'Hi everyone my surname contains the word ass.' I'd be thrown out of the O2. Sorry I'd be wanged out of the O2. (lol)

Not Phil Wang of course he's a lovely and funny man but it is funny what people laugh at and find entertaining. There's a play, a franchise now called *The Play That Goes Wrong*, and it's a play… that goes wrong, but the clever thing is it's supposed to go wrong, it's supposed to be shit. But the other thing you need to know about this play… it is also shit. It's a shit play. And it sells out every night like ha ha ha what a shit play. I'm sorry the people behind this are evil geniuses. I went to see this play and I left before the interval and I I've never done this before but I went to the Box Office and I said this is the worst thing I've ever seen can I get some money back please. And they half laughed at me and said 'but sir, it's supposed to be the worst thing you've ever seen'. They had me over a fucking barrel. You can't complain can you about a show called 'This is supposed to be shit'. It reminded me of a kid called Daniel Goodchild at school who for his GCSE did a shit piece of art and the teacher said that's completely out of perspective and he said but sir it's called 'completely out of perspective' and they gave him an A. I was so annoyed. It's like these comedians who bill their shows under theatre and then start getting 5 stars now they're called 'The show that was never supposed to be funny'. Bullshit. I know what you're thinking I'm getting this completely out of perspective. That what it's supposed to be!! Anyway I hope you enjoyed this one which is called 'this one was supposed to be shit' which I hope gives you a completely different perspective on it.

DAILY NOTES VOL I

February 28th 2023
Rihanna & Calvin Harris – This Is What You Came For

I've always been of the viewpoint when it comes to sex – don't miss the point. The point is pleasure, not pain – pleasure. The point of sex, unless you're having babies is to pleasure each other – God, or Jesus or whoever has provided us with more sensory receptors on certain parts of our body, tip of the penis, clitoris, nipples, lips, neck and most importantly inside the asshole, touch those bits and then after a few minutes have an amazing orgasm. An orgasm, the best feeling in the world, it better than sex. It's orgasmic. It's easy. This is what you came for. So can anyone tell me why people are constantly over complicating it? Oh let's get the whips, the handcuffs, lets cause you pain, lets humiliate you, no, I get enough of that in my day to day life, let's walk you round on a lead, bark like a dog, let's sit there in a nappy and you pretend I'm a baby – no, fucking no, I'm not a baby I'm an adult, and because I'm not a baby I'm clever enough to realise this is what I want - touch my penis and my asshole and make me cum. It's as simple as that.

Do it slow if you want or quick whatever you want. I don't want you to whip me, I don't want a lead round my neck, in the same way that in the middle of sex I don't want you to start cutting my toenails, ooh can I cut your toenails, no! Why not I'm into that shit. Stop it. Yeah and then vomit – I'm an emetophiliac I want to have sex with you covered in vomit – stop it – the vomit just gets in the way, and that goes for licking chocolate or cream off me – just touch my penis and stick a finger in my asshole, I'm not a gateaux. Touch my penis and stick a finger in my asshole and feed me chocolate and cream. Cool. Just stop being weird about sex.

There's huge swathes of women that don't have orgasms and why – because their partners are doing the sexual equivalent of cutting their toenails. Sex is like any other household chore – there's a way of doing it and a way of not doing it – you're not gonna stick your dick in the dishwasher are you? Oh I am, mm the dishwasher, I'm into that shit, yes please, stick a lemon fresh tablet in my slot – well grow up then. Grow the fuck up.

DAILY NOTES VOL I

March 1st 2023
Carin Leon X Grupo Frontera – Que Vuelvas

I don't know what this song is about because I don't speak the language because I wasted my childhood learning unnecessary things that I would never need again. We all spent our childhoods learning things we would never use, and for every lesson in art, English and comedy that was actually usefully there were a hundred lessons in mathematics about the use of sin cos and tan – whatever the fuck it was – sine cosine and tangent. I spent 2 years learning sine cosine and tangent, of course there will be engineers that need to understand sine cosine and tangent but kids know at 15 whether they are going to be engineers. The world is going to shit, kids are coming out of school without basic life skills , my son can't even sign his own name – or indeed co-sign – sorry this is going off at a… what's the word - and we are all wondering what's going wrong. Every kid still has to do 2 years of sine cosine tangent and it's a complete waste of time at an age where they could be doing something important – like starting a successful podcast - called I don't know Triggernometry.

Straight out of University I got a job working out angles of triangles from the length of the opposite side and the length of the adjacent side. Of course I didn't I got a job in a Bank where there were no triangles just squares and cunts. And the square on the hypotenuse was equal to the sum of the cunts on the two adjacent desks. It was awful. I did banking for a few years because I needed money to get a house in London and all these other twats seemingly earned money so they could get more expensive watches. Everyone was obsessed with what watches they had back in those days – people started getting coloured watches, these Rado colour watches two grand a pop and Rolex – my watch is worth ten grand – it keeps time within a millionth of a second – no one is asking you for that time – have you got the time please… let me finish - to within a millionth of a second please? Because I'm meeting my mate to go axe throwing and I don't want to be a millionth of a second late. And I'm like we all hate our jobs, we are only doing the jobs for money, why are you guys spending that money on a device that tells us exactly how much time we're all wasting? I've just spent 13 hours shovelling shit I hate my life. Erm that's not true actually… its 13 hours and a millionth of a second… Oh God that's so much fucking worse.

DAILY NOTES VOL I

March 2nd 2023
Harry Styles – Keep Driving

Stand-up comedy is of course the best job in the world. And that's why thousands of people every year try to do it but can't. And I see comedians all the time and it's not quite working for them, and they can't understand it so they get agents and PR and writers to try and improve their stand-up comedy and it's still not working, and audiences aren't finding them funny, they still win major comedy awards and get on TV but they're not funny and they know deep down its not working - and they finally come to me and say Nathan, how come you're so good at comedy and we're not as good at comedy, what can we do? And I always say the same thing to them, it's easy to be funny, go back in time…

And you know your rich parents who sent you to boarding school and so you had feelings of detachment mixed with immense privilege you spent Summers in Hawaii - so you developed a brain that you thought was a comedians brain but it actually isn't because you had no real struggle, yeah, go back in time and get everyone around you to treat you in a very specific way – how can I explain it – don't let them overtly abuse you but definitely get them to never tell you that you're loved, ask them to never say that they love you and get them to never act like they love you apart from if you tell a good joke and then they'll laugh and you think that must be love, and get them to not overtly again but without saying it say that you're not worthy of success, there are successful people and then there is you, you're never going to be successful and this is the important one, again without knowing it ask them to convince you that even though you're fine looking and many parents would say beautiful because they're your children and you're seeing the faces through a lens of love, get them to convince you, again not overtly that you are ugly, that you are worthless, have no money so the only time you felt good was when they laughed at you, get them to treat you like this and then you are ready and one time at university you won't be able to leave your room and so you end up shitting in a Tupperware box. Then you'll be able to write a joke. Until then, get out my fucking lane. Yeah it's the slow lane but that just means I'll get exactly where you're going but I won't fucking annoy everyone on the way.

DAILY NOTES VOL I

March 3rd 2023
Wild As Her – Corey Kent

There's one subject I would never go near in my comedy, in comedy you can say anything can't you, and the people that focus on the fact you can say anything often forget to make it funny, but the one thing I don't talk about is because I'm gonna struggle to make it funny – my daughter. I love my daughter of course just like I love my son, but notice I will call my son an asshole, thick as shit and what have you and of course I'm half joking but not really, and I never say the same thing about my daughter - and why – well she isn't an asshole or thick as shit but say it quietly neither in reality is my son, they're both equally gorgeous and talented. So why do I feel that I can joke about my son and not my daughter?

My daughter is more placid , less wild than my son for sure, so she does fewer stupid things, but you'd think I'd be able to find one funny thing to say about her. But I can't, and the reason isn't writers block, it's a mental block, she's got the same name as my grandma number one, so it's like she's carrying on her legacy, so if I feel like if I call my daughter names I'm calling my grandma the name too, and she's such a good sweet girl. But the ultimate reason why I don't joke about her I guess is… I'm sexist, I'm sexist towards my kids. And it's not just me its most of society – boys – thick as shit, assholes, muppets, while girls are sweet, lovely, nice. And I know it's not true because some of my daughter's friends are very annoying, not lovely, never shut the fuck up. But it's something about your own kids, you are sexist towards your own kids, and I have to admit I'm sexist towards my kids, and as sexism goes its often directed towards women isn't it and yes I'm sexist towards my daughter, I do not include her in many of my jokes, and I apologise and I must make up for that, starting now.

Because there must be something funny I can say about my sweet gorgeous, lovely talented special beautiful daughter. Oh God, it's so hard to do this, my son it's so easy, he's such a muppet. My daughter, aaaah, I just love her. OK here's something I joke about with my daughter, I took her to Disneyland Florida when she was 4 years old, spent about £2000 on her that week, she doesn't remember any of it, yeah I know that's not funny because why would she remember, but it's still annoying. Parents, do not treat your very little kids to anything more than a trip to the local park, they do not remember anything and its annoying no its not annoying because she's the most beautiful gorgeous talented thing and true story even her farts do not smell. I've got nothing, I've got nothing on my daughter, what can I say, my humour has been shown up to be the load of old sexist rubbish that it is – what can I say? For some things all I have is love.

DAILY NOTES VOL I

March 4th 2023
Harry Styles – Grapejuice

I love America – my favourite place in America – Nevada. And not just because of Vegas, I love all the bits around Vegas - Red Rock Canyon, Hoover Dam but mainly the desert and you can drive for hours and see nothing but the land and the sky. So I was driving through the desert on my way to Vegas from Yosemite which is quite a long drive, 50 degrees outside and the air conditioning breaks and we are nearly out of petrol and we are out of water – we could die if the car breaks down - but thank God there suddenly appears this little café in the middle of nowhere. And we go in and we say just any cold drink please and he says… we're not open. And I say I'm dying here, and he says no this is being built its not open, we don't have any drinks, there's not even any running water connected here yet – and I said have you got personally got anything? He says with a southern drawl… All I've got is whisky and red wine. And I'm like - this isn't a country music song? I'll bring the whisky, I'll bring the wine, I'll get my guitar and I'll just die. Whisky and red wine. And then he said… I'm just fucking with you, English right? Monty Python right? Oh yeah that brilliant Monty Python sketch where someone batters a café owner to death with his bottle of red wine – what shall we call the sketch – dead claret or dead prat?

There's a time for joking around. People joke around on cards all the time as you get older, you'll see it for cards for older people above 50 ha ha ha thank you for being my much older friend ha ha ha , your joints are stiff - you're rolling them too tight ha ha ha you old cunt that kind of thing and one of my friends since I was 30 every birthday says like '20,000 more sleeps' as in until I die. He's got me dying at 70 and last year it was like 7000 sleeps, that's gone down significantly - he's the death clock that nobody wants. 7000 sleeps. That's not many sleeps. Every time I go to sleep, most people count sheep I just count sleeps. 6999 more sleeps. I fear every birthday – misery misery misery. People obsess over your age as you approach what they call a big birthday – oh it's a big un they say, why, because it has a zero in it? Grow up. Stop thinking about age as the number of years since birth and start doing it as the number of years before you die. And factor in how healthy you are. There are 15 year olds whose health is so awful they're gonna be dead at 50 if they don't get up off their arses, and whatever age you are, you'll be dead before

me, and anyway, I'm on glorious borrowed time anyway, because I could have easily died on that day in Nevada, if I had clubbed that café owner to death for doing undoubtedly the worse joke of all time, apart from every single joke on every single greetings card ever....
'In dog years you'd be dead...' ha ha ha ha.
'One year closer to the grave'.... Ha ha ha ha, yeah sure mate, send me that card if I can also send it to your two children. If it's funny to me, it's equally funny to your three-year-old daughter.

DAILY NOTES VOL I

March 5th 2023
Ed Sheeran – Don't

There were some heroic final words on 9/11 and the most famous was 'Let's roll' said by the bravest man in the world Todd Beamer on flight 93 before he stormed the cockpit and brought the plane down in Pennsylvania saving countless lives. Less heroic was I used to do a stand-up act at the turn of the millennium - I'd been doing it for about 2 years, and it was a silly improvised act, the joke being I had no jokes and I also carried a keyboard on stage and the joke there being I couldn't play it. And it was silly, one liner jokes no connections type of act. And 9/11 happened and I knew instantly the world has changed. So I gave up stand-up comedy which some people still say was the biggest tragedy of 9/11, in that everyone was a victim.

And that's the thing – you can do stuff, but also, you don't have to do it if it's not working. Don't. Society insists that everyone has a can-do attitude. No. If you can't do it, don't. I couldn't get proper laughs after 9/11 with no depth one liner comedy, I mean proper laughs not groans, proper laughs where it's in your gut, you're moved and affected, I couldn't do it so I was the hero and I said, no, I don't have to flog this dead horse. Don't. And I only came back to it when I'd developed an act that the world needed which is of course sardonic, insouciant and droll.

But what is more tragic is in the 22 years since 9/11 the world has got progressively worse hasn't it – financial crisis, wars, breakdown of society and then the biggest tragedy of all, there are entertainers that continue to goof around doing one liner cracker jokes with no depth no heart no soul and I honestly think awful stand-up comedians are my terrorists. And they should be yours as well. These are the people we need to stop. Because people think that it's all just harmless fun, when the host of *The Masked Singer* says 'Back after the break it's Scotch egg, I'm sure that will be egg-citing…' But it's not harmless is it, it harms me, and it also harms society, because people sitting at home think that it's good enough, and there's no point trying to do better, so they just sit there watching this shit and then go back to their phones and watch people fall into wet concrete, and 9/11 conspiracy videos. Let's all do better. Let's roll.

DAILY NOTES VOL I

March 6th 2023
Robin Schulz – Titanic

My partner lives in Manchester and we're both working class, although I never mention that on stage, we work for all our money and can't really do things that are that extravagant but she knows someone that works in one of the if not the swankiest hotels in Manchester – the Dakota hotel – and on Valentine's Day this year ago she got us the Balcony Suite for free, this is usually £463 a night top floor suite of this beautiful hotel, her manager said I'll treat your friends - and we turn up and she says I'm so sorry, Leonardo de Caprio has just turned up and my manager has given him the suite instead. I'm so annoyed. And we said no that's fine, to be honest a £463 room isn't our style, a normal room is more than enough. And she says well that's the thing, it's Valentine's, the hotel is full. So there was no other option, we had to have sex with Leonardo DiCaprio. Of course not, that would never happen, we're in our 40's.

We are instead led to the basement, you know that area of a swanky hotel where you have gone down the wrong lift and they've just stopped painting. Looks like the lower decks of the Titanic – the decorators think fuck it we don't need to do this bit – a corridor of staff bedrooms, so we're in this dingy badly lit corridor – and we think shall we just go home - we can't her friend would be devastated so we have to stay here for her. And there's this common room of staff in the basement and we walk in and they're all talking about Leonardo DiCaprio, and I thought dear God this was supposed to be a romantic evening and it's turned into a weird kind of James Cameron Titanic experience, a load of working class people sat around drinking and smoking in a basement while the upper classes quaff champagne on the upper decks.

I half expected Leonardo to join us any time and we'd all start doing an Irish jig. But of course he didn't because he was having sex with a model in our Balcony suite. And some people would be bitter with Leonardo getting the suite, but I was very understanding - Leonardo's girlfriends are all of a certain age where the only thing they respond to are suites.

March 7th 2023
Ed Sheeran & Rudimental – Lay It All on Me

You've got to stick together, brotherhood, like the song says – when you're hurting, lay it all on me. I'm there for you. We're here for each other, support. And that's a great thing right, well it is and it isn't, because when you're there in a little gang supporting each other, you're often not there for anyone else, and of course you can't support everyone, but people naturally support their closest friends and in so doing distance themselves from anyone else. Think about what you would do for you closest friends – I would do anything for them, lay it all on me. How about someone you don't know – well, I'd do nothing for them I don't know them. But you only don't know them because of chance and lack of effort in getting to know them, in another circumstance they could be your best friends and your best friend could be someone you don't know.

Sure… but that's not the case. I know but what I'm saying is maybe it shouldn't be 100 and 0, give your best friends maybe 90% of your effort and leave some left over for people you don't know. No, I hate people I don't know. Why? They're just people you don't know. But people I don't know can't be trusted, they're not my friends, fuck them. But can you hear yourself, your friends are just chance, circumstance. No they're not we all went to the same university. What - you're basing who you like based on university?! Well we're like-minded people that's how friendships work. What's your point.? My point is *Knock at the Cabin* the new M Night Shyamalan film, you would rather save someone you know over the entire world… Yeah fuck the entire world, and fuck *Knock at the Cabin*, shit film made by shit director.

You know the film I associate with, *Texas Chainsaw Massacre*, family and friends are all good, and fuck everyone else, I wanna take everyone else out with a chainsaw. I wanna fuck up all those comedians I don't know who went to a different university with a chainsaw and as they're dying they will say oh wow this is a bloody mess and a TV exec who went to the same university will laugh then as they're dying, they will be asked to say that joke on a panel show and the audience won't laugh but laughter will be dubbed on, why have this hatred for people you don't know? And secretly Nathan you don't want to be Leatherface do you, you want to be in the gang, frolicking in the countryside, having sex with the cool kids, don't you Nathan. All hatred is born out of love not being allowed to blossom. Let you love in, let your love in. And lay it all on me.

DAILY NOTES VOL I

March 8th 2023
About Damn Time – Lizzo

Wouldn't it be great to go back in time and be young again? No. Who wants to be young again really? Not now anyway. The youth are stupid. My son was cutting strawberries and nearly cut off his thumb, he said it will be fine. I said no you have to connect the bits, it's not gonna stop bleeding. And your thumb will fall off. And he said I don't want to go the hospital. And I said you're going to the hospital. And he said I hate hospitals. As a kid he had problems with his back and head and teeth etc and was in and out of hospitals, I get that but it's also stupid your thumb is hanging off. 'I don't want to go to the hospital daddy'. So I pulled out my trump card. I said George, look, if you lose your phone how will you be able to open your phone and swipe up? 'Take me to the hospital daddy'. 'Na hitch a ride cunt... and good luck with that munted digit.'

When you're young you want to fight, I'm done with fighting. And it's freeing. Have you seen *The Whale*? Extraordinary film and one of the themes is I don't want to be saved, and I love this. I just want to eat chicken and chocolate and Maryland cookies I don't want the hospital. I don't want to be saved I don't want to do better. My life isn't going to be extraordinary. This is who I am. I'm not someone else. And perhaps I don't want to fight. I am who I am and I don't want to fight. And when you realise you can be who you are and that is good enough, then that truly is transcendent. Fuck self-help, fuck self-improvement and fuck comedy courses, be who you are and if you are who you are and you don't want to fight and scrap and beg then that my friends is a great stand-up comedian. I don't want to fight I just want to be. In stand-up comedy there are those that want to make Marvel films and those that want to make *The Whale*. And the difference – those that make Marvel films are rich and successful and popular and happy. And those that want to make *The Whale* are so broken down and so helpless that they can never win any fight, they will lose every battle and yet they will still be considered the greatest. That is a stand-up comedian. Whenever I oversee two comedians arguing about what they can and can't joke about my only question is why am in a situation where I am hearing this debate, I must float higher, I must strive to float even higher. And the less you fight, the higher you float into the dazzling white beyond.

DAILY NOTES VOL I

March 9th 2023
Watch The World Burn – Fallin In Reverse

Watching the film 'Look Up' again last night on Netflix, very funny, particularly Jonah Hill and there's a moment towards the end of the film where the comet is in plain sight and there's a meme 'look up' and then there's a counter meme from comet deniers 'don't look up' and it's a great bit of commentary on where we are in the world now. The truth is just one of the available options now. And because so many people believe things that blatantly are not true, they become true from the sheer number of people that believe these things and act upon those things.

Everyone believes they are right, we know that others can be wrong but we more than ever before believe we are right and our opinion needs to be heard. You watch any show on TV that involves debate and everyone with totally opposing views believes they are right and they have to be heard, and also heard until the end of their point, making the most common phrase on this kind of television – 'can I finish? If you'd let me finish, can I finish?' when someone tries to interrupt them, like it's the rudest thing in the world to not let them finish a sentence which is simply their opinion and who are you to tell others when your opinion has finished or whether you opinion is more valid than someone else's opinion? All opinions are important and all opinions also are completely irrelevant, who cares about your opinion, truthfully, let me finish, if you say all opinions matter then watch the comet fall on our heads as half the world argues that it hasn't fallen on our heads.

All debate is irrelevant if there is no end point to it, and 99% of debate has no end point and so is pointless, let me finish. No, I will not let you finish you vacuous, self-important pompous prick, and if I had my way I wouldn't let you start either, get down from this bleating high horse, stop debating and start living. The end is coming and it's in sight, stop looking inside yourself for an opinion that nobody asked for and nobody wants, that half the world believe and half don't, it's utterly pointless to spend your life trying to change the unchangeable, which is humanity's inherent belief that they are right and others are wrong. So stop trying, and instead… look up.

DAILY NOTES VOL 1

March 10th 2023
Ed Sheeran – Subtract

Ed Sheeran's new album subtract is not out yet , it's not out for a few months but he's released a trailer with the sound of the sea and him messing around on a beach, and presumably the album won't sound like that it won't be just the sound of the sea but even it was billions would buy it, he's brilliant and he's so popular now he could take a shit on the beach and spoon feed it to all his fans who would kneel down with open mouths. This is Ed Sheeran's chance actually to release an album of sea noises and noises of him taking a shit and it would still be the best-selling album around the globe. Because when you reach a level of fame, you can still keep releasing stuff for many, many years and people will stay with you.

When I was a kid and a teenager because it came after the Beatles, Paul McCartney was regarded as a bit of a joke, oh he can't sing and he's releasing *Frog Chorus*, and then he croaked on *Hey Jude* at the Olympics and everyone agreed oh he's rubbish, but they carried on buying his records, at least his old records, and a few with Wings, but all his solo albums sold absolutely zero, not even his own family wants to buy them. But then *Get Back* came out and everyone thought oh fuck – you actually are a genius, and so all his solo albums started flying off the shelves, even the ones of beach sounds and him taking a shit. And this is necessary of course because fame brings money and opulence and isolation and a complete dry well of inspiration for musical genius, and that's why Ed Sheeran apparently binned scores of songs that he was going to put on a new album - he suddenly went through a really hard time and wrote some better songs and so has binned the songs he was going release – but I want hear those songs – because I bet you they're just sea noises and the sound of him shitting on the beach.

Tragedy is bad for your life, but it sure is good for inspiration. I'm happy right now, but for God's sake and the sake of my art, keep that tragedy drip, drip, dripping in. And I guarantee the next tragedy is just around the corner, that's why it's so exciting being an artist, you are never short of inspiration, because one thing is for sure – your life is only ever a few hours away from turning to complete shit. And I love it, my life is awful, brilliant, now is the time to right that killer routine.

DAILY NOTES VOL 1

March 11th 2023
Die For You – The Weeknd & Ariana Grande

My favourite book about getting old is *The Old Man and the Sea* by Earnest Hemmingway – 'Dreamers they never see the riptide coming, but then who can really blame them? Better to sail in an ocean of hope than a sea of despair.' That's what sustains us hope…even when we know there is none. We're all going to be taken by the tide so soon.

I have a vision that I'm going to end my life on a beach, not in this country obviously. People have a tendency in the UK to retire to the seaside in the UK - don't do that - the seaside in the UK is absolutely depressing for all but three weeks of every year. No, I will end up on a beach, in the sunshine. With my little finger wrapped around the little finger of my partner and we'll die at the same time in bliss. A lot of couples have a vision of dying together. But you know that's both optimistic and weirdly pessimistic. Right I'm dying… I need you to die too. You have to die now, come on, hurry up, die for me! People are obsessed with dying together. It's like cumming together – sounds great but ultimately who cares - I'm finished it doesn't matter whether you finish or not, I'll be asleep.

Often the fantasies of growing old sadly do not come true, even for the best of people. Even my grandma who I loved so much and was such a beautiful, generous person… the truth is that for the last 20-30 years of her relationship with my grandad they slept in separate beds and they used to bicker all the time, the most awful bickering, and my grandad was the archetypal downtrodden husband, there was no dying together romance for them – and if the truth be told, my grandad once called my grandma at a family party THE rudest of words to her face. I won't go into detail about this incident but if I was to write a book about it I'd probably call it *The Old Man and the C.*

True story, but my grandma is always an inspiration, right up to the end. On her final day she was sitting up in bed and I said 'fight grandma, please fight.' And she said 'Nathan, there comes a time where we stop fighting.' I used to worry about dying, but after that, I stopped worrying. There's no time for worrying about something that is definitely going to happen. We only have time to dream

DAILY NOTES VOL I

March 12th 2023
Dawns – Zach Bryan Featuring Maggie Rogers

We're all looking out for dawns right now, just a scattering of sunlight, we're not even looking for sunshine, we're just looking for dawns across the world, and we have to maintain hope, but hope fades that you'll ever see the sun if you never even see the dawn. But then again the worst thing is if you see dawn and think the sun is coming up and then it never does, so maybe the lack of hope is a good thing. So here's what I do, and maybe you can find this useful. I know that the sun is never going to rise, metaphorically, I don't live in Northern Sweden or whatever, I know almost for certain, no if I'm pushed - for certain - that the sun is never going to rise, however I have convinced myself that I am constantly seeing the dawn, I have convinced myself that something good is always about to happen, and it has created within me a constant state of excitement that something beautiful is over the horizon. And that is truly the best state to be in, because let's face it even if the sun did come up it's just annoying, probably too hot, you're too exposed, you're going to get burned. Far, far better to be in a perpetual state of excitement thinking that the thing that is definitely not going to happen is going to happen and when it does its going to be amazing when in reality it would be rubbish even if it did happen which it's never going to.

So... the big question, how do I stay in this perpetual state of dawn? Well its easy - I'm selfish, I'm doing what I need to do, I'm thinking the way I need to think to make me happy, and some people would call that deluded, but I call that genius - I have come up with a thought pattern that keeps me in a consistent state of excitement that something great is coming over the horizon which I know in my heart isn't there. So am I mad? Or is it mad to be depressed thinking it's never going to happen or depressed when it actually does happen and it's not how you thought it was going to be. Everything is shit, everything that will be, will be ultimately shit, all we have is our hope, and luckily that's the one thing we can control. We can live in a perpetual state of hope, we can literally live our dreams.

In short it's like this this - believe you can win the lottery, when you haven't even bought a ticket. That right there my friends is the secret of happiness. Or mental illness. But am I mad, or are you?

DAILY NOTES VOL I

March 13th 2023
In Ha Mood – Ice Spice

You know what – I'm really happy in life – but I have a kind of grumpy, insouciant demeanour… and many people say to me 'are you happy Nathan?' And I say yeah … and they say 'tell your face'. Tell your face. Makes me so angry. My face is nearly fifty, I can't tell it what to do. If I could tell my face what to do it would be look like Leonardo DiCaprio and appear to give a shit when the millionth person says they have ADHD. Ooh you can't concentrate on stuff - when I was a kid that was called being human. My mate got married this year. And it was his third wedding. He's fifty. And the most shocking thing happened on their wedding day – they genuinely looked happy. My mate was happy and he'd told his face to look happy and his face looked happy. You can't tell my face shit. It doesn't listen. I think it's got ADHD.

Every young person has ADHD - of course they do, their brains are wired that way now by TikTok. Oh I cannot understand why I can't concentrate on things – hey look at this daddy he's fucking a turtle – yeah I have real trouble concentrating on – now he's being fucked by a dog ha ha ha. Who wants to be young again really? Not now anyway. The youth are stupid. But maybe they're not, maybe they're cleverer than they look, more clever, cleverer, I'm not sure which it is. Because maybe they've realised life is shit, the world is awful, so they've chosen instead to scroll on their phones, and watch people fall over, into wet concrete. Because it is funny, and if you look up, life isn't funny. They've given up. And they're happy. Maybe that's the secret.

Maybe that look on my friend's face wasn't happiness at all, of course it wasn't, people can't be happy. What it was, of course, after two marriages, was the face of someone who had given up – this will do – I'm done trying – I've given up and now I'm happy. Of course, if only I could give up. That really is the secret of happiness, give up – if you can be content with nothing then your face is always smiling. But I can't give up, I'm constantly trying, constantly moving – you know what, I think I've got ADHD. Constantly trying and knowing constantly that I will ultimately fail. And that's why even when I'm happy my face tells the truth. So stop telling my face to smile, it gave up listening many years ago.

DAILY NOTES VOL I

March 14th 2023
NLE Choppa & 2Rare – Do It Again

Comedy is hard, it isn't good for your mental health. And the main issue with privilege in comedy isn't the comedians in their little gangs, it's the audiences, it's you… that's right Toto, we ain't in Kansas anymore - some of you, the ones in gigs that laugh the least, yes comedy is subjective but is someone finds me subjectively not funny then they are objectively wrong, if you haven't laughed it's probably because you're privileged - you've had it all from birth, so privileged, why should you laugh at me, I'm scum to you. When I see you guys in the audience I can spot you a mile off because even in the funniest show when everyone else is laughing, you're sitting there like you're in the film *The Quiet Place*, you think that if you make a sound that someone will kill you, when in reality you are just slowly killing yourselves with your inability to find joy in anything but money, which was really your parents money anyway.

It's like Trump, it's not a talent to make money off a load of money. You are cunts. Not the parents, you. Your parents made their own money, you guys are just self-made cunts. But what is really going on Nathan? Have you just had a bad gig where nobody laughed. No, I just had a gig where one table refused to laugh because they are these type of people. But shouldn't after 15 years in comedy you not give a shit about things like this? Are you bitter Nathan? No, I'm not bitter. Isn't the truth Nathan you criticise the gang, but that's all you want isn't it, to be in the gang, chainsaw in hand nobody stands a chance. It would make it far easier wouldn't it Nathan, and the added benefit of that would be you'd be rich and then you'd totally understand the people not laughing because they have never needed to make an effort to do anything, it just lands on their laps. Wouldn't you secretly like that Nathan, everything landing in your lap? No, no I wouldn't. Give me one good reason why you wouldn't want to make it easy for yourself if you had to do it all again? OK, here's the reason. Because I'm excited about my next joke, I'm excited about my next show. I'm excited about the struggle. The struggle is the only thing that makes the success completely and utterly fulfilling. It's something the gang will never feel. That show that I've worked so hard for. And when that joke is done, when that show is done. I'll do it again. And again and again and again.

DAILY NOTES VOL I

March 15th 2023
Going, Going, Gone – Luke Combs

The Queen Consort (Camilla) – it's not the Queen Consort is it - it's Camilla Parker Bowles – Camilla The Queen Consort is appearing on *Antiques Roadshow*. Now if you don't know this programme it's not where they drive round all the oldest people in the country and ask them whether they had anything to do with the death of Diana Princess of Wales, it's where old relics are discovered and they are asked to take in any antiques they own to be valued – lol isn't it funny to joke about being old because the good news is it's not gonna happen to me or anyone that I love, and I mean that as a joke and not as it sounds., fairly fucking sinister. Anyway, the Queen Consort Camilla Parker Bowles bringing in a couple of old family heirlooms to be valued on *Antiques Roadshow* – bit of fun isn't it – no not really – it's a bit of a smack in the face to the people that work all hours trying to make ends meet really. You, technically the actual Queen of England getting stuff priced up as if the crown you'll wear at the Coronation isn't actually priceless, no amount of money could buy it, so what are you gonna bring in to be priced up – The Crown Jewels or are you actually gonna do what we half expect you're going to do - bring in something that's not worth very much, and they're gonna say oh that's only worth £300 and you'll walk away like a woman of the people like yes I'm struggling too, into my waiting horse and golden carriage back to actual Buckingham Palace.

But the thing is there's no winning for Camilla because she's not Diana and whether or not she had anything to do with her death, did she buy Henri Paul the wine we don't know, she will never be in the Nation's heart because the thing is there's only two things that you can't put a price on – The Crown Jewels and love, you can't buy love, not proper love anyway, and you can't choose love, love will just happen, you can't be blamed for who you fall in love with. So when you get it, hold on to it, because it's the most precious thing, and you'll never need to get it valued because it's not for sale, and if you treat it well, it can be passed down from dad to daughter from grandma to son and it literally is the one thing that will make you feel better, when you're told that old coin you had is literally worth fuck all. Really, fuck all? Fucking hell, I'd been saving that for years thinking it was my pension. Ah fuck.

No matter, I've got you. Charles my darling, love is all you need.

DAILY NOTES VOL I

March 16th 2023
Harry Styles – Matilda

So Roahl Dahl was in the news recently as his books are being rewritten to take out any mention of potentially triggering words. So Augustus Gloop in *Charlie and the Chocolate Factory* will no longer be called 'fat' but will still, curiously, be called Augustus Gloop. Instead, he will be described as enormous. Ever more curious, fat people out there, do you want to be described as fat or enormous? Just checking fatty. Other words scrapped are ugly, crazy and female, female being the most contentious of the lot – how dare you call me female you fat fuck? So ugly has been removed as a reference to *The Twits*, Mrs Twit is no longer ugly she is now beastly and fit, like proper fucking fit – I mean she's dirty but like a hot homeless person now, like a twit I like to fuck. A TILF. The word crazy has been removed because people don't want to refer to non-crazy people as crazy because that's a slight on actual crazy people who you don't call crazy now, so the question is – why is crazy still a word? Is it just for crazy paving?

In *The Witches* they were referred to as a bunch of dangerous females - this has been changed to a bunch of witches, because witches is preferable to females just in case those crazy sorry those silly witches don't want to be called females by a man that is now of course dead. Sorry, not alive. What do you know anyway mate you're dead, you're literally passed it. You don't know what we want any more, because you're dead. We don't want mothers and fathers we want parents we don't want cloud men we want cloud people, we don't want tiny men we want – 'it doesn't matter what size they are' people, and I cannot tell you the number of people, who were coming up to me before these changes not crazy but certainly furious because these books were ruining their lives, but now they can read them in the knowledge that they will not be triggered and they can relax, put their feet up and read one of your safe as fuck, mother-cunting books. Because I tell you what's more important than anything – I've always said it, words – as the saying goes – 'we want words not actions', the world will never change through actions, it will change through words. I'm right aren't I? I knew I fucking was. And if you think I'm wrong, you're crazy, and fat.

DAILY NOTES VOL I

March 17th 2023
American Pie – Don Mclean

This is my grandma's favourite song, American Pie and it was released just before I was born and my grandma says she has listened to it nearly every day for her whole life she loves it so much, which is all the more remarkable as its 8 minutes long. And even more remarkable as it is about something fairly depressing - the plane crash in 1959 that killed Buddy Holly, The Big Bopper and Richie Valens. The day the music died. Certainly for my grandma who has listened to this song virtually to the exclusion of all other types of music. What's your favourite genre of music grandma – I like Don Mclean American Pie – that's not a genre of music – it is to my grandma. My grandma came from a generation that was happy with nothing, they had nothing and they expected nothing, so when they got one thing they were happy with that. We've all heard stories of our parents or grandparents going on holiday to the same destination every year, find one thing that makes you happy and stick with that.

And there's something in that, the world gets too bored too easily now, how much better would the world be if we could be happy with just one thing – one partner, one house, one car, one holiday, one love and one song – American Pie. And my grandma never wanted one thing – money, because she knew how to cope without it. When asked what American Pie meant, McLean replied 'It means I don't ever have to work again. If I don't want to.' I love that because he wanted to, of course he did, the money was never the thing, it was the music. Don't let the music die.

I've inherited so much from my grandma, for example her extensive vinyl collection of one Don Maclean song. But the main thing I've inherited from her is this notion of one thing, one house, one car, one love, and the notion of not desiring anything material, because material is unimportant, I care about nothing material, I really don't, I couldn't care less - when the plane crashes for us all, are we thinking of anything material, of course not, and the great thing about investing in non-material things is they can never be destroyed, they will never die.

DAILY NOTES VOL I

March 18th 2023
Sure Thing - Miguel

So many things I grew up believing were sure things turn out to be lies – you can't see the great wall of China from space, a penny dropped from the top of the Empire State building will not kill you and the guy in the Guinness Book of Records who grows his nails to be the longest in the world isn't an arsehole, he's just the most unforgivably desperate human being imaginable - the only way he can feel like he's left his mark on the world is by growing his nails to like 20 feet or something you know when they all go brown and start curling round themselves, its fucking disgusting, on one hand obviously so he can wipe his arse with the other hand.

The last one I saw was a guy in India and I've actually recently moved next door to this prick, so I can track him, he's nearly dead and he never leaves the house because of his awful left hand, anyway you may not have seen me recently but I too have been growing my nails long and now mine are the second longest nails in the world behind this guy so on the day this guy dies I'll celebrate, I'll get the Guinness Book of Records round to measure my nails and I'll be like yes you have to put me in the book now I've got the longest nails in the world I've achieved something with my life, yes I could have been helping the sick but instead I've been lacquering my 19.99 feet nails so I can get a 2cm square picture in a book which 100% of the readership will look at and wretch - that's my life's ambition.

Anyway once they're measured I will cut off my disgusting nails and I'll dance around at the funeral and then I'll slam the nails into his grave, they'll literally be the final nail in his coffin. A couple of days later the Guinness Book of Records will call me up and say 'oh hi Nathan, I hear what happened at the funeral' ... 'whatever mate at least I'm in the book' ... 'yeah it's about that Nathan, are you aware that nails carry on growing after you're dead?' 'No that's not true mate, that's something that everyone that thinks is true but isn't.' 'Well no you're wrong because the base of the nail retracts when you're dead and we measure from the tip to the base, so anyway, cut a long story short since he's been dead the guy in the coffin has regained the record from you.' 'No worries mate, do you wanna just stand at the bottom of the Empire State building, I'm going to throw a penny off the top attached to myself.'

DAILY NOTES VOL I

March 19th 2023
Big Love – Fleetwood Mac

So congratulations to Brendan Fraser for winning best actor for his performance in *George of the Jungle*, sorry for his performance in *The Mummy: Tomb of the Dragon Emperor*. Hello Imhotep how are you? Thanks for asking no one asks how I am. Well you do kinda bring that on yourself Imhotep. How so? Well, you're kind of… what? Well… mardy? I'm not mardy, I'm happy, well tell your face. Don't tell me to tell my face, I haven't got a face to tell… you see you're at it again. Sorry, Brendan Fraser's amazing, spellbinding performance in *The Whale*, of course he won the Oscar it was an incredible performance in an incredible film that left me sobbing uncontrollably, wow!

And I looked online afterwards to read all the reviews and many were glowing, but then many were not - 2 stars – 'a contrived disappointment'. Peter Bradshaw (basically Imhotep manifest) writes 'it's a vapid, hammy and stagey movie'. Is it Peter, is that a fact Peter, is it fact or is it opinion as you're writing that the film I and millions others and the Academy and Venice that gave it a 6-minute standing ovation, you're writing as if it's fact that it's shit – 'the writing clunks'… Does it Peter? Yes it does – 'the narrative is contrived and unconvincing'. But I'm convinced by you Peter – 'and the whole film has a strange pass-agg body language'. What the fuck is 'pass-agg body language'? Oh passive aggressive, who says pass-agg? I looked it up Peter, no one, no-one but you. You're use of pass-agg is strange, it's contrived and unconvincing, how can a whole film have passive aggressive body language, sorry pass-agg bod lang?

Isn't the truth of it Peter and everyone else that didn't love this stellar performance in a stellar film, that you will never be impressed. For fuck's sake guys let yourself enjoy something, be moved by something, let something impress you for goodness sake, love something, love anything in your God awful, pass-agg existences. Brendan Fraser talks about his time in the wilderness, where he felt no love, don't let that happen again people, to him or anyone just trying to do their best. When something's good, tell them it's good. And if everyone else thinks something is good and you don't, well, as my grandma says, if you don't have something nice to say then don't say anything at all. Is that really so hard Peter? I mean probably yes if you're a film critic and don't like something. I get it, sorry if this has come across as pass-agg. Love you Peter, and if I ever star in a film that wins me Best Actor at the Oscars, don't be a cunt.

DAILY NOTES VOL I

March 20th 2023
Encanto – All Of You

One more on the Oscars, where *Encanto* won best animated film in 2022 of course, that's the link, this year it was won by *Pinocchio*, a reimagined adaptation set in Fascist Italy during the interwar period and WW2. Really? Sounds a bit heavy – keep it light mate – when he lies his nose grows is that the story? Stop making everything political - anyway haven't seen it because Ewan McGregor is in it and er... anyway, if you can't say something nice don't say anything at all. So, erm I won't... but have you seen the film *Impossible* starring Ewan McGregor about a tsunami, I only got about ten minutes in, I didn't even make it to the tsunami, all I'm saying is... no I can't say it.

People talk about wooden acting and I'll just say... have you seen *Pinocchio*? Am I lying? Is my nose growing? Anyway, I love you all, all of you, you're all amazing and as I said yesterday just allow yourself to enjoy things and be nice to people. And on that note, lots of people are having a go at Hugh Grant for apparently being not nice in an interview with Ashley Graham who asked him as all Oscars interviewers tend to ask what are you wearing and he said – well just my suit. He wasn't being rude! That is the answer, he was wearing his suit, made by his tailor, not everything needs to be an advert for Dior or Top Man. And then he was asked about his excitement to be in Glass Onion the film and he says well I was only in it for 3 seconds, which again is pretty much the truth, not everything has to be amazing.

When I say be nice to everyone, don't be disingenuous. Hugh Grant was operating within his right to say nothing at all to questions that he thought were nonsensical, have some perspective – this is a man who got a blowjob from an LA prostitute – that was rude. Was it though? Not really. But Hugh, Hugh, how did you feel being in Divine Brown's mouth was it exciting? I was barely in it, I was in it for 3 seconds. Great Hugh, and what were you wearing for the blowjob? I was wearing just a striped T shirt, you know what I'm saying Hugh, who made it? Well I believe it was Top Man. Oh that's amazing Hugh can we see it? Well you can but it's covered in spaff. You lied about seeing prostitutes didn't you Hugh? But did every time you lie it got bigger? It happens man, it happens.

March 21st 2023
Everything I Love – Morgan Wallen

Ooh one more on The Oscars, and the film *Everything Everywhere All At Once*, the best film, everyone loved *Everything Everywhere All At Once*. Not me, I hated it, 30 mins in I had to turn it off. Nonsense, waffle, too much, what the fuck's going on? Just my opinion of course but you tried to do too much, you tried to do everything everywhere all at once – and for me it was like the film equivalent of TikTok, which has everything and then nothing. You know what I mean, if you have everything you also have nothing, it's too much. There are moves to ban TikTok, already happened for government employees in the UK and Joe Biden talking about it in the US, because of security and other concerns but the main concern people should have with TikTok and the reason it should definitely be banned is it's everything everywhere all at once and it's too much.

It's babies falling over, it's dogs fucking, it's people kissing turtles, it's planes landing, baseballers baseballing, it's basketballers basketballing, it's tits appearing it's cars crashing it's fatties diving, it's some twat with a thousand ping pong balls sitting on a flight of stairs trying to bounce a ball on to the base of a pan on to the base of another pan on to the base of another pan and then into a plastic cup and then he cheers and applauds as if he's achieved something. The only thing you've achieved mate is the status of humankind as moronic.

There is no hope anymore, we have everything everywhere all at once and so we vote *Everything Everywhere All At Once* to be the best film because there is everything going on but essentially nothing. I mean I don't know for sure, I switched it off after a few minutes but that's what you want right, you want me to swipe up, what's the next thing, what's the next thing, I never want this thing I want the next thing, I wonder what the next page of this book will be about, I'm not thinking of this one I'm thinking of that one, I think it will be called *NewJeans*. Swipe up, read that one, that one will be better, you're bored of this one aren't you? Who would have thought - you're bored of everything because you have everything. And no one saw it coming.

DAILY NOTES VOL I

March 22nd 2023
NewJeans – Ditto

People always say to me Nathan, why are your jeans so tight, are you trying to look young Nathan? Are you? No, how is that a thing? Young people don't wear tight jeans, they wear baggy jeans hanging off their arse so we see the entirety of their pants, at least in London where I live, young kids, boys walking around with their jeans pulled down so low we can see the entirety of their pants. When I was that age if your trousers fell down so people could see the entirety of your pants it would be like Oh my God how embarrassing you will never believe what happened to me the other day my jeans fell down so people could see the entirety of my pants, now it's are you ready son, yeah I'm just pulling down my trousers so people can see the entirety of my pants, oh right, do you want me to check whether I can see the entirety of your pants, yeah I can, cool, I'm ready, let's go.

Anyway, what I'm saying is I don't wear tight jeans to look like the young. So why do I do it? Well in truth, I think I look good, I think that's the best looks for me, when I wear baggy trousers I think that doesn't look as good on me, and that's the reason, I want to look good, shoot me. However, I do get it, when I see tight jeans on other men my age I do think, that doesn't look good, are you trying to look young? Are you? That's a bit sad, trying to look young are you? How tragic. So maybe I need to reflect that strange loathing back on to myself and think maybe people are right, maybe it's time for baggier jeans, maybe not even jeans - chinos or chords, or maybe even a fucking tracksuit. Because that's right, you get to your late 40s and you have to stop having your own mind and bow to the opinion of everyone else who says you're old now, give up, no one wants to see the outline of your legs and your bollocks because you're old, wear baggy fucking trousers just don't let them slip down because then we'll see the entirety of the nappy that you're wearing because you're in your 40s and are totally past it.

Na fuck you, this is the beginning for me. I'm off to buy another pair of skin-tight jeans and dust off the leather jacket and get that earring and tattoo that I've always been threatening. And I'm gonna be wearing exactly the same thing well into my 90s, when my jeans will be even tighter as my legs will be skin and bone. I cannot wait to disappoint you all, you judgemental, baggy trouser wearing pricks.

DAILY NOTES VOL 1

March 23rd 2023
Last Night – Morgan Wallen

So last night I did something I've never had to do in 15 years of doing comedy, and that's pay someone to leave a gig. 15 years in comedy I've seen everything - shouty, gobby, drunk people, stag do's, people that won't shut up and you either shut them up or they eventually fall asleep or leave of their own accord, it often detrimentally affects the night but whatever, there are assholes everywhere, that's life. But last night, and you can see this incident on my Instagram and TikTok that's thenathancassidy but even preceding your name with the word 'the' on your socials does not even come close to the arrogance of this woman who I had to pay to leave the gig last night.

So I come on as host and say everyone excited to be here and everyone is apart from this one woman who says well let's see how it goes, let's see whether it's worth £10. Ten pounds – if you're not from the UK this is nothing, you get 5 comics, ten pounds, let's see whether it's worth £10 – ok prick, maybe, and this is the way I let most people off, maybe you're just trying to be funny – I get it you're at a comedy night, and you think I'm funny, my cunty friends think I'm funny so I'm as funny as these professional comedians who have been doing it as a job for 15 years playing to stag do shouties and pricks like me, but I'm funny too and here's me showing how fun I am by saying 'let's see whether it's worth £10'. There we go, whatever, you're a prick, let's move on with the night.

Then the first comedian comes on, everyone is laughing and I come back on as host and this woman in the crowd passes some shitty comment about her with her still in the room, so I say that's a cunty thing to say and she says give me back my £10 and I'll leave. Abso-fucking lutely. Oh my God abso-fucking lutely. I couldn't get the ten pound note out quick enough. Bye bye. And I was filming the night for my thenathancassidy socials and you'll see as she leaves I shout into the camera in celebration, one of the best things ever to happen in my career, when the cock voluntarily leaves the room.

'Amazing', I shouted and as I shouted because I'd been ill you'll see me shouting I'm losing my voice but I don't care, this is the best thing that's ever happened. Anyway, next morning, I had lost my voice, completely. It's been a week now and its only just come back so this gig wasn't last night but my voice feels like it was, I've had to cancel work, lose money, and then I get notification from the producer that this woman requested a refund on her ticket and that of her friend who stayed behind by the way, so she got paid £10 to leave. I mean full credit to the privileged prick. Proving once and for all, that you can't ultimately beat the privileged entitled twats, but you can celebrate when they stumble and fall, particularly when it's out of your sight at least for one night.

DAILY NOTES VOL I

March 24th 2023
I Wrote A Song – Mae Muller

Seriously who is doing PR for Eurovision? You may not be aware of Eurovision where you are in the world it's a competition to choose the shittest song in Europe. That's unfair, but it is totally fair to say that up to this time last year, the competition was seen as an absolute joke in this country, the UK, mainly because we hadn't won it for years as everyone around Europe hates us. The biggest joke, not taken seriously, then last year a singer Sam Ryder came second, well technically first beaten by Ukraine who would have beaten The Beatles with John Lennon and George Harrison coming back to life to stage a one off performance of Frog Chorus with Yoko Ono on the pots and pans. But even Sam Ryder's success does not go anywhere to explain the sudden turnaround in how we view this contest in the UK with tickets changing hands for thousands of pounds to the event which is happening in May in Liverpool, a perfect place for that Beatles Frog chorus reunion by the way. The whole country cannot get enough of this thing that only last year was universally regarded in this country as a massive pile of glittering shit.

And now we have the UK's entry for this year's contest just been announced and it's Mae Muller – I wrote a song, I haven't listened to it but from the title it's the kind of self-referencing thing that Eurovision loves like a comedian doing a joke about writing a joke, it's all nonsense and very soon the bubble will burst and we'll all go back to thinking the whole thing is a waste of time, so why the turnaround? Well it can only be down to one thing, the quality of Sam Ryder's song notwithstanding, it explains the rise and fall of virtually everything and anything in entertainment – PR bullshit, we are told what to like and what not to like, PR bullshit, because of PR bullshit people are paying hundreds thousands to watch the rehearsal for the Eurovision Song Contest, the fucking rehearsal – to put that into perspective I went to see the opening ceremony of the Olympics rehearsal for free, because it's the fucking rehearsal and it should be free. PR bullshit is like a magic potion and its very soon going to run out for Eurovision, and I'd imagine for many its gonna happen about twenty minutes in to the rehearsal which they've paid £1000 to attend and, as a couple that could have been in Vegas, they instead turn to cach other and say – well this is shit isn't it – yes it is my friend, yes it really is.

DAILY NOTES VOL I

March 25th 2023
Valerie – Amy Winehouse

I'm not sure Amy Winehouse would be successful in today's market, because we don't want tortured souls any more do we? And the young people ask what's a tortured soul Nathan is that an app? No it isn't an app it's someone that says 'Is this it? Is what we're fed as entertainment the best we can do?'. 'Is TikTok the best we can do? Car crashes and people falling over?' Yes it is Nathan and fair enough it's not for you because its aimed at 10–18-year-olds, its infantile – of course you won't like it because it's not for you, it's for infants. If you want to be the comedy equivalent of Amy Winehouse then that won't be successful any more, you need to be Miley Cyrus, not even Miley Cyrus, you need to be Hannah Montana, the kids show where she lived a double life as a pop star by disguising herself with a wig.

Disguise yourself with a wig – that's all it takes now to fool the morons. That's what the cartoon character He-Man used to do – disguise himself with slightly longer hair and a tan and no one knew who he was. The more dumbed down shit we are fed the more we get a taste for it – and like any junk that we eat it tastes good for a few minutes and then it instantly makes us feel awful – because it fills our bellies but not our souls. So what is *Valerie* about, how did Amy Winehouse write this, well of course it wasn't Amy Winehouse it was a cover of a Zutons tracks about a girlfriend of the lead singer Dave McCabe, celebrity make-up artist Valerie Star. Which makes the soul of this song even more remarkable, a world away from the original version, she found the soul in a song that didn't on the surface have any and wasn't her story, but it was about a long distant relationship that couldn't be, she found the tragedy in it and it adds to the picture of a tortured soul, when in reality it was written by someone else, about someone else who liked dressing up and creating a new character with her ginger hair and the way she liked to dress.

That's the thing about being a tortured soul – they can take the simplest story and find the tragedy in it, and is that a good thing or not I don't know, but for some of us, no different haircut will make us change, we can't fool anyone that we're anything but tortured souls.

DAILY NOTES VOL I

March 26th 2023
Ed Sheeran – Salt Water

It's not out yet, the song *Salt Water* by Ed Sheeran so this is just my guess as to what it will sound like – it will use the four chords of Ed Sheeran Em C G D. He's promised it's going to about sad and difficult moments in his life though so the tears will I'm sure flow, they are not flowing yet, salt water has not been released just yet. That's what tears are of course, they are salt water – well in detail they are a salt water layer sandwiched between a layer of fat and a layer of mucus. No, tears are salty because of electrolytes and our bodies use electrolytes to create electricity that helps power our brains, and that's why when we cry our brains stop working don't they, they do, most times when someone cries, they've temporarily lost their minds.

Stop crying and you get your minds back. Stop crying basically, it's not good for you. Excess salt in too many tears can lead to serious and life-long eye damage and eve loss of vision. So next time you hear someone say 'it's good to have a cry, it's good to have a bloody good cry', quote this podcast at them and tell them no it isn't, it's not good to cry, so stop listening to songs that make you cry presumably like the *Salt Water* by Ed Sheeran.

We're all very sad that Ed went through a hard time but I'm not sure we need sad songs, life is hard enough and I find myself doing this, oh let's listen to *Time to Say Goodbye* so I can be reminded of my grandad's funeral and have a really big cry because crying is good for you - no it isn't, sadness is not the best medicine it's laughter, laughter releases endorphins that power the body, crying just makes the body feel worse and can have long lasting damage on the body if you do it too much.

What I'm saying is, are you going to the theatre to get upset this week, or are you going to the cinema to watch *The Whale*? Don't – yes its remarkable but at the end you'll be bathing in a sea of your own salty tears, I cried so much I was drowning it was like I'd been hit by a tsunami, that can't be good for you right, and it's not, just buy my Amazon specials and have a laugh, the only crying you'll be doing is when you see how much they are.

DAILY NOTES VOL I

March 27th 2023
Somewhere Only We Know - Keane

I'm getting old and I need something to rely on, I'm getting tired and I need somewhere to begin. For the first time this week I have definitely felt old and tired. Three days ago I went ten pin bowling, I played 2 games, no not on my own, with my son, my 15-year-old son. And as these things come to pass, he beat me at ten pin bowling for the first time ever, over two games he beat me by one point, I mean it was one game all in reality that's how these things are measured actually, but technically over two games he beat me by one point, one game all whatever, so there was that that made me feel old, when your kids start beating you at stuff but it's what came afterwards that has made me feel properly old.

The next day and for two clear days afterwards I feel broken, my body aches all over… it feels like I'd been working for 30 years in a factory, and the worst factory as well, a factory making ten pin bowling balls, and I had the worst job in that factory, I'd have to take the ten pin bowling balls off the production line and chuck them into the back of a lorry, and the lorry was always really long. I would have gone on strike but every time I called a strike they just cheered. So I went part time by the end I was just ten pin.

You see these are the jokes you get if you don't support proper comedy, it will die off. As will I. I listened to this Keane album over and over again when I was in my early 30s, I was in the States, driving for hours, constantly doing stuff, football on the beach, basketball, and I never ached and it's that simple thing, not aching, if you're young listening to this and you don't ache, that is the simple thing that you have that you should cherish above all other, because when its gone you'll be longing for it back. Whatever the benefits and the gifts of getting old that is the one thing you'll want back, I just want that ache to go. But I know you won't listen to the old, but let me in, because we know, the old, you should listen and cherish every day that you feel young, because if it's one thing the old know about it's how it feels to be young. The young don't know how it feels, only the old. That place, being young, is simply somewhere only we know.

DAILY NOTES VOL I

March 28th 2023
I Wrote The Book – Morgan Wallen

I wrote the book *Resurrection by Boris Johnson*, a spoof post covid diary by our UK Prime Minister Boris Johnson – half of it was true and half of it was made up about what was going on with Boris Johnson and the Government over the first few months of the Pandemic, and when you're reading it, it becomes tricky to separate the fact from the fiction as the fact was so ridiculous, did that really happen, yes it did, did they really have so many boozy parties at Downing Street when they were telling the country not to socialize and have parties? Yes they did. But it's just come out that Boris Johnson is not to blame for these parties, and what he says is he misled MPs when he said there were no parties, but he did not do it intentionally or recklessly. Which I think is fair enough, as long as everyone is allowed to use that defence for everything we ever do.

I've recently got a speeding fine, I want to get out of it, can I simply say that I did not speed intentionally or recklessly? Because it wasn't reckless, it was 72MPH on a motorway (speed limit 70, I may have not noticed that they temporarily had brought it down to 60) and it was not intentional, in a way. I mean it wasn't my intention to get fined, but seriously, if you're listening to this in Germany you'll be wondering what I'm talking about, speed limit what's that? 70 MPH, I know it's crazy, most of London has a speed limit of 20MPH, to put that into context most of you will be doing that kind of speed in a car park, 20MPH – I once got flashed for doing over 20 when I was pulling the car out of a parking space. They are reducing the speeds everywhere, cameras everywhere and it's to control us, but now we all, in the UK at least, have the ultimate defence, we did not do it intentionally or recklessly. So let me off.

I did not burgle that house intentionally or recklessly, I did not call the policeman a cunt intentionally or recklessly, it's now the ultimate get out clause, if he gets away with it. But of course they always ultimately get away with it, because they have intention and are reckless, and we just watch on like speed cameras saying they're going too quick, they should be fined, they're breaking the rules, they should be fined. And occasionally they get fined, they get sanctioned. And who's won then? It's them isn't it? They're speeding, intentionally and recklessly while we sit, suffer and judge.

DAILY NOTES VOL I

March 29th 2023
Nicki Minaj – Red Ruby Da Sleeze

Ah the lyrics of this song are remarkable, it's Shakespearean in its details, so much going on, at one point she says she hasn't fucked with horses since Christopher Reeve, pulling out that reference, it's incredible, extraordinary. And there's even a chorus that basically goes na-na-na-na-na. It's a very good and very complicated song and you should check it out because I don't feel like I've truly done it justice here.

But it reminded me of the other song with the chorus na na na, *Hey Jude* of course, na na na, famously butchered by Paul McCartney at the Olympics. But it's the simplicity of those songs versus the complication and the lyrics and the ferocity of this that shows how far we've come. The Beatles and Paul McCartney are held up as geniuses and of course they are but it's the simplicity of their music that actually makes it so beautiful. Paul McCartney is not a great pianist and what he said is you can teach kids chords in ten minutes to write a song and he's right, some of The Beatles songs are so simple – C G F Am. *Let it Be*. Perhaps the most beautiful song of all time.

And then you come forward 50-60 years and what we have is this song *Red Ruby Da Sleeze* - I haven't seen the video but presumably Nicki Minaj shaking that ass and writhing over a python or some shit. You know what the videos were for The Beatles songs – they didn't have any, or at most it was them singing the song, standing there and singing the song. Because ultimately that's all that's needed, keep it simple, a few simple chords and stand there and sing the song. Simplicity is the key note of all true elegance, who said that - Coco Chanel.

Don't over complicate things, don't look too deeply into how Coco Chanel collaborated with the Nazis and Churchill's intervention to get her off spy charges, stop over complicating things stop reading and stop writing, keep it simple, that's the key to beauty and that's the key to happiness, when someone asks you to get too complicated, tell them this – na, na na, na na na na.

DAILY NOTES VOL I

March 30th
Ain't That Some – Morgan Wallen

Yes, I've separated from the mother of my kids, But we've stayed friends. We don't have the time for enemies. Time is so short we don't have time for enemies. people throughout history battling enemies, dying because they could not avoid their enemies, and now we think we can't avoid our enemies – yeah you can put your phone away, because all our enemies are self-created. And on our phones. If you put your phones away, you don't have enemies. So many feeding the trolls online, 'oh look at my enemies everyone and the hate they're spreading.' You're spreading the hate too, you're feeding the trolls. And it does not make them go away, because they will never go away, there is nothing you can do. Oh yeah there is, put your phone in your pocket.

Because your enemies aren't real, they don't affect you looking up to the sky, out to sea, being surrounded by your friends and family that love you. Real enemies would stop all of that, don't feed the trolls. And whatever you do, don't get enemies in real life. You can avoid that. Just because you've split up from your partner, unless they've done something awful to you, don't forget when you've split up that you once loved them, you once thought that the sun shone out of their genitals so much that you were willing to suck them. Don't forget that when you inevitably split up. You don't hate them, it just appears that way, because the love hate coin has turned the other way. Don't forget love is on the other side.

My friends were getting divorced and in court my mate genuinely said to the judge – she's a nob, ask her who she fucked when we were married. I said to him afterwards – yeah went quite well mate, right up to the point where you said 'She's a nob – ask her who she's fucked'. I mean imagine if she answered, you're paying for the court's time, in my experience that would take forever. Just halve the money, halve the house and move on to your next love. Because if you don't do this, next time you meet someone you'll think – oh my God, this is the one, this is the one in the future I'm going to hate. Then you'll never be able to suck it.

Get down there, and love.

DAILY NOTES VOL I

March 31st 2023
Dying Man – Morgan Wallen

As soon as you're 40, in terms of stand-up comedy some people think you are a dying man. There was a sitcom in the UK called *One Foot in the Grave* and the lead actor Richard Wilson played a very old man with one foot in the grave and he was 4 years older than me when he first started on this… one foot in the grave. Of course Hollywood actresses know how this feels, with one foot in the grave at 35, or child actors, one foot in the grave at 10, dog actors, one foot in the grave at 3. Getting older is seen as a sign of weakness, particularly in stand-up comedy. When I was 40 I was told by industry people to lie about my age and tell people I wasn't 40. Seriously a well know PR person – came up to me, she was in her 40's by the way - easily, she said you can't name your show after your age in your 40's. I said why not - and I quote her, 'you have to be aware of Adele. She names her stuff after her ages but that works because she's 19, 25, 30 – no one wants an Adele Album called 48'.

You can't tell an audience your age Nathan if you're over 40. Why not? So no one suspects I'm actually good at it? Stand-up comedy is one of the many things that you get better at as you get older, it's only sport where suddenly and depressingly you become shit at it when you're 37. And this is nothing against young stand-ups, I was one too remember, and you think you're great, and the industry think you're great - but you're not, you're awful. So when the next new big thing breaks and you read in the press, oh you've got to see this person, this is the hot new thing, they'll use the following marketing… fresh new face, hotly anticipated debut… those are the words you really need to look out for – hotly anticipated debut, bullshit, no one but no one is hotly anticipating it, because we all know it's going to be average at best, unless you're Adele. Average toss full of air, padding and empty words with no life experience to back them up and make them real, make them truly funny.

Singing and sport, yes, you're great when you're 19, 25 and 30. The albums you need to be looking out for in comedy, 42, 48 and best of all, 70. That's when you see the good stuff from stand-ups. So exciting right, only 51 years to wait for me. Because I'm 19, and my hotly anticipated new show is coming soon.

April 1st 2023
Randy Newman – You've Got a Friend in Me

I have many friends in stand-up. So many friends. And we are a particular type of friends because we are in a small group in the world who know what it's like to stand up in front of people and try to make them laugh and all the joy and terror and heartbreak that can bring and that cements us as very, very special friends. And I want to illustrate what our friendship means. If any one of them steps up on a microphone ever and says anything that could be conceived as offensive in any way and you are called out on it by the public whether in a justifiable or a totally over the top way I'll tell you where I'll be as a friend - nowhere fucking near you. That's what friendship is - I'll be nowhere fucking near you in person and I'll be nowhere fucking near you online because friendship on this level or indeed any level is utterly meaningless. Me saying I'm your friend is the same as saying I'm your total fucking stranger.

The only people that matter in this world are your partner, your parents your grandparents, your siblings and your kids. You don't truly care about anyone else. Oh that's not true Nathan – I'd die for my friend. Bullshit. On a 'I'd die for you' scale your friends are in the same bracket as your cousins. You wouldn't die for your friend you wouldn't even tweet for your friend if you thought it was going to affect your life or career in any negative way. This is the truth. You would die for your partner I believe you and how do I know you wouldn't do the same for your friend… when you split up with your partner or your wife or your husband when you have moved on or want to move on when the love has completely gone, when the feelings you have for them are stone cold dead, what is the best thing you can say to them. How do you let them down gently? But … we can still be friends. Bingo. You've lost all love, all affection for them, you don't really care about them at all, you definitely wouldn't die for them are you fucking crazy? And yet you could still be friends, because ultimately, friendship means fuck all. That is the truth and it's shown to be the truth again and again.

The word friend may as well not exist in the dictionary it may as well skip direct from foe to fuck off I never knew you at all.
But that said, it doesn't have to be like this. We could instead live in a world where friendship truly mattered and where kindness is the

cornerstone of existence. And all that we need to make that nirvana a reality is for us all right now to delete Twitter. Who's with me? I knew it. You were never my friends anyway.

DAILY NOTES VOL I

April 2nd 2023
Eyes Closed – Ed Sheeran

I love sleeping, I'm probably the best sleeper in that I can fall asleep within 30 seconds anywhere and everywhere. And so it's very tempting to fall asleep more than once a day because it's such a skill of mine. I'm sometimes in a situation where I can easily fall asleep like on a date in a cinema but it's wrongly I think frowned upon in this country the UK, if I was in Spain they expect you to fall asleep in the afternoon unless you're flying a plane, well let's face it you don't need a pilot to land a plane it's all automated now but people would stand over you if you were a pilot and asleep, they'd nudge you and tut.

And that's how I feel if it's the afternoon and I'm sleeping, I feel the worlds eyes on me tutting, I feel my grandparents eyes on me tutting, they never slept in the afternoon, I mean they did when they were in their 80s that's all they did I mean when they were my age, they didn't have the option to sleep they were slogging it, sleeping in the afternoon is a luxury and I will never ever take it for granted, I love it and I'm very, very grateful I get to do it. There are downsides, one main one – I think because I'm feeling guilty about my occasional afternoon nap, I'm falling asleep (within 30 seconds remember) with some anxiety so this transfers to some of the most fucked up dreams. I can be asleep for just 20 minutes, power nap, and some of the most hideous thoughts can enter my head, real nightmares. I wake up sometimes feeling refreshed but utterly terrified – I mean fucking hell, that dream was brutal.

Some dreams are fucking brutal, and often you can't remember dreams can you? And there's a good reason for that – if you did remember the detail of some of these brutal dreams, they would haunt your thoughts forever and you'd never be able to sleep again. But no terrifying dream could keep me from my sleep, I'm good at it, I love it and it's one in the eye for one of my good friends who has worked out I'm dying at 70 and so sends me birthday cards with for example… '7000 more sleeps', that was my card last year – 7000 more sleeps, well I've got news for this MF, it's at least 14000 more sleeps, and I'll have more naps if I can. And as I keep saying, because of this lifestyle, I know one thing. Whatever age you are, you'll be dead before me. Sleep nice.

DAILY NOTES VOL I

April 3rd 2023
All Of The Girls You Loved Before – Taylor Swift

Andrew Dice Clay – the Diceman – he's in *A Star is Born* the Bradley Cooper version as Lady Gaga's father. Blew my mind when I saw him in that, apparently he beat Robert DeNiro to the part, let's say that again - he beat Robert DeNiro to the part, and Ray Liotta. Anyway he's a standup comedian that wouldn't get anywhere near mainstream TV with his act because of past content regarded as offensive but he's popular, 1990 first comedian to sell out Madison Square Gardens for two consecutive nights.

Anyway, interesting character, divisive, one of his bits he goes up to a couple in the audience and he's generally sexist and offensive but they're both laughing because they've gone to see The Diceman that's what you expect when you go to see the Diceman, anyway he says to the guy – first time you banged her, was she good? And he says yeah pretty good, and then he says let me ask you one more question, how do you think she got good, and they both laugh, and then he says you know what I'm saying, stretch marks round the mouth. And they laugh more, they belly laugh. Now I'm not saying that I think that's good comedy but the belly laugh is missing from so much comedy now and we have to get that back, I laughed at something the other night that was so offensive but it was hilarious and I laughed in a way that I'd actually never laughed before, I was howling laughing, and it was upsetting and hilarious all at the same time. Let's not lose that.

Because if you turn up somewhere and pay to be offended then it's not offensive is it, no one turns up at the Diceman and doesn't expect him to be offensive. That's what you pay for, that's what you like, that's what sells out Madison Square Gardens twice. Here's the interesting thing, the only way Diceman could be offensive to you at a stand-up gig, is if he wasn't offensive. Work that one out. It's tricky because I get it kids can be influenced but my kid gets it, he knows what's offensive, let's not sanitize let's educate. Because when I saw the Diceman in *A Star is Born*, a load of people thought that's fucking cool. More people I'd imagine that if it was DeNiro. DeNiro the safe choice. Diceman the interesting one. Let's not stop being interesting.

DAILY NOTES VOL I

April 4th 2023
Miley Cyrus – Flowers

I can buy myself flowers – you can write my name in the sand – we've all done that, talk to myself for hours yeah, well, no actually, don't talk to yourself for hours I'll start to worry about you, I mean I'll start to worry about you after about fifteen seconds, ten seconds really that's the cut off for talking to yourself, hours of talking to yourself that's a serious issue, what are you doing both sides of the conversation? Hey Miley how are you, I'm fine Miley how are you? Are you fine Miley you're talking to yourself. But I guess she can get away with it as she's also Hannah Montana so could just take the wig disguise on and off. Anyway, no don't talk to yourself for hours and hours it's not healthy.

I can take myself dancing yeah, yes you can, better, that will make you feel good, release endorphins, I can hold my own hand… na Miley, again don't do that, what does that even mean, if you mean it literally then no don't do that, that's not gonna make you feel better, but maybe metaphorically, you mean you're going to masturbate, fair enough, that is often so much easier than falling in love and the logistics of bussing back and forward to dates – yeah I can love me better than you can, well probably not better, but almost as good, and when you factor in all the other hassle, the buying flowers, the dancing, the talking for hours, so dull, I think you're right Miley, I'm down with it, you're talking sense. We should go out for dinner maybe, oh no, that kind of negates the whole self-gratification thing cool, but let me buy you some flowers. As a thank you for cementing what I've always thought – because flowers fill you with so much love don't they, and they look beautiful, and they smell beautiful, and then they start to rot don't they and you try and trim and tidy but you can't hold off the inevitable and after a relatively short time they die and you have to throw them in the bin and try to forget about them and just go upstairs and masturbate.

And sometimes they say after masturbating you feel low, well I've got a little trick for that, after masturbating, just do what I do, and talk to yourself for hours. And I can now reveal this is what this book is, it's me talking to myself into a Dictaphone after daily masturbating, hope that makes you enjoy this more now.

DAILY NOTES VOL I

April 5th 2023
Whitney Houston – Greatest Love of All

Learning to love yourself is the greatest love of all. Oh Whitney, if only you practiced what you preached. Because we know we should love ourselves, but it's hard isn't it, and unfortunately the enjoyable things in life often cause us the most damage. And I'm not talking about the extreme things that did for Whitney, I'm talking about food. I was at the dentist again this week and they're done with telling me to drink juice through a straw like I'm 7, they're done with telling me to stay off sweets, now I have a weakness in a tooth I had a root canal so now its avoid eating any hard food. Avoid eating any hard food! That's what you say to someone in their 90's for fuck's sake. And do you get food stuck in your teeth Nathan? Well yes doesn't everyone? Show me your teeth mother fucker, how good are your teeth? What are you eating with all the millions that you're earning?

Anyway so the hygienist told me to get a Waterpik flosser, have you seen these things, have you used them, they're the next generation in flossing, new technology and what it is basically it's a water pistol, the water blasts out and shoots through the gaps in the teeth and expels all the bits of food, and yes it really works but it's humiliating because here I am, a man that's now not allowed any sugar, anything chewy, anything hard, so is pretty much on the kind of food I was on when I was weaning. What kind of restaurant would I like to go to? Maybe a weaning restaurant, the kind of restaurant you'd go to if you were weaning – yeah stewed apple no sugar, gravy that kind of thing. What would I like to drink? Breast milk through a straw please.

Anyway using this Waterpik is humiliating, standing there over the sink, water shooting everywhere, bits of old broccoli, there's no dignity, there's no getting ready for bed any more like Tom Cruise and Nicole Kidman in *Eyes Wide Shut*, it's gross. I'm gone, I'm a spent force. But at least I have my kids, and as Whitney says, the children are the future, and last night I walk in and my son has been having a water fight in my bedroom using my Waterpik flosser. Water everywhere, the little cock. So ignore this song, it's all bullshit, I know what I need right now, cocaine and a bath. Because that is undoubtedly the greatest love of all, and honestly there's no better way to clean your teeth.

DAILY NOTES VOL I

April 6th 2023
Ariana Grande – Break up with your girlfriend

My son is really into Ariana Grande obviously and he said if he went out with her he'd never split up with her, even if they didn't get on. And I'm like sure, you're fifteen of course you think that way, but looks aren't everything. And he said but daddy it's Ariana Grande, and it's a hard thing to explain but if Ariana Grande is annoying and I'm sure she isn't I'm sure she's really nice and the millions of pounds are nice as well, but if she - I don't know - if she ate with her mouth open or stank - I'm sure she doesn't - if she whistles like my stepdad, used to drive me actually insane, she can do one. And my son said well she does in a way her voice is so high – he's into singing – it's called the whistle register, the timbre of the notes is similar to a whistle. And I'm like bingo right there, however attractive she is, however many millions she has, if she started whistling around the house like my stepdad did for 8 years as I was clawing at the wall make it stop - you'd have to break up with her.

And he said bullshit and I said stop swearing you're 15. And he said you'll see, and I was like what does that mean? And I can only think he means that he's a wannabe musician and singer so maybe when he's 20 he's gonna meet Ariana Grande, she will have long separated from her current husband Dalton Gomez, she doesn't stick with people for long and come on, Dalton. Dalton? Anyway – he'll bring back his new girlfriend in 5 years, he'll be 20 and she'll be like 34 and he'll say look daddy Ariana Grande and I'll be like whatever, cool, I know celebrities I'm Nathan Cassidy and she will say oh my God, you're Nathan Cassidy, aren't you the star of Amazon Prime Specials Observational and Bumblebee? Yes I am, and she'll say, God this is awkward but… and I'll say let me stop you there Ariana, are you still doing that whistling register shite, no thank you, I've only invited you here tonight under the express conditions that you do not whistle, annoying. And my son will say stop it daddy you don't know what you're talking about and I'll say I do know what I'm talking about – whistling, scratching, coughing, clicking, picking, chewing, biting these are all things that scratch chew pick and bite into your soul and even if its Ariana Grande leave me alone, get out of my house, and son break up with your girlfriend. And she'll say oooohh – and I'll say was that a whistle? Get the fuck out!!

DAILY NOTES VOL I

April 7th 2023
I'll Be Waiting – Cian Ducrot

When I was 20, I got ill with an ME type thing, and I was unable to move for a few months, I lay on the bottom bunk and I would gouge words into the wooden slats of the top bunk. And they would say things like hope and dream, it was really the first example of the inspirational positive thinking quotes that people have on calendars and the like, that thinking back if I'd monetized would have made me an absolute fortune. Do one thing every day that scares you, that's a popular one. When I had this illness I went to a doctor and he said 'Nathan you might never get better'. That scared me to be honest, I'm not sure I want to be doing that every day, but I went home and I gouged the word 'hope' into the top bunk. And over the months I ran out of wood to gouge and I got a bit of strength and I started to write and I also was inspired by an episode of *Blue Peter*, a kids programme that I'd seen, about a time capsule, they were very big on digging up the earth and putting a box in there, a time capsule, telling people about how life used to be, and I thought that's good, but if I'm not around in the future to see if anyone spots it, then essentially I'm just burying rubbish in the ground.

So what I thought I'd do is what many people did back then I'd write letters to myself, about how I was feeling and what I wanted to achieve in my life and I thought I won't open them til I'm 50 and by then I will have got out of this bed, I will get better, and I will have achieved all the things I wanted to achieve, and it's a motivation isn't it, self-determinism – if I write it down, it's more likely to happen. Write down how low I am and high I want to be. And its 30 years later, and it's come to the time where I'm going to head into my mom's loft as I know she's still got all these things from when I was a kid and I'm going to open this door into the past - do one thing every day that scares you they say, well this absolutely terrifies me, because I really can't remember what I said, and what happens if I've achieved absolutely nothing off the list? What then? Well if that's the case, easy, I'll just do it again and write a load of new notes for when I'm 80, and this time I'm gonna make it easy for myself - eat raspberry magnums and cuddle someone you love, there's nothing else that matters. I'm saying that to make myself feel better when I read from these notes and discover I've achieved nothing. And that in a nutshell is what positive thinking is all about.

DAILY NOTES VOL I

April 8th 2023
Tiesto Featuring Tate McRae – 10:35

I watched a lot of TV when I was a kid, far too much, but my parents were never ones to say stop me watching too much TV because life is about just getting through the day and not dying that's all that really matters, there are people dying in the world, and as long as we're not one of those people dying then we're fine. Forgetting of course that one day death is inevitable so you have one chance to fill the non-dying days with more interesting stuff than consuming television. And of course there's good television but I'd say 98% is pointless, it's an industry paid vast sums to make shit to feed to people to keep them lazy, its McDonalds. And when I was an older teenager, and I was off school, or at University there was a programme called *This Morning* and it started at 10:35 and it would take you all the way through to 12:15, so that's nearly 2 hours of programmes every day, and there's so much television like this, and what were the things on this programme – I have absolutely no idea, I can't remember one thing I watched because of course it washes over you – it's an interview with the latest vapid celebrity flogging their latest perfume, it's a cooking feature with someone making spaghetti bolognaise because we're all morons, it's a quiz where you get to win your gas bill and worst of all it's the gurning, grinning presenters pretending that life is ok. It isn't ok, I'm watching *This Morning*, and you're trying to trick me into watching bullshit so I can watch the adverts that are paying for the bullshit that will make me buy more bullshit.

And back in the day there was a presenter Judy Finnegan and I was obsessed with her, because she bucked the trend completely with this kind of television, she never once looked comfortable, she never once looked like she wanted to be there, and it came out later she hated it, really she was only there because her husband Richard Madeley was the co-presenter but the more I watched her the more I thought the person feeding me this bullshit knows it's wrong, knows it's pointless, you could hear her silently screaming 'switch off, don't listen'. And to this day, she is probably the only genuine presenter I've ever seen on television. Because every day she said silently 'This is bullshit, and you only have to look as far as my face to see it.' Everyone else feeding us bullshit with those plastered on grins - you're lying, get real, you're fooling no one.

DAILY NOTES VOL I

April 9th 2023
Superhero (Heroes & Villains) – Metro Boomin, Future & Chris Brown

It's my birthday, and I really feel like a superhero. What a very, very, very special day it is. And as you get older the worst thing is the comedy birthday cards… 'in dog years you'd be dead' – that's anything over 17 you prick - one I genuinely got last year from a friend – 'one year closer to the grave' – I said sure mate, I'll let you send that to me if you also send it to your 2 children, because if it's true for me it's equally true for your three year old daughter. Happy birthdays sweet pea, one year closer to the child sized grave.

And it's not a big birthday, you know what I'm saying there, a birthday with a zero in it – one decade closer to the grave, so say it quietly, I don't give a fuck it's my birthday, really for the first time this year any residual giving a fuck has gone, because it's just one year closer to the grave – why are we celebrating that? But of course you have to pander to everyone that wants to buy you stuff, which as you get older is usually stuff that reminds you you're getting older – here's some moisturiser, some hair thickener, I was given a running magazine last year with the headline – 'run your belly off'. Fuck off.

Aging is an inevitability and I do not fear it, I welcome it, I'm lucky to age but that does not mean necessarily I want to celebrate it with a shit cake where the only thing I'll get out of it is the next day having to run my belly off. But all that said, if people didn't make an effort, I'd be mortified, I'm counting my Facebook happy birthdays of course I am, it was less than last year - is that just people don't love me or is it the fucking algorithm? Love me, buy me a card, I don't care what it says it could say 'happy birthday statistically you could die of old age this year' and it would be fine, just love me.

This is big, it's not a big birthday but it a big birthday because every year is a big birthday, I might only have a few left, I'm one year closer to the grave remember, so don't waste your chance, there's still time to give, go to my website, there's so many ways to give me money, buy my shit, don't delay, people were giving generously to me all the time during the pandemic, and fuck all recently. Get back on that. This is bigger than a global pandemic, this is MY FUCKING BIRTHDAY!!

DAILY NOTES VOL I

April 10th 2023
A Hundred Miles – Heather Morgan

Series 3 – Episode 100. And the quality keeps up doesn't it? Quite remarkable. All killer hardly any fiiiilllleeerrrrrr. Filler filler filler filler filler filler. And people say Nathan after 2 series and 100 episodes, 830 episodes in total, how on earth are you generating ideas? Well I'll tell you it is getting more difficult, in fact today I have run out of ideas completely which is disappointing as it's the special episode 100 of episode 3 and as I said yesterday on my birthday everyone loves a round number don't they? But in today's world, you can never run out of ideas because of Chat GPT, the AI text generator, give it anything and it spits out auto generated content, it's a marvel.

So I went to chat GPT today and I stuck in my email and then password and lo and behold it came back with something I could never have come up with myself – it said, in red letters 'Sign-up is currently unavailable, please try again later'. Genius right, the world is talking about it and now I see it in action I see why – 'sign-up is currently unavailable – please try again later'. Good God that's good, just when I thought I had nothing left in the tank, Chat GPT to the rescue. And you know what, I don't think I'll be going back for another try.

Because do we want machines to take over the one remaining thing we have - independent thought? Of course we don't, and when Chat GPT failed me I realised that was a sign, to re-energise myself for another 830 episodes, and double down on this podcast, I don't mean make the episodes twice as long, remember in the first season where the episodes were always 10 minutes or more, how the hell did I do that, literally how on earth did I do that? What I mean is today to mark the 100th episode I'm launching today a new service where you can sign up to it and like on *Only Fans* I'll send you a personalised video message completely naked. Completely naked, you'll be able to see everything – knees, penis, whatever you want.

The only bad news is that sign up is currently unavailable, please try again later. That's sign up is currently unavailable please try again later, tomorrow and the next day, forever.

DAILY NOTES VOL I

April 11th 2023
Thinkin' Bout Me – Morgan Wallen

My comedy has become introspective, and that's not good maybe, the issue becomes when I'm trying to make it about you and what you think and feel it becomes for me a bit hack, because I'm automatically generalising, I don't know what you're thinking, and even if 99% of people think this way then I'm going to be leaving people out and I don't want to leave anyone out, and I feel that if I talk about me then that's not leaving anyone out but is it in fact leaving everyone out, because I use this podcast and most of my stand-up to tell you how I feel about stuff, what about the way you feel? That's what I think. And then I watched a quiz show today, and the host asked one of the contestants, they were in couples, what do you do in your spare time, and she said, well we mainly do escape rooms. I'm like oh fucking hell, really, that's what we do is it, he didn't ask you what you both do, what do you do, or have you stopped being an individual now you're married, ok what you both do, the main and seemingly only thing you like doing is escape rooms - what being put in a locked room where the only way out is by solving puzzles, or just by sitting there for an hour or whatever your allotted time is and then being let out, because you're gonna be let out aren't you, there is no jeopardy, oh we really like the horror ones, the Saw ones… great, get back to me when there is any chance in any of your rooms of your foot actually being sawn off, then you'll have an anecdote, then you will have a story my friend, and that's why I can't make these about you because I seriously do not know who you are, what motivates you, because you might be listening to this thinking ah you're being a bit harsh about that lovely couple that just love doing escape rooms - no you don't get it, this is why I do this about me, because its sometimes only me that gets it but I hope you do too, we are all living in one big escape room, of which there is no escape, we get to live in this fun scary glorious horrible horrifying beautiful escape room for real, you do not need to manufacture and pay for a miniature version, I will never understand you and I need to escape and be alone with my own thoughts, I need to escape, but I can only escape if I solve the riddle if I can work out 9x9 divided by 2 and times that by the amount I give a shit about what you morons think. Oh I know the answer - zero. It's all my thoughts I'm afraid, from that there is no escape. Apart from this one is finished now, you're free to go.

DAILY NOTES VOL I

April 12th 2023
Toosli – Favorite Song

My favourite songs to listen to are often the slow songs, when I listen to music I want to be what we all secretly want to be, depressed – give me *Tears from Heaven* any day – give me a song about death that makes me imagine death in the saddest possible way – that's what music is for me. But not when I'm driving of course, particularly on the motorway, because like many of us I need fast music to keep me awake. Ah the motorway, the interstate, the autobahn, huge tonnes of metal hurtling down a runway at 100mph driven by people falling asleep. Most people are just desperately trying to stay awake on a motorway, motorway of course short for monotorway – hours and hours of monotony mixed with a real sense of danger so you are only ever seconds from death. So of course, to decrease the chance of falling asleep you play fast music. However that is what you shouldn't do as fast music makes you want to drive faster – and that's what I learned on my speed awareness course this week when I was caught doing 72MPH on a stretch of motorway where the speed limit is 70MP – indeed, lets concentrate on the serious crime guys – listen to slow music to slow you down, so in short they'd rather want me asleep and dead than speeding.

But I get it, we all need to slow down on the roads, they're very dangerous, we could die, but if I was to be in an accident, heaven forbid, you know they say your life flashes before your eyes, mine would and I know what I'd see, I wouldn't see my children's faces, all my many awards and to a lesser extent people I love, I'd see all the faces of all the people in all my speed awareness courses who wouldn't shut the fuck up - shut the fuck up, I want to get out of this, yes I get it go slowly on the motorway, but in the speed awareness course go as quickly as possible, keep your head down and drive and we'll be out of here – it's like these people are sitting in their houses waiting for this opportunity to talk - no I do not want to know your driving playlist of slow songs you boring bastard, this is more monotonous than route 66.

Stick Queen's *Don't Stop Me Now* on, I'm nodding off but let's hope for the best. That said, I've been on about ten of these courses now, drive safely, go slowly, don't be a dick and listen to *Tears from Heaven* on repeat.

DAILY NOTES VOL I

April 13th 2023
Hozier – All Things End

One thing I've not really talked about in all 832 episodes of this podcast is my love for the game of snooker. I love it, you may be aware of the World Championships of snooker I travel there most years and watch games, I always watch the matches on the TV, I'm slightly obsessed. And what I'm obsessed about are the personalities, because snooker players more than any other sportsmen, like great musicians I guess, you know they had to spend a hell of a lot of their childhoods doing very, very repetitive things on their own, which develops a certain personality – these people have spent most of their childhoods in dark rooms trying to get balls into pockets with a stick, and now they are paid hundreds of thousands of pounds to do that.

They are treated like superstars and given nicknames like boxers that they can never live up to – some can, famously Hurricane Higgins and Whirlwind Jimmy White, they lived up to their names, fast around the snooker table and fast in life, but for example Mark Selby, his nickname is The Jester from Leicester and as far as I'm aware he has never cracked a single joke on or off the table. He doesn't have time for jokes because he's dedicated his whole life to potting balls into little pockets with his big wooden stick. But most fascinatingly of all for me, is when these top sportsmen and that's what they are, they get to about 40, 45, they suddenly become completely shit at snooker. They're terrible at it, they couldn't pot a cow's arse with a banjo, and of course most sportsmen go this way in their 40s but with snooker it's particularly cruel, because there's no physical reason why you should stop being good at it, it should be like stand-up the more you do it the better you get, but for some reason with snooker they suddenly get shit, but because it's all they know they keep playing for another ten to fifteen years, getting beaten by teenagers who are often ten times better than they ever were, its horrific and beautiful to watch, its hopes and dreams, aging, refusal to give up and above all, an absolute assurance that all things end.

And that isn't sad, that's just life, and after all, life is just a game.

DAILY NOTES VOL I

April 14th 2023
Elton John – Goodbye Yellow Brick Road (Live)

Last night I was at the O2 watching Elton John's farewell tour Goodbye Yellow Brick Road and it's an amazing concert, his final big arena shows, a retrospective of his career, oh my goodness what a show. This is your last chance to see him in a big arena like this, incredible, and we were lucky enough to have great seats with a perfect view of the stage on ground level, and he's on stage from 730 to 10.15 - 2 ¾ hours of brilliant entertainment, and then about 20 mins before the end the couple in front of us just left and the guy said yeah that's about it we can beat the rush and they just left, they missed the final 15/20 mins, what the hell? What are you doing?

We've all waited about 4 years for this concert because of Covid and his hip problem, to even get the tickets you'd have paid £100 or more and you'd have had to be first in the queue to get them and you're leaving before the end because you want to beat the rush – the rush is a like 10 minute delay – that's the rush – let's call it what it is – it's not the rush it's just a queue to get down the escalators for the underground, no one is rushing, there is no rush, what you're avoiding is a 10 minute wait for an escalator by missing the end of the concert and anyone that knows anything about anything, the end is the best bit, the end of everything is the best bit, that's what it's all leading up to, it's the end bit, the emotional bit where he says it's the end, I mean obviously he's got lots more of these concerts around the country but to you it's the end, goodbye yellow brick road, and you've tapped out before you've even seen the wizard – oh I can't be bothered to see the wizard, and why, because I don't want a heart, or brains, or courage I just want to vegetate in the long grass, the only thing I care about is beating the fucking rush, oh the rush, the awful, evil rush, the wicked witch of the rush, that terrifying 7-10 minute wait to go do the escalator that I can avoid by never doing anything special in my life.

I just want to get to my grave quicker, no passion, no excitement, just get me into that grave, I just want to beat the mother fucking rush.

DAILY NOTES VOL I

April 15th 2023
Whitney Houston – I'm Your Baby Tonight

You're having a baby – oh that's brilliant, that really is brilliant, and you go to all the NCT pre-natal classes and they tell you what it's like to have a baby and you go oh that's great we're having a baby and you read the books and you make friends with people that after a few years you'll never see again because the kids have moved schools and you're only friends because the kids went to the same schools and here you are ready to have a baby. And then one afternoon you have the baby, I mean I don't but you do, and you're panicking and on the way to get something from the car you come as close as you ever have to dying in a car accident, I mean that would have been a story wouldn't it worthy of a soap opera, anyway you have the baby and it comes out and it's like what the fuck is that and you think to yourself no this is it, this is what having a baby is, this is the baby, and the nurses are all great and act like this is the first time this has ever happened in the hospital as opposed to what it is which is basically KFC for babies, a big old baby fast food factory chucking out endless stupid babies, and after a couple of hours they stick you in the back of a cab and say fuck off and never come back until you inevitably have a second and if you're mental and want to guarantee your relationship is fucked a third and then you get home, and you're knackered and overwhelmed and then the first night you lay the baby on a mat between you on your bed, because you want the baby close and you lie down next to your baby and everyone I guarantee has the same feeling – what the fuck have I done, what the fuck have I done, my life will never be the same again, fuuuuck!

I'm your baby tonight. Fuuuuck. It gets better after that, and worse, and better, and worse, but that first night I will never ever forget. I've forgotten almost the entirety of my children's childhoods, you have to, you have to block it out because it's so awful and boring, but that first night you will never ever forget. Your entire life has been a lie, you thought you knew what it was about, and then there's this, that instantly becomes your life. The only thing that matters is keeping this thing alive. Everything else can die – your hopes, ambitions, certainly your relationship that's already dead. The only thing you have left is this screaming little warm bundle of shit and tears. Fuuuuuck

DAILY NOTES VOL I

April 16th 2023
I'm Still Standing – Elton John

One more thing on Elton John. And I love Elton John I really do. But the merch. The merch Elton. Do you really need to charge so much for the merch. And it's not just the merch at the concert, he has a pop up shop in Selfridges in London – box of chocolates £40, sunglasses £200, rugs £500, t-shirt £300, purses £1700, luggage £1900, robe £1750, suit £3500, and worse a candle for £250, a show candle for £250 which of course would not still be standing once you've used it because once you've used it its gone, it's something for £250 you literally set fire to it. I mean I don't get candles generally, people spend a lot of money on candles but surely not £250, Jesus Christ, you better hope that candle is in the wind so it blows out and lasts a bit longer. Oh but don't be silly Nathan it's so special I'd never use it as an actual candle – then why are you buying it then you silly prick? How much money do you have? You're burning your money, well you're not burning it but you know what I mean. And then again, as I said to someone the other day in quite a shitty way I can spend my money on what I like thank you very much, so many people drink and smoke, I do neither, 90% of people spend all their money on booze and fags, if the remainder of us want to spend our money on wax that we burn into a pool of hot waxy broth then fair do's, and yes there are people dying in the world but they are not gonna be helped by wax, if anything they'd be disappointed because they'd think oh look at that lovely shoe, finally I can have shoes on my feet and look they're lovely, they're like Elton John's shoes and they're white and oh fuck they're candles, why are you taunting us Elton, we need food and not a £40 box of chocolates I don't give a fuck that the box is shaped like a piano, you don't keep the box do you, you burn the box with the candle. You know what fuck it, I need to calm down, I'm gonna buy some booze and fags and just set fire to my remaining money with my lighter, I'm gonna buy that £3500 suit, pack my £1900 suitcase and turn up at Elton John's house and just stand outside, yeah I'm still standing outside your house Elton, look at how ridiculous I look, in this garish suit with my feet wedged into two shoe candles – but this is what you get when you charge the world for stuff that you burn – you get me mad Elton, and I'll still be standing here until you refund me and take this shit off the shelves – don't you have enough money and don't mention your fucking AIDS foundation, fuck me sideways.

DAILY NOTES VOL I

April 17th 2023
Next Thing You Know – Jordan Davis

Whenever anyone says 'next thing you know', they are about to wildly speculate and probably say something a bit racist. You let some of them in, next thing you know, they've taken over, they've got our jobs, next thing you know, they're governing us, next thing you know they're our facking royal family. And always of course the next thing you know never happens as its always a worst case scenario in some reactionary prick's head that just wants to mouth off and control their little corner of the world.

And we need to stop these reactionary racist bigots because if one of them says something racist or whatever online then the next thing you know, all their friends start to do it, and the next thing you know, the whole country starts to do it and then the next thing you know, the whole world is full of hatred and you really don't have to look too far for the reasons for all the world's problems as it's all around us and it's more than probably within ourselves – hatred for others based on an inherent fear, an inherent loneliness, a basic and fundamental unhappiness about our own lives that makes us take it out on others.

So how can we turn this around? Well we can look at our own lives and think, there are 9 billion people on this planet, what makes us special, and the answer is nothing, the chances of us being anything special are by the nature of odds billions to one so pretty much zero, so once we accept that we are not special then the next thing you know if you can convince your friends that they're not special, you know all your friends that ponce around pretending to be someone, they're really nothing in the great scheme of things, and then the next thing you know you've convinced the whole country they're not up to much and the next thing you know the whole world realises that they aren't going to amount to anything so the next thing you know they stop being bitter about others and shut the fuck up. So we have to start somewhere and so I'm here to tell you today you aren't special and all that angst and bitterness about not achieving what you want to achieve, its wasted effort, you were never going to be anything anyway. Oh my God how freeing, how liberating, you suddenly hate no one because you are no one you are free. And now you're free, the next thing you know, you really could be someone.

DAILY NOTES VOL I

April 18th 2023
Drake & 21 Savage – Spin Bout U

I've never been to a spin class, but I can imagine how awful it is. Ooh let's turn the lights out and put neon on the bike wheels and then all get on our little exercise bikes and cycle along to music and the chief cunt shouting at us. Really truly dreadful. There were no spin classes 100 years ago of course, our ancestors would have thought we were totally mental, and of course we are. They would have said about exercising – just get off your arse, walk around, go about your life, eat sensibly and you'll be fine – and if you want to ride a bike, I've got a good idea, ride a fucking bike, it sounds crazy but if you want to ride a bike then ride a fucking bike. And I know what you're thinking, some people don't have a bike, well if that's the case, don't ride a bike. Don't ride a bike and have a walk or a run or if you want to go on an exercise bike buy an exercise bike for the price of one session at a spin class.

Oh no but I do hot pod spin class – what's that – that's spin class in a sauna. Is that right – yeah? Well you're a dick as well aren't you? These aren't real things – they've just been made up to give people a reason to spend money. I tell you what my grandma spent her money on - getting to work, coming home and food. That's it – she is my ancestor, and her and all my ancestors before her that's what you spent your money on and in 40 years we've come so far down the road to hell we're are willingly recreating hell for ourselves by cycling on the spot while someone shouts at us in a furnace. Stop it. Just grow up and stop it

And people say oh Nathan you don't know what something is like until you've done, true, but I know something is shit without doing it – I've never jumped off a cliff but I know that would be a bit shit, but not as shit as spin class, unless it was at night, the cliff was lined with neon and someone was shouting at me jump, jump, come on keep it moving jump. And that's, as they say, what's coming next.

Next thing you know it will be 'jump off a cliff' classes and we'll all sign up like the useless brain-dead lemmings we are.

DAILY NOTES VOL I

April 19th 2023
One Too Many – Keith Urban & Pink

So there's one too many morons isn't there wherever you go. This week I went to watch a brilliant new musical *The Secret Life Of Bees* at the Almeida theatre London and it's a brilliant new musical, really great, the songs were great, the choreography, the acting, the directing and it was mainly women but there was this great guy in it who had a recurring funny storyline of asking someone to marry him and the person he was asking would always turn him down, and it was sweet, set in the 1960s, and it got to a bit where at the end of the musical he has one last shot, he sings this brilliant song and he gets down on one knee and she's wavering and he says so what do you say, and there's a dramatic pause, there's tension, and then someone's phone goes off – the loudest, worst possible alarm tone, apart from if it was Crazy Frog. The crowd gasps, and the guy is there with his partner and its awful for the twat in the crowd too of course as he scrabbles around his pockets more panicked than he'd ever been in his life and seconds go by and the cast have paused and its excruciating and eventually he stops the alarm. What is the cast going to do – are they going to mention it?

Well they didn't and I wished they had, because there are documented examples of someone stopping a performance to have a go at an audience member, I mean this wasn't even a phone call remember, I mean that would be bad enough, you're given countless warnings and you just know don't you by now, there really are no excuses, but this was an alarm, going off at 10 o'clock at night, why is his alarm going off at 10 o'clock at night, does he work nights, is he a drug dealer, both could explain why he's a dopy cunt that has left his alarm on in a theatre show. I mean he was unlucky, this was the worst possible moment, and the pause that seemed like it was going on forever was finally pierced with her saying yes I will marry you and they embraced, and all was well again, and I looked over at the couple in the audience, and the woman, eyes of daggers, staring at her partner, and I wondered just in that moment where actually we had two people on stage getting together and two people in the audience splitting up, because for me there would be no way back. If you're going to leave your alarm on in a theatre show, what else are you going to? You're stupid, you're ignorant, and it's over. That's what I would have done, I'd have waited til after the show, got down on one knee and said you're a twat, you're dumped. One too many dicks in my life. Alarm bells indeed.

DAILY NOTES VOL I

April 20th 2023
Whitney Houston – I Have Nothing

My favourite place in America – Nevada, the deserts of Nevada. Because you know what I love most – nothing – that's why I'm growing to love this book – you're essentially reading nothing – brilliant isn't it? That's what you're doing looking at TikTok – you think you're looking at people falling over and jiggling tits but actually you're looking at nothing. But I don't need Tik Tok I just need a straight desert road and I can close my eyes and scroll through in my mind what I would be seeing on TikTok and all the times I've seen people fall over and jiggling tits.

The nothingness is awesome isn't it, what would we do without nothing? It's like oxygen – it keeps us alive. When I'm very, very old and in my final years I want to be near a beach. I know now why people want to be near a beach when they get close to death. Because in those final years you know nothing is coming so you want to prepare yourself for nothing. I want to be like Jonny Utah and end up in a beautiful Beach in Australia, looking at nothing, doing nothing, not even a facial expression – nothing, I'll be like Keanu Reeves in any movie.

It's gonna be so beautiful. Me, an old man, on a beach. I'll probably fall over and my old man droopy tits will jiggle, it will be hilarious and at the same time it will be nothing. Everything is over-rated apart from nothing – and if you have nothing you have everything. Think about all the poor people that have nothing, they also have everything. Because nothing has value, all the wealthy people are striving for everything and will never get there so they will have nothing. It's only the people that have nothing and are happy with nothing that will ever be happy in this life.

And that is why I constantly strive for nothing, and don't get me wrong, its hard work, because if you have less than nothing then that's the worst feeling in the world, just get me back to nothing and keep me there forever. Because only nothing truly lasts for an eternity.

Read this last sentence carefully, it's nothing, but it's beautiful.

DAILY NOTES VOL I

April 21st 2023
Wait in The Truck – HARDY Featuring Lainey Wilson

You know the job that fascinates me the most – lorry driver, truck driver, I've met a few in my time on speed awareness courses and they're a particular type of human, very matter of fact, but more than that they talk about other stupid drivers on the roads, and of course there are many, but the few that I've met seem to delight in the fact that because of the weight of their truck or lorry if someone cuts them up or whatever then they've got no chance of stopping and will just plough into them and kill them. Now I'm not saying they want to kill people on the roads, but they kind of get off on the fact that they can.

I mean look we all feel more powerful behind the wheel don't we, get out of my fucking way, fuck you, suck my dick etc, imagine what it's like driving a massive truck, with a big trailer on the back. For those that have never done this, have you ever driven a slightly bigger vehicle than the one you're used to like a van or whatever, it's weird isn't it, it's hard, imagine driving a truck, or a bus, we don't give these people the credit they deserve, they're driving things that look like they should be on the set of *Star Wars*. And this will blow your mind – these people are just human beings, they're human beings like you or I but they have been given these huge pieces of machinery that weigh a tonne and they are legally allowed to hurtle them at speeds that the vehicles definitely can't cope with, knackered and almost certainly pissed down a motorway. Is it really any wonder that they develop a God complex and delight in the thought of killing people?

But just like God who kills lots of people every day, they don't seem to mind - as God would say, shit happens if you're a prick. Shit happens, that's what God would say. They are powerful people just like God, it's understandable, people may get killed and if you're a lorry driver I mean particularly prostitutes, I've said it before and I'll say it again, the shocking and true percentage of lorry and truck drivers that kill prostitutes – 100%. It's what they do and it's what God does, they kill and kill again - bow down and respect them, truck drivers are our Gods.

April 22nd 2023
Eat Your Young – Hozier

Lots of animals eat their young, lions, hippopotamus, hamsters, spiders, toads, praying mantis, and scarily our closest animal relatives, chimpanzees. Oh yeah, our closest animal relatives can be brutal as fuck. Who would have thought that, because us humans aren't hideous at all are we, we've evolved so far that we don't in the main kill our own young. However, there is very little otherwise that we don't kill. We kill fucking everything don't we the humans, because we have found a use for every single living breathing thing on the planet – we either wanna eat it, wear it, sit on it or fuck it.

Oh we don't kill and eat our own young – how civilized are humans? Not civilized at all. Jesus, there is a thing you may or may not have heard of where you are in the world called The Grand National where about 40 horses are run full pelt at fences until several of them crash into the fences and break their bones and have to be killed on the track, and the one who's left not killed by the end of the race is the winner. Mental. And the people defending this race, the humans defending the race say that well all sport is dangerous – not sure that's true I haven't seen many people dying in snooker, or darts, or football hardly ever. The Grand National stands alone doesn't it – those horses get killed every time, and they say no I mean Formula 1 that's dangerous isn't it we can't make everything safe, yeah I get that but that would only be analogous if the Formula 1 drivers tied their pet dogs to the car bonnets, because of course horses don't have the choice do they, they are told they have to do this, they can't tap out they have to run full pelt at fences and hope for the best.

But you know what, if they weren't doing that we'd be eating, wearing, sitting on or fucking them so maybe horses have got the best of all of the options, at least we don't eat horses in this country generally, or wear them, or sit on them, like we do with everything else. But humans are still the most civilized animal because we don't eat our young. I swear this is true, if we all ate a baby or two, and stopped The Grand National, the world wouldn't necessarily be a better place, but it would be just a tad more pleasurable for horses, but who gives a fuck about horses anyway, not me, because I'm a fucking human. Anyway in short, I've lost my bet again. Total fucking waste of time.

DAILY NOTES VOL I

April 23rd 2023
ABBA – Honey, Honey

What do you call your partner, your boyfriend, your girlfriend? Babe, honey, pooky bear, or by their name? When you've been someone for any length of time, the name goes out the window doesn't it, absolutely irrelevant because we all have a different name for someone, it's usually baby, let's not think about that for too long, but that what it usually is, baby, and that works for everyone doesn't it. And I'll tell you why it works for everyone, because it totally gets rid of the chances of calling the most special person in your life by the wrong name, which many of you will have done and is the very worst thing you can do to your loved one.

And it's made all the more hard because everyone has a similar name don't they – I was talking to a 20 year old the other day, he's got 3 girls on the go at the moment, I think it's all fine, everyone knows about everyone but the names are Mollie, Millie and Ellie – I mean that's a fucking minefield isn't it, you don't wanna go near names when the names are Mollie, Millie and Ellie, it's like an impossible puzzle that you can never win - there is only disaster with Mollie, Millie and Ellie. But the names don't even have to be similar, the name of the previous person you were with is burning a mark in your brain and you're desperate to shout it out aren't you, but it's a name that would be the death knell of you current relationship, so that's why you go with baby every time isn't it, so next time you hear I love you baby – know what they are doing – they are calling you baby so it avoids mentioning the name of the previous person that they also called baby and never referred to them by their name but now their name is the name in their head when they're about to call your name its on the tip of their tongue and your relationship will stand and fall based on whether they say this name or not.

Know this baby, know this honey honey, know this pooky bear that your relationship is always hanging by this thinnest of thin threads. And you know what, how about you just do it anyway, call your loved one by your ex's name and see what happens, fuck, what a ride, you can fuck things up forever at any second – do it, do it baby, baby baby baby, what a rush.

DAILY NOTES VOL I

April 24th 2023
Reach – S-Club7

Well it was very sad that one of the bands of my younger years S-Club 7 lost one of its members recently Paul Cattermole and it's very sad when anyone dies young and they'd just announced a new tour this band and of course they should go ahead with it as a tribute to Paul and obviously the songs will be nothing without Paul and the concert will be rubbish without Paul but all the fans should pay their money and sit through a bad concert with bad singing as a tribute to Paul.

And a lesser person would say that Paul not being there would make an almost insignificant difference to the songs and I am that person but that's not to say that an almost insignificant positive difference is an irrelevant one. Because the other reason the fans should go to these concerts with S Club 6 if they go ahead, is because first time around this band and bands like them, there were loads of bands like this 20 years ago, they made fuck all, they were incredibly successful, hits everywhere but the management took all the money and they should be ashamed of themselves and if band members get fucked up over the years and suffer bankruptcy and mental health problems partly due to a lack of money and then die then these ex-managers have blood on their hands.

How much money do you need, how much money is enough that you don't give a fuck about the people earning the money for you? Surely once you have enough money to do everything you want then it will make you feel better wouldn't it to give a bit back to the people making it for you? But no of course, because these people don't want to reach for the stars, they want to fuck up the stars, they want to create stars and then fuck them up. On the next clear night, look up to the stars and if you can get off your phone for 5 seconds, look at the stars and then realise how insignificant you are in this universe and how privileged you are to be involved, and all we can do, is try in a very small way to make the universe a better place, to make a tiny almost insignificant but positive difference.

And if you can do that, that's when the rainbow will shine on you, and only then will all our dreams really come true.

April 25th 2023
ICU – Coco Jones

Covid's over isn't it, we're done with that now aren't we? We're done with Covid right? Someone I heard had Covid the other week. I'm like, how do you know? Are you still testing for Covid? It's a cold Goddammit, people still wearing masks, grow the fuck up. But of course the scars still remain for many, those who saw their loved ones taken into ICU and didn't make it or even worse couldn't see their loved ones taken to ICU because they weren't allowed into the hospital because of, well the rules. Remember the rules. Remember we all followed the rules apart from the people that made the rules, certainly in this country but probably in yours no doubt too. The people making the rules, the people enforcing the rules don't follow the rules do they?

And since Covid's over this hasn't been tested has it, but it will, and I'm waiting for this moment with bated breath. Because next time I'd imagine we will all say as one - fuck the rules - and it's gonna be an interesting moment isn't it, when the governments try and tell us what to do – er fuck that, how did that work out last time – we couldn't go see our loved ones dying as you guys partied and fucked your bit on the side in a corridor – fuck that – ICU, ICU my friend, I see what you're trying to do and this time we won't have it

I cannot wait for collective rule to tip the balance against the authorities, then we're gonna have some fun, because governments are what a few hundred people, the police a few thousand, we're millions, you literally can't stop us doing what we like if we're all or most of us are of one mind, you won't be able to stop us. And I pray for that, because it doesn't even have to be violent, it doesn't even have to be angry, if we all agree, next time this shit happens, we can all just say calmly but firmly - no, not this time, no ICU, I see what you're trying to do, but no.

And this is why I do not fear another Pandemic, and nor should you. The tide has turned, I just wanna see the waves crashing now into the people that deserve it the most.

DAILY NOTES VOL I

April 26th 2023
Niall Horan – Heaven

You're heaven Niall Horan, always the one least likely to have a sexy solo career off the back of One Direction, the ginger Irish one, is he ginger? He's certainly Irish. But here is he with another almost hit single, Heaven and a new album out in June called *The Show*. And it's not just a show to call your song Heaven because Niall is of course a good Catholic boy and is godfather of his nephew. Oh the godfather, the godmother, it's a choice that many parents have to make when their children are born even if they're not religious at all, it's something you do isn't it, it's a big deal, who's the godfather, the godmother? Oh my, you're asking me to be godfather, oh my God that's so special, that means so much. And of course, without any level of cynicism at all, it also means fuck all. Absolutely fuck all, its meaningless. Oh no Nathan it means that in the event of death of both their parents, carry on with this happy story, in the event of the death of both the parents the godfather or godmother would take the kids – no they wouldn't – that's an absolute fallacy – let's face it if you have parents they would take the kids, there ain't no friend on earth that would want to bring up your kids, that ain't gonna happen.

So then why have a godfather or mother, well it's a nice thing isn't it, it's a way of later in life saying to someone you are my best friend, or at least the best friend I have that I could theoretically even though as I say it's never gonna happen, look after my kids. I have another best friend, but they are too cool to be trusted with my kids, you because you're boring and have kids already I can trust you to be bestowed with this pointless honour. But there's another reason why you choose someone isn't there – come on, you know what I'm talking about – they're minted right. The godfather or godmother is minted and you're saying to them you're a special minted person, come on, let's have some bigger presents from you. Yeah, right, in my experience that lasts about a year and then they couldn't give a fuck about your kid, they couldn't give a fuck about their godson or goddaughter, the only thing they love about their godson or goddaughter is they don't have to bring them up and there is absolutely no chance of bringing up another person's kids, which would be a fucking nightmare. So next time you think you're having a bad day, remember this – you're not bringing up someone else's kid. And you're not listening to Niall Horan – heaven.

DAILY NOTES VOL I

April 27th 2023
Golden Hour – JVKE

What's the sweet spot in your life? The golden hour? Where everything slows down and you're in love and you're having the best time of your life. Well we all know the answer to that don't we, it's when you're 20. Oh fuck it's when you're 20 isn't it, being 20 is fucking amazing – you've left home, I mean back in my day you had, now you're living with your parents until they die and you're in your 40s but in my day you'd left home, you could do all the things adults do, you could have relationships and you could fall in love, that golden hour, where time slows down and you're in love and you realise you've got your whole life ahead of you.

It's 20 isn't it, not a care in the world, you're at University, money is free, it is – money is free – you don't have to sit in an office or work on a lathe to make money – money is free from the government isn't it – they give you free money, yes they call it a loan, a student loan but you never have to pay these things back, grow up, this is free money, and its free love, it's the golden hour, time stands still, the light shines upon you and you're free.

Now, let's not dwell on the fact that as soon as you start work and your relationships goes to shit that you realise the golden hour is just that, an hour of your life, and the majority of your life is hard and rubbish, let's not dwell on that, we all know that's the case, let's look back at that golden hour and work out what was so golden about it – you were in love, you didn't have a care in the world, you had free money and you had your whole life ahead of you. Well, good news, this can be recreated, whatever time in life you are – you can be in love for today - just lower the bar, give that person a call, get out there, no care in the world – get drunk, forget about your cares, free money – stick it all on a credit card, it's fine, free money is there for you today and your whole life ahead of you. Well that's the thing you see it's a fallacy isn't it, when we were 20 we thought we had our whole lives ahead of us, we didn't know that, a few of my friends didn't make it to the end of their 20s, it's just a feeling you have, and really what have we definitely got, we've got the next hour haven't we, and that's all we ever really have – this hour. Who knows what happens next. But we definitely have this hour. the next hour can be golden, if we let the light in.

DAILY NOTES VOL 1

April 28th 2023
The Letter – Made in Dagenham

This is a lovely song and you know what I think I can play and sing it pretty well, and I know that's what you might not want from a comedy piano podcast, all piano no comedy but sometimes you've got to take a pause haven't you and think I'm happy there, I've achieved something. I know you can't hear me singing it through this page, but really, listen to the podcast for this one, I do play and sing it phenomenally well, really.

Ten years ago I couldn't play the piano at all, obviously I'm a phenomenal singer I've always been a phenomenal singer that's always been without question but I couldn't play the piano and here we are and I have done this on my own. You've got to take a pause sometimes haven't you and think I'm happy, take a pause, gratitude isn't it, if you're feeling that odd funny feeling what is that, why do I feel so, hang on its happiness – what the hell is that? I don't feel that all the time – no you don't – so take a pause and reflect on why you're feeling happy – maybe because you've learned the piano or you're a phenomenal singer or maybe it's something simpler like you've made yourself a nice dinner or it's a sunny day or you've had a great shit.

It's often the small things that can make us the happiest, not small shits, small shits never make us happy, it's those big beautiful shits that come out clean, we feel clean, its beautiful and it should be celebrated, not everyone can do that, and not everyone can do what you do, so whatever you do today, whether its fixing a tap, taking a shit, killing a rat or just putting love out into the universe in some small way, celebrate that you have done something good today, and more than anything celebrate if you've listened to the words of this song and realise that marriage doesn't work, you don't need anyone to in quotes be your wife, stop signing contracts for love and just let love into your heart and throw it back out.

And that's the episode over, let's flush that one away and see what tomorrow has in my horrible and always surprising bowels. Did you listen to me singing it on the podcast? What do you mean it was shit? And anyway, like shit is bad. Have you not been paying attention, shit is to be celebrated, every single day.

DAILY NOTES VOL I

April 29th 2023
Happy - NF

Things we do now to make us happy we couldn't do 30 years ago. Imagine if 30 years ago in the early 90s you spent your day staring at your phone, you'd have been sectioned. 'What's Nathan doing? He's staring at the phone again, we would call the doctor but Nathan is staring at the phone, we only have one between all of us.' There was no binge watching in the 90s, even when you got a DVD of 6 episodes for Christmas you'd watch one episode then put it away until tomorrow, '2 episodes back-to-back? I have a fucking life!'

Now you don't need a life, a life is over-rated. I remember when Netflix started they used to post DVDs to you and you'd have to subscribe and send the DVDs back and then you'd get another one a few days later, giving you a chance that they don't give you now to go outside. I remember them trying to flog shares in Netflix and I remember very clearly thinking no, you sad little dweebs, posting films to people are you and getting them to post them back and then you'll post them another one. Get a proper job you losers. But the thing is I was right, they didn't turn profit for like 10 years or more, they were making losses. Its only because you're rich can you get away with starting a clearly shit business, it was still a shit business.

Forcing you to go the fucking post office to watch a film. I don't want to leave my sofa and I don't want to choose a film. And that's why I liked the 'surprise me' feature on Netflix – remember this – you didn't even have to choose a film. – because you had this feature – surprise me. I will watch whatever you choose for me because I am a moron. And you know the worst thing to happen this year, this was axed in January by Netflix, you can't get this option any more, which is bullshit, asking me to choose my own programme, what next Netflix, force me to go the fucking post office and wait 3 days you pieces of shit. I wanna binge watch – binge is a bad thing – yeah in any other context – you binge anything you need help – binge TV that's cool. I binge watched – I mainlined *Succession*, I had to have my eyes pumped for *Jeffrey Dahmer*. Cool man. Have you never been outside? That's so so cool.

DAILY NOTES VOL I

April 30th 2023
Ed Sheeran – Supermarket Flowers

Has anyone noticed outside is getting scarier? Outside is scary now. I mean maybe it's mainly where I live but no it is everywhere. People walking past you like the opening scene of *Shaun of the Dead* – aaaaargh – they're not mentally il they're just beaten down by food prices. Supermarket flowers £20. Take me back 30 years when a packet of crisps was 10p. A packet of Walkers crips £1.25– that's not a corner shop rip off, that price is on the fucking bag, it's in the design – there's a star around it – they want to draw your attention to it - they're proud of that price at Walkers. Only £1.25 – come get it – what a bargain - £1.25. Guys there's half a fucking potato in there.

£1.25 – you don't even get the footballers name on them any more – Salt and Lineker, Cheese and Owen, Crisp Akabussi - £1.25 for a non-celebrity endorsed half a potato and that's why it's scary out there, because we're all on the brink of rioting but we just haven't bought the balaclavas yet, but we're angry enough to do it now – aaaaarrrghh.

I mean thank fuck Netflix has evolved since the early days of posting DVDs back to them. Imagine if we had to queue at the post office to return DVDs every time we wanted to watch a new episode of Jeffrey Dahmer – aaarrgh! I'll stick your head in the fucking fridge. And people always say the same thing – cut down Nathan, you don't need flowers, you don't need crisps. Occasionally you do need flowers, if someone dies a text isn't enough, and let's face it, you always need crisps, I'm sorry life wouldn't be worth living if it wasn't for crisps.

I had a guy in my gig the other day who had eaten two bags of crisps every day of his life for 30 years and everyone was like WTF and I made a big thing of it but when I got home I realised – I think I've done that but I get the big bags from the supermarket that are like 5 packets of crisps in one and eat like half a bag a day, hang on those bags are £1.20, fuck, things are cheap actually, life is good, and let's face it with the amount of crisps I eat it will be over soon, and when I go, don't waste your money on flowers for goodness sake you're gonna need it for those balaclavas.

DAILY NOTES VOL I

May 1st 2023
Forever – Lil Baby Featuring Fridayy

Life doesn't go on forever, death comes to us all. Benjamin Franklin said the only two certainties in life – death and taxes. Pessimistic. It's very surprising to me that people don't talk more about cryogenic freezing. And even more surprising that more people haven't chosen to do it. Only 250 people have frozen themselves. 250 people, they've cheated death. Is everyone else insane? Well it's the cost Nathan – no its 28,000 dollars, that's it – one off price, nothing more to pay - fuck leaving that to your kids, most of us will have 28,000 dollars to our name when we die, stick me in the fucking freezer.

I won't have died technically and there will be no taxes to pay. Fuck you Benjamin Franklin your witty quote means shit. But there's no evidence that it will ever work to unfreeze you. Really, if I'd come to you in the 60s when Austin Powers was walking around fucking everything that moved and said in 60 years' time there will be none of this, people won't be fucking each other, we'll all be staring at our mobile phones watching people fucking each other. That ain't gonna happen, it has happened. Along with 3D printed food and smart toilets that play songs as you shit.

And who's to say in 60 years' time we'll be unfreezing 250 people and they'll be like, where's all my mates? They didn't choose to freeze themselves, what did they do instead, cremation? Idiots. There ain't no coming back from cremation dickhead. $28,000 one off fee, why aren't more of us rolling the dice? The lack of foresight is astonishing. Well when I die Nathan I don't want to come back as my old as fuck self. Come on if they've invented thawing a dead human body they would have probably invented reversing the aging process, but secondly, yes you would, think about it, you're 90, you die they unfreeze you and you're alive again, it's the year 2223, 200 years later, you look up and everyone has mobile phone attached to their eyes, ah fuck - stick me back in the freezer, let me know when humans have been wiped out and its only us 250 left who actually have some get up and go and will to live, then unfreeze me. And that's why for most of us one life is enough, the older you get you really do think, na one life is enough to be honest with you useless cunts. Cremate me.

DAILY NOTES VOL 1

May 2nd 2023
Adventure of a Lifetime – Coldplay

And it happens again. That dead feeling inside when Ronnie O'Sullivan gets knocked out of the World Snooker Championships. It's ridiculous. I recognise it's palpably ridiculous. But that feeling is undeniable and it's always been like this and it just gets worse. I don't get this feeling from any other sport, from national or international football, from any other sporting figure losing. It's disappointing sure when England get knocked out of the World Cup but when Ronnie loses in the World Snooker Championship it hits me hard, I feel it hard, and now I really need to question why this happens.

It's history of course, it's 30 years of supporting one player in a game you love, but what is 'supporting' in the context of snooker? It's not like a football team that you perhaps watched as a kid, I've never seen Ronnie play live. With snooker you are supporting a way of playing, a personality. As a kid it was Jimmy White and I had exactly the same feeling when he lost, it just transferred to Ronnie in the 90s. The way of playing, the personality – the anti-establishment, fuck it, unorthodox attitude that I identify with. But Ronnie this year was beaten by Luca Brecel, who has the same playing style as Ronnie, perhaps even more maverick, and arrived at the Championships with only 15 minutes practice, so why do I hate that he beat Ronnie? Can't I transfer my joy to Luca? And Ronnie wants him to win now, and loves watching him, why can't I? Why do I not care about anything now Ronnie is out?

Is it about Ronnie's age? We are a similar age and do I reflect it back on myself when he's beaten by someone younger - is it over for him and therefore over for me? He's won 7 World Championships, is that not enough, why can't I be happy with 7? I care about him, I worry about him, and when I hear an interview with him afterwards that he's fine and he's looking forward to 'going running again' do I believe him? Or is he lying like my son lies sometimes when he says things are ok when they're not. And is that the key? Do I feel the same way towards him as my son, do I love Ronnie O'Sullivan? I think that's it, yes, I love Ronnie O'Sullivan. The reason I feel awful is I'd feel the same way if my son lost in the World Snooker Championship, I'd feel awful. Because I love him. And then I'd

92

wake up the next day and it would be ok again. The pain of love must be replaced by hope. We must carry on. Life is an adventure. And we only have one life. Blink and you'll miss it.

May 3rd 2023
Careless Whisper – George Michael (from Deadpool)

So we must strive to do better, and I want to inspire you right now – I want to truly be inspirational and potentially turn your life around. And I think it's good when you're doing this to have someone in mind to aspire to, so for my son it's Elton John because he wants to be a singer songwriter. And for everyone else I think it should be Ryan Reynolds, he's a good person to aim for, because I don't know you all, but I know this, compared to Ryan Reynolds you're not quite as good.

If you're an actor compared to Ryan Reynolds you're not very successful, it's a goal isn't it. If you think you're happy in a relationship then 10 years with Blake Lively, 4 children, you're not as happy. If you're a business person, he's taken over Wrexham football club and has just got them promoted and has made a billion dollars from mobile phones and gin - if you're a businessperson compared with Ryan Reynolds you're a cunt. If you think you help people out, care for the sick and dying, compared with Ryan Reynolds – he has given millions to Ukrainian refugees, clean water projects in Canada, invited a dying man to the set of Deadpool 3 – you're again an asshole.

If you fancy any celebrity, Ryan Reynolds had had sex with them all - Alanis Morisette, Sandra Bullock, Charlize Theron, Scarlett Johannsen, Ryan Reynolds (he's masturbated) compared to Ryan Reynolds you're a cunt. If you're a fan of Pokemon he starred as the titular character in *Pokemon Detective Pikachu* a live action film adaptation of the Detective Pikachu video game – you're a cunt - and if you think you're sexy Ryan Reynolds was named People's sexiest man alive in 2010 and compared to him you're a troll.

And if you think well I'll never be as good as Ryan Reynolds I've got mental health issues, if you read Ryan Reynolds' Wikipedia page which I clearly have for this one, if you scroll to the end past all the people he's fucked, the films he's been in, the billions he's made, it says right at the bottom and I quote… 'Ryan Reynolds has had a lifelong struggle with anxiety' - so compared to Ryan Reynolds you haven't got mental health issues you're a cunt. And if that's not inspirational for you, nothing will be.

DAILY NOTES VOL I

May 4th 2023
Eladio Carrion & Bad Bunny – Coco Chanel

Coco Chanel – Nazi sympathiser and informant. It's a pretty big thing that people tend to gloss over, and the world is now full of things that people gloss over and things that we choose not to. I get it in my industry all the time – I could never work with that person and here I am on a public forum wailing that I'll never work with this person because of something they said 10 years ago. Pardon, misheard you. Something they did? No something they said. What to a loved one, no in a comedy routine. What? You're not working with someone because of something they said in a comedy routine 10 years ago? That's a fairly high bar. Yeah and he apologised for it as well. What? Yeah but I still wouldn't gig with him. What on stage at the same time? No on the same line-up with him? So you wouldn't even see him? Potentially, no. But you'd wear Chanel? Yeah what have they done? Oh nothing doesn't matter.

It's how we pick and choose what we're going to be offended by and what we gloss over, and it's totally performative – it's not what people feel it's what people feel will look good. That's right people don't feel anything anymore, what they feel is how will it be perceived by others, and that's fair enough is you're pandering to good people, but often the people you're pandering to are the most divisive backstabbing awful people around, the strange abhorrent gatekeepers to a moral code like St Peter being a paedophile and still choosing who gets in and out of heaven.

Oh I could never do a gig with that person who apologised for a joke told 10 years ago, but absolutely I'll work with this other person who has done and said far more awful things but the morality police have let that one go because they're famous or middle class or generate money for the system, so that's fine. Wearing Chanel is fine just as long as she never made a joke that she immediately apologised for 70 years ago. Because that in my mind actually in someone else's mind not mine, would be unforgivable. Grow up everyone and realise… play the game all you want, you still won't win, this game cannot be won, we are all heading for inevitable defeat. So knowing that, why are you all sticking to someone else's rules?

May 5th 2023
The Look of Love – Burt Bacharach

Watching the film *Austin Powers* with my son - he goes from the 60s to the 90s and all his attitudes are outdated, those who practiced free love are now slags and a slag in the 90s is now a bad thing etc. They should have another *Austin Powers* film where he goes from the 90s to the 2020s and all his attitudes that he re-learned for the 90s are now really fucking offensive and wrong. Tony Blair is cool! Cool Britannia. Things can only get better. That was their theme music Things can only Get Better – that dated badly - D:REAM, one of the band members Brian Cox now is an astronomer, has spent his life looking for other planets as he knows this one is fucked.

Bill Clinton is the worst president ever, how could he get away with being sucked off by his intern. That's why hating on slags in the 90s is now the most outdated thing of all. In the 2020s we love slags again. If you're the president now and you're not fucking the intern or prostitutes what are you doing old man? Everyone saying Joe Biden is too old to be President it's like if you're not young enough to fuck the intern how are you gonna fuck Putin? You say you're ambitious for the country we don't believe you, you don't even have the ambition to fuck someone that's not your wife. Uurgh! Joe Biden has been having sex with the same woman since for nearly 50 years, how is that someone we can believe in? That's disgusting.

Bring back Bill Clinton, differentiating between a blow job and sex by making up his own definition of sexual relations live on television. Boris Johnson's 7, 8 or 9 kids. These are the men we want, these are the men we vote for. There is a pattern, the public like a slag. We vote for a whore. We're all swinger voters. They say there will never be a woman president, yes there will never be a woman president until one is prepared to step up to the plate and admit she's a slag. Where are the slutty candidates? The best we've had is Hilary, ooh my husband's a slag – stop relying on your husband love, who have you fucked? Which males have you fucked? What you've deleted all you males? Just your husband? Jesus – you want in to the oval office, who has been in the oval orifice, if it's just your husband, jog on virgin.

DAILY NOTES VOL I

May 6th 2023
Henry Carey – God Save The King

What else could we talk about today than the coronation of King Charles III, the marvellous occasion where the whole country no the whole world comes together to celebrate something that we all love and we all believe in the Monarchy and I don't mean that sarcastically of course, just for the coronation even those that don't believe in the monarchy will be watching, you watch them, well you can't because you'll be watching too, everyone will be watching because everyone for that moment will come together and celebrate. And you're thinking no I won't Nathan I don't believe in the – stop, just stop what you're saying and here's my plea to you – have a day off, have a day off the negativity, give the man his day. And whatever you do, don't protest today, either in your own home or by chucking soup or whatever at Prince Andrew. Prince Andrew has done nothing wrong in the eyes of the law because he paid off Virginia Giuffre with 16 million dollars, 3 million of which was from his mom, but Charles has done nothing wrong for goodness sake and that's a fact, jeez some of the people you talk to they act like he's killed someone. Prince Charles has not killed anyone probably. Not directly. Stop it, stop the protest, and they say no this is the day to protest, this is the exact day to vent my dissatisfaction, well yes and no, because the thing is, lots of people have a different point of view, they like the Royal Family, they love the Royal Family, so remember you're not right, I might agree with you but you're not right, this is just you opinion, and really, venting your negative opinion on this day, over these few hours, I don't know, it strikes me as a bit neggy, a bit opportunist, a bit on the nose, a bit uncool, protest the rest of the year, but for today let King Charles III have his day, let him celebrate, let the world celebrate, come together, love each other, park the neggy just for one day, because knowing what we know about King Charles, who knows he might actually agree with you, he might actually agree that the millions of pounds, the pomp, the ceremony is all ridiculous, but just for this short time, let's love, let's party, and let's forget just for a moment that it's all palpably ridiculous. In short let your hair down and don't let your heir down, who's the king now, you know what I mean. Love, forgiveness, no murders, no nonces, just light, love and Queen Camilla. I swear allegiance to the King and I swear allegiance to Camilla Parker Bowles. Kiss the ring, and love the King.

DAILY NOTES VOL I

May 7th 2023
All Night Long – Lionel Richie (Live)

Tonight is the night – it's the King's Coronation Concert to celebrate the Coronation of the King, the brightest and best stars from around the world, those that want to be associated with the monarchy and establishment, gather like 15th century jesters to entertain the King who is hungover after the Coronation yesterday – I mean can you just imagine how much he drank last night poor bastard. I mean we all have a bit of a drink when we get a new job don't we – can you imagine what you'd do if you became the fucking King – shut the fuck up I'm having another pint Andrew I'm the fucking King, and can you imagine how much he fucked last night, how hard he was, I'm the fucking King, I mean many of us have said that in bed but how many of us have actually been it, he is it, he's the fucking King and he will be watching this concert tonight with a head like a chewed arsehole.

And I pity him to be honest because there's gonna have to be a whole lot of pretending going on as Take That, Katy Perry and Lionel Richie are paraded in front of him and he has to pretend to enjoy them. Because nothing against these artists and bands but anyone appearing at this type of thing are not by their very nature exciting anti-establishment figures, they are the establishment, they are the bland. I'm with the bland. I mean you know you're in trouble as anything exciting and cutting edge when opera stars Andrea Bocelli and Sir Bryn Terfel take the mic, I mean again nothing against them but fucking dull, these people have just won the lottery and been plucked out of what would have been Sunday teatime church choir obscurity to be elevated as something we all need to listen to, it's nothing is it, it's bland.

Hugh Bonneville is on hosting duty again lovely chap I'm sure but the blandest of the bland. Nobody wanted them but it's just what fits with the event – bland – even King Charles didn't want them he wanted something more exciting – Ed Sheeran and Adele, who turned it down due to an unspecified reason – I love that, we all know the reason, its bland as fuck, and the way King Charles was fucking last night and now hanging out of his arse I'll be amazed if he stays awake – you watch as he nods off as the opera twats warble out their musical equivalent of carbon monoxide and it wafts over everyone and starts to send the King to sleep. It will be magical television and I for one will be glued, God save the King from this all night long avalanche of utter boredom.

DAILY NOTES VOL I

May 8th 2023
Tyler Hubbard – Dancin' In The Country

How big a problem are potholes in your part of the world? I've been up in the country with my mom for a day or two and all she can talk about are potholes, the danger of potholes, and how when you're driving it's all a dance around the potholes because the local councils don't have enough money to fix them. And I thought, really, is this the biggest problem in society? Potholes? Don't you have anything else to worry about? My mom is a worrier, constantly warning me about the dangers of parked cars. 'Be careful down that road Nathan – there are parked cars down that road – there's nothing more dangerous than parked cars.' Really mom, what about moving cars, aren't they more dangerous than parked cars?

And now its potholes, be careful of the terrifying potholes. Mom, you should try driving in London or LA, no potholes there but there are assholes, lots of assholes, I know what I'd rather be avoiding – potholes or assholes – potholes you can avoid, assholes you have no chance. Anyway, this is what I thought, mom, think about the bigger things in life to be worried about, or better still stop worrying, you're in a nice house you have what you need, these potholes are not going to get you. And then there were the local elections in this country last week and the Conservatives got a trouncing as the incumbent party often does in local elections held between the general elections and one of the reasons they got a trouncing - they said in the run up to the election – one of the things we are going to fix in this country are potholes, they made a huge thing of it, we are going to fix the pothole problem – they were talking directly to my mom and people like her where the biggest concern in this world are potholes, but sadly for the Conservatives, everyone else can see through it, the whole world but seemingly this country in particular, there are massive holes in society that we are all slipping through and you can't cover that by talking about the tiny holes in the road, and I can hear my mom now – they're not tiny Nathan they're massive. No mom massive is the economy, it's Russia, it's Brexit, it's refugees, the biggest problem in this life is not potholes. Well try saying that Nathan when you're stuck in one. Noooooo! No more, the time for being fooled is over now. We see through the bullshit, we are not falling down these black holes ever, ever again.

DAILY NOTES VOL I

May 9th 2023
Set Me Free, Pt. 2 – Jimin

So *Austin Powers* someone frozen in the 60s unfrozen in the future - this could happen in reality one day very soon. The first person to be cryogenically frozen was James Bedford in 1967 who is frozen at the Alcor Life Extension Foundation in California – note, Life Extension Foundation, James Bedford is technically not dead, those people that have been cremated they are dead. James Bedford is clever, he paid fuck all as he was the first one - to have his life extended. He is still alive. Blood and semen survive freezing. That was an awful visit to the ice cream van. Frogs and viruses have been revived after freezing, who's to say James Bedford won't be revived in a few years' time, maybe this year, we don't know. And what would he think, what would he do when he was set free? Would there be any fucking like Austin Powers? Probably not he'd still be in his 70s and he'd be knackered, and freezing – put the fire on.

But how would he feel and think with his 60's attitudes in today's society? Well James you'd have to learn very quickly what you can and cannot say. Many comedians say you can't say anything anymore, and those comedians never say anything of any interest ever, which kind of proves it But when James Bedford was last around you could say anything. You could literally say anything and it wouldn't be regarded as that offensive. As long as you didn't swear. Swearing in the 60's you couldn't do it on television, career over, but you could say anything else. So when James Bedford comes out, someone have a word in his hear before he shouts his mouth off and says the wrong thing. If someone doesn't write his 'you've set me free' speech for him it will be no doubt liberally littered with racism, misogyny, mis-gendering.

And there we go you see, James Bedford is coming back to life and the thing we're worried about is what he's going to say – he's taken both feet out of the ice is he about to put his foot back in it. But are we worried of course? This is a made-up scenario. James Bedford is dead and his head is now a block of ice, there's no chance of this happening, probably. But what we learn from this of course is you have your attitudes and you believe what you say and feel is totally the right thing to say and feel because it's now, it's right now. History has taught us that within 30 years and certainly within 60 years most things you say and feel will be outdated and much will be taken as offensive. But, and it's a big but, and I love big buts and I can't lie (you can't say that since the 90's either) this represents an absolute miniscule fraction of what it is to be alive. You can't say anything these days – no – you can say a million, billion unlimited things because you are alive and there's one or two things that you think and feel that might offend others so I've got an idea… just don't say these things, live your life, live your one life before you freeze yourself and come back to life in 30 years' time and find out you can't say cunt any more. Will you want to be killed again because you can't say cunt? No, because you're alive. So get on with living, because you'll soon find out, when you're dead… that's really the time that you can't say anything anymore.

DAILY NOTES VOL I

May 10th 2023
Heavyweight Champion of the World – Reverend and the Makers

Be like everybody else, be like everybody else, just be like everybody else. My son has just bought a new pair of trousers, so he can be like everybody else. Which is fair enough, when you're his age you want to fit in. But when you fit into a jigsaw, no one notices you anymore. The only way of being noticed is the piece that won't fit in, the piece with the rough edges, the broken piece.

It's fine if you don't want to be the heavyweight champion of the world, and most don't, and I get, because you're not going to be the heavyweight champion of the world more than likely, it's almost impossible, so why bother. You're not going to win the lottery either so why bother? Well you bother because you're not entering the lottery to win it, you're entering the lottery to be in it, because believe me when you're not in it, life is dull. You have to be in it, and to be in it, don't be like everybody else, because one thing's for sure - if you're like everybody else you won't be seen. And when I say that I don't mean stick out like an annoying cunt, people think they can stand out by being an annoying cunt, no, sorry, if there's one thing that will make you blend in with everyone else, it will be sticking out like an annoying cunt, so many people are annoying cunts - that is the majority now - you can be different, you can stand out, without being annoying. Just go your own way.

One thing links all heavyweight champions of the world, they've all gone their own way, they're all one-offs, and if they'd blended in then instead of being world champions, they'd have been bouncers on nightclub doors, stopping people coming in because they don't look like everybody else. The nervousness I used to feel getting into nightclubs – will I get in? Other people are cooler than me, I need to look like them to get in, I need to look like everybody else.

That's a club nobody wants to be in, but nearly everyone is trying to get in. Why?

Even if you get in, no one will notice you anyway.

May 11th 2023
Ed Sheeran – No strings

Well I've been very much enjoying the Ed Sheeran documentary on Disney, I mean he's just so lovely, his wife is lovely, his friends are lovely, he's suffered the awful loss of his best friend, he's so talented, what can I say, I just want to say I love you Ed Sheeran with no strings attached. And while watching it you know what I thought, I thought oh no, have I ever said anything about Ed Sheeran in any of these Daily Notes which was derogatory as a joke? And I don't think I have thank goodness, because for me Ed Sheeran is one subject I think is beyond humour, you know some comedians make jokes about certain things and you think that can never be funny, such as egg puns, well for me after watching this Disney documentary, Ed Sheeran is one of those out of bounds subjects where it is impossible to make jokes about them, because he's just lovely and talented and I love you Ed Sheeran no strings. He's had the same friends since he was a kid and he travels the world with him, they work with him I think or he pays them to be his friends, no that sounds derogatory, I missed that bit, but yeah he pays his friends to travel with him, I just wanna say Ed, I would be your friend for free, because I love you, no strings.

I was at Wembley, I'm not sure you remember me I was the one in row ZZ with an open-mouthed son who wants to follow in your footsteps and he just might do that if he can get off his phone long enough to work as tenth as hard as you did. So yeah, if it doesn't work out with my son can I travel the world with you instead please Ed? As I say you don't have to pay me like do your other friends to like you, I love you - no strings. And I tell you what I'd do for free, I'd be the guy that keeps handing you different guitars, I'd be that guy, I saw you say thank you to that guy and that's all I'd want, a smile from those cherry lips as you say thank you as I pass you another guitar, and I'll try not to get pissed off when you just give yet another guitar to a kid in the crowd because you're a Saint and although that creates more work for me as I have to get a spare guitar from the van, I don't care because I love you and if you'll have me, I'll keep passing you guitars until we're 70 and beyond, and you know what Ed just for you, every guitar I pass you – it will be perfect - no strings.

DAILY NOTES VOL I

May 12th 2023
Karma – Taylor Swift

Who would have thought Chat GPT would delete the need for virtually every single job. It's happened and its hilarious, who would have thought that my job is the only job Chat GPT won't get rid of - comedian. Looking back on my banking days when I started out in stand-up comedy 15 years ago, I remember you John, I remember overhearing you at that pub in Islington where you told other bankers that I wasn't funny and that wasn't like it was your opinion you said it as if it was fact John, and it wasn't fact, comedy is subjective and if you think I'm not funny then you're objectively wrong. Well John, I've always been looking for karma for you because as well as slagging me off you were also the one that bullied me and you were also the one that bullied my friends, you were a nasty piece of shit John and you also did a job the need for which was basically non-existent, you were a manager without portfolio, and I looked forward to the day that for you and people like you your jobs would become obsolete, what you thought was so hard and deserved your 100k salaries could be replaced by the touch of a button by Chat GPT and here we are John that day has come my friend, karma.

I'm sure it has done for you like it has done for so many other bullying useless bastards. And to celebrate this day I've got my friend to write something to you – you're a cunt John, the biggest cunt in the world, and Nathan just wanted me to say that we are all so happy you are now unemployed and probably sitting at home in a pool of your own piss and regret, maybe you've put on one of Nathan's Amazon Prime Specials *Bumblebee* or *Observational* or *Fifty* and noticed how many awards he's won in the last few years and realised that he is funny to some people, not you we understand that because you are a black hole of joy that cannot be filled and the only time you will ever be taken out dancing is the day that you die and Nathan and all his old bank colleagues who you bullied turn up to dance on your shitty grave.

Who am I John? Well, I'm the guy that took your job John, I'm Chat GPT, Nathan doesn't write these any more, he gets me to write them, I'll have his job soon too.

Eh? What the fuck?

DAILY NOTES VOL 1

May 13th 2023
Euphoria – Loreen (Live at Eurovision)

Well there is Euphoria in Liverpool tonight as it's the big one – it's the final of the Eurovision Song Contest in Liverpool which here in the UK we have dutifully taken over from Ukraine who won the contest last year fair and square and presumably will win it again tonight but it's not about which song is best, it's never been about that, it's about celebration, it's about Euphoria. And Ukraine's entry is Heart of Steel by duo Tvorchi and you'd have to have a heart of steel not to say that even in advance of them doing so, congratulations on Tvorchi for winning the Eurovision Song Contest 2023. It's about togetherness, this was never a contest for songs, even though it's called a song contest, this was a contest for hearts, and Ukraine has won our hearts and we in the UK have bravely taken on Ukraine's responsibilities for hosting this heart contest saving them millions of pounds, so maybe we deserve second place in the heart contest that's all I'm saying just like we got last year when we came second, technically first, you know what I'm saying.

I don't know if you do know what I'm saying really, it's about fairness at the end of the day, Ukraine says it's fighting for fairness and justice but is it, is it really? If it's going to win the song contest, it is a song contest, with a sympathy vote and presumably do the same again this year… and 12 sympathy points go to Ukraine, you know, all I'm saying is we could shoot down one or two cruise missiles over Liverpool if it meant we were bound to win. That's all I'm saying. Putin said earlier this week the world is at a turning point and you know what, I kind of agree with him, it is at a turning point, for are we to judge a song contest on its songs or on sympathy? All I'm saying is there should perhaps be two contests - the Eurovision Song Contest that we would win just like we technically won last year – Space Man – and the Eurovision Sympathy Contest which would go to whichever nation Putin is trying to destroy. Anyway, it's not about the winning, because winning it is now a travesty of justice, its about taking part and coming second behind Ukraine so technically first, and it's about euphoria, getting swept up in the euphoria of the whole thing and forgetting just for a moment about fairness and justice. Do whatever you think is best world. As always - you do you.

DAILY NOTES VOL I

May 14th 2023
Ed Sheeran – Dusty

Hi again Ed, further to what I said about you the other day in that I would never ever say a bad word against you because you're clearly a brilliant human being and so talented I love you, I saw something on Facebook yesterday and it hurt me. It will never hurt you because you'll never see it but it said and I quote 'I think Ed Sheeran comes across as a lovely guy, it's just a shame that his music is so terrible'. And whatever, I'm sure you don't give a shit and these pricks that pass comments as if they're facts rather than opinions deserve the little air time that they will inevitably always get, but I just want to say that I will never do that Ed, I will never pass a sarcy comment on your music because it's pathetic quite frankly, not your music the comments - who cares what my opinion is?

And as I said the other day me and my son came to see you at Wembley and you rocked it and every song was brilliant, and you've been through a hard time and so binned the songs you were gonna do for this album and instead produced this album and I get it, I get it, I really do, I get it. I went through some shit 5 years ago, and I wrote a show all about it, its cathartic isn't it, and I did the show but I performed it once, and it went well and I said to my producer afterwards I will never ever perform that show ever again, because I knew if I played my bad times over and over again then that would keep them alive. And a brilliant person in my life taught me how to grieve, how to let go, and part of that was not playing the tracks of that grief over and over again, and indeed, never again.

Let those tracks be, let them gather dust, and never ever put the needle on dusty. You can't control your dreams sometimes, but you can control what you play out when you're awake, so after this I'm going back to the *Shape of You* and *Bad Habits* and *A Team* and *Perfect*. But you do you Ed, release this music if it makes you feel better, as I say I am not one to pass judgement, who cares about my opinion or anyone else's? Anyway, my point being - I think Ed Sheeran comes across as a lovely guy, it's just a shame that his music is so terrible. Not all his music, just this album. I love the other stuff though Ed, all the other stuff. Don't mind me, this is just me thinking out loud. And no one wants that, it's just a copy of *Let's Get it On*.

DAILY NOTES VOL I

May 15th 2023
Princess Diana – Ice Spice & Nicki Minaj

Well I tell you who didn't get a look in over the Coronation weekend – absent friends. I love that bit at an occasion where a glass is raised to absent friends and they unnecessarily introduce sadness into an otherwise happy event. Yeah I know you're all having a great time but can we stop for a moment to think about all the people we loved who have died and remind ourselves that this good time won't be going on forever and indeed it won't even be a bad time it will be no time at all because we'll all be dead, we'll all be dead real soon, so charge your glasses and lets all remember that soon we will all be dead. We'll all be dead!

But that said, I was slightly disappointed that the late Princess Diana didn't get a mention at the King's Coronation. Maybe, I don't know, her brother could have made a speech, Elton John could have sung a song and maybe there could have been a drive past of Mercedes something like that. But the truth is that for most there, they wouldn't know what I'm talking about, because it was 30 years ago, it was 1997, and 30 years is around the time when no one gives a shit any more do they, because anyone under 40 doesn't remember and anyone over 40 realises there are more important things in life like their own impending death to be bothered any more about something that happened 30 years ago.

Never has there been a more dramatic representation of time healing than the fact that pretty much no one thought about Princess Diana as King Charles and Queen Camilla got married in the very spot that Princess Diana had her funeral with Queen Camilla smirking away, I mean literally what the fuck? Was I the only one thinking what the fuck? Yes I was, because you've all forgotten about something you all never thought you'd forget about. So next time you have any awful tragedy in your life, just cheer yourself up and think well in about 30 years' time I won't even be thinking about this at all, so maybe I should be less bothered about it now, I think that will help you. But of course there's some things you never get over, and King Charles and Queen Camilla being crowned in the exact spot where Elton John sung *Candle in the Wind 97*… Jesus, there are some things I can never unsee. Goodbye England's rose. I never ever forget.

DAILY NOTES VOL I

May 16th 2023
Search & Rescue – Drake

Where's Osama Bin Laden? We all know where he is he's in the sea, he's in the Northern Arabian sea. And what did the SEALS do in the back of that helicopter? Well as we all know and as we all accept wholly, his body was shrouded in a white funeral grab, he was gently eased below the waves in accordance with Muslim funeral rites, a military officer read prepared religious remarks which were translated into Arabic by a native speaker... a US defence official said. Cool, yeah, US defence official, who has got a defence for everything apart from his bullshit!

Anyway, that said, a body in a weighted bag in the middle of the Arabian sea, obviously that's the end of that right? No of course not, because there's always one nutter isn't there, there's always one nutter that thinks he can find the needle in the haystack, and that nutter is treasure hunter Bill Warren who in 2011 went looking for Bin Laden's body in what he called 'the most exciting and maybe dangerous project' to and I quote 'prove one way or the other that he is in fact dead'. Now, why would we be sceptical that this could have succeeded? This guy, Bill Warren, has spent his life looking for buried treasure, not that Bin Laden is buried treasure, he's more buried terror, but Bill Warren has got previous in finding the unfindable and making millions of dollars in the process from the loot. So what was his plan if he found Bin Laden? Well it was fairly loose, he said 'we would take photos, video, a DNA test maybe on his gair or his beard'. Cool yeah. 'I know his family lives in Arabia' he continued like a nutter. Cool, nutter cool.

So what was his motivation? And this is gonna blow your mind... it's money, there was a 25-million-dollar reward to hand Bin Laden's body in dead or alive, and that reward still existed! Ridiculous, stop encouraging these nutters going out in the Arabian sea with fishing nets. However, at the last-minute Bill Warren discovered that obviously this reward no longer existed. So you know what he said? 'I'm still gonna look for him anyway'. Of course he did, because Osama Bin Laden knows this more than anyone else, there is always one nutter in the world prepared to go further than everyone else.

May 17th 2023
I Wrote a Song – Mae Muller

So then I wrote a song – oh it didn't do very well did it, it wasn't great was it – a song about writing a song, it's like *Inception* folding in on itself, these things never work. I mean I never start a joke with 'so I was writing a joke the other day and it was about writing a joke, the joke was like – when you're writing a joke about writing a joke, if the joke in the joke in the joke had a good punchline does it matter if the joke about the joke just fizzles out without any punchline at all?' Nonsense. Self-referential bell-shit. And the trouble is the UK entry needs to be so good now doesn't it because after Brexit Europe hates us, it was only because Sam Ryder was so lovely last year and the song was so good that we came second, technically first. If the song is anything but amazing which this song about a song wasn't, we're never gonna win. Please stop these self-referencing songs about songs they are never gonna work.

Like I was planning this podcast in my head just now and I thought what will it be about, and I thought what it should really be about is not the Eurovision Song Contest, it shouldn't be about Brexit and everyone hates the UK now and the UK is going down the toilet washed down the S-bend along with all the shitty songs we've entered into the Eurovision Song Contest over the years, no this podcast should be about writing this podcast, because that would be clever, and meta wouldn't it, it's a podcast about how I wrote this podcast... well it's not that clever is it because I just thought in my head before I started this what I should talk about. I can't spend 5 minutes saying this song was shit because that would be cruel, so I'll bury that under layer upon layer of meta shit to disguise the actual shit that is this song. But the thing is, the clever thing is, if you listen to the lyrics of this song carefully, Mae Muller says she wrote a song about how you did me wrong, but it wasn't this song was it, the song that she actually wrote was actually great, it was well written and it was sung really well, but we only heard the bad song didn't we, not the song she wrote. You get me? The Eurovision audience didn't get it - they gave her fuck all. But what do they know, they wouldn't get a self-referencing song if it jumped up and kicked them in the balls of their dad as he ejaculated into their mother and thought 'and then I'll make a kid'. Or some shit. I should really write these down then they'd be better, and that's in short how to write a podcast.

DAILY NOTES VOL I

May 18th 2023
NLE Choppa – Slut Me Out

I mean people talk about the great poems but I like to think of songs as the greatest poems, take this song for example, slut me out…

Yeah, ETB
Why you being weird to me?
Ayy, rip off my shirt if you love me (love me)
Spit in my face when you fuck me (fuck me)
Play with my gooch, while you suck me (suck me)
Eat the dick like you was ugly
I mean, hold on, wait
Where your friend? Bring your buddy (your buddy)
I don't think that you enoughie (enoughie)
Her favorite thing to say is, "Cuff me"
Slut me out (out)
Slut me out (out)
Slut (slut), slut (slut)
Slut me out
Rip off my shirt if you love me (sexy)
Spit in my face when you fuck me (come sex me)
Play with my gooch, while you suck me (don't text me)
Eat the dick like you was ugly (don't text me)
Big dick energy, I give it (I give it)
Don't believe me, then come feel it (come feel it)
Gon' put this here in your kidney, please (please)
And hush it like some kidney beans
Suck my balls, come chickpea me
Why you being weird to me? (Weird to me)
Put your ass in my face 'til I get pink eye
Fuck you anywhere, I'm that type guy (that type guy)
At the church, on the plane, at the basketball game
I don't care, I'm a bust my nut 'til I die ('til I die)
What position do I like? All of 'em, baby (Baby)
Put it on camera, masturbate to it later (to it later)
Ever sucked a vegan dick? Baby, come taste me
Promise that my nut taste like sugar gravy
Don't cum quick, I control my bladder (control my bladder)
Dick real big, come climb my ladder (my ladder)
Fat coochies, little coochies, all coochies matter (they matter)

DAILY NOTES VOL I

Ass real fat, I can make it get fatter (fatter)
Wanna see a magic trick? Bend over backwards (Over backwards)
Meat to meat, wall to wall
Coochie to my balls, dawg
Ayy, rip off my shirt if you love me (love me)
Spit in my face when you fuck me (fuck me)
Play with my gooch, while you suck me (suck me)
Eat the dick like you was ugly
I mean, hold on, wait
Where your friend? Bring your buddy (your buddy)
I don't think that you enoughie (enoughie)
Her favorite thing to say is, "Cuff me"
Slut me out (out)
Slut me out (out)
Slut (slut), slut (slut)
Slut me out

It happens so infrequently, but sometimes, something is so perfect that if you add anything to it at all, you'll ruin it.

DAILY NOTES VOL I

May 19th 2023
A World of Our Own – Westlife

Where the hell are Westlife? Well, the boys are back on tour this year – Mark Feehily, Shane Filan, Nicky Byrne and Kian Egan – I'm Feehily excited for Mark, I'm Filan wet for Shane, I'm burning me Nickers for Nicky Byrne and I'm keen and Eager for Kian Egan… I mean those names have to be made up don't they – sexy boy band – feehily, filan, nicky, byrne, Keen, Egan, Mark me, feel me, Filan me, Byrne me. Anyway, probably one of the reasons they couldn't have someone in the group called Brian – Brian, probably the last person on earth to be called Brian. Brian McFaddyen famously left the group in 2004 after 4 number one albums, ten number one singles, so much success – he left because he wanted to spend more time with his wife Kerry Katona, who he split up with and divorced from a few weeks later.

And there is the number one lesson, never stop anything really enjoyable and successful to spend more time with your partner - are you actually mad? We are in a world of our own here, and by that I don't mean two of us, I mean we are on our own. Sure invite other people into your life, spend your life with someone but don't give up what you really want to do for them, oh my God is there any bigger mistake? Brian!! Can you imagine him arriving home – 'Kerry I've got some amazing news, I've given up the band'… 'What?' 'Westlife love, you remember, the band I was in - the four number one albums, the ten number one singles, I've given it all up so I can be with you, in a world of our own… Right, what shall we do tonight?'…

Erm, watch TV? Eat pasta? I need a poo, sorry if it stinks.

Oh God no – this is shit isn't it? Life is shit. So many people say all I need in life is love. It's just not true, your partner is not your life, your partner is who you choose to live a life together, you need to look at more than just your partner or they will drive you to divorce within weeks. Life is not about your partner, it's about looking up, looking north - north life, south life, east life and westlife. Give all that up and you'll be divorced and overweight and on drugs within days, your life will be in the muck-fadden. 'Brian!! Clean that shit out of the bog Brian!' For fuck's sake. You silly, silly man.

DAILY NOTES VOL I

May 20th 2023
Jealous – Nick Jones

Are you jealous of your son Nathan, he's at Brit School, he's young with all these opportunities, aren't you jealous? Someone asked me this the other day. A ridiculous question, I mean yes when I was his age, I was given no creative opportunities, my son goes to a weekly dance class with this street dance collective called Zoo Nation, the most renowned troupe of its kind in the UK, kids come from all round the country to train with these guys, my son just does this every week, it's round the corner from him because he lives in London whereas I at his age lived in Birmingham where I only did one dance class it was over the road in the little room above the flower shop there was me a 13 year old and five or six old people doing what looking back I now realise was a movement class for pensioners to get their blood flowing and keep them alive which I now realise put me off dance forever, the awful and crushing embarrassment

Anyway where my son has a studio in one of his rich friend's back garden to practice music, I had a piano in the hall of the sub Post Office where I lived and I wasn't allowed to play it in the daytime because the Post Office was open and my step brother wouldn't allow me to play it in the evening because he'd pin me down and call me 'shit-bag', not all the time, but I do remember that it happened lots of times. My son goes to Brit School where in every lesson creativity is encouraged, I went to an all-boys grammar school where the only thing that mattered was 9 grade A's at GCSE - what an utter and complete waste of time. My son has got two parents that love him, I had an absolute clusterfuck as a kid I don't wanna go into detail here because yes what a ridiculous question, of course I'm jealous, my kids have got everything and I had nothing, of course I'm jealous, I mean thank goodness the economy has tanked and the world is fucked making it almost impossible to move out let alone achieve anything in this world, thank God for that, so he can live with me forever and he'll just be waiting for me to die but I never will because my body has not been able to get tired or grow old because I didn't actually do anything because I was given zero opportunities to do anything, and even at 140 years old I'll still be keeping myself alive by going back to that dance class above that flower shop – remember me? You will, someday… I'm gonna be someone.

DAILY NOTES VOL I

May 21st 2023
Arctic Monkeys – Do I Wanna Know?

Do I wanna know if I've got a life limiting condition? Well hopefully not in the middle or even the start of a so-called comedy podcast. But you know you have the option now don't you of doing a test for many things that might kill you, and the thing that might kill me because there's a lot in my family, dementia, and you can do some early tests for that which might tell me that I'm gonna get it. Do I wanna know? A lot of people say oh I don't wanna know – to me that's crazy, that's like jumping in the car for a long journey and ignoring the traffic reports and the sat nav telling you to go another way - na I'm going that way anyway, even though it's a standstill, I'm gonna carry on regardless.

Crazy, of course I'm gonna listen to the satnav and if the satnav tells me that I'm gonna get dementia at 70 then great I'll go a different direction, and the different direction I'll go is to live even more now than I do, live every day like in 20 years' time it's gonna be my last because it will be my last and then aged 70 when I've spent all my money my kids will be getting fuck all, I'll show the first sign of dementia. Daddy do you know where all my life savings have gone? Er no I forgot… didn't you spend them in Vegas? Vegas? Have I been to Vegas? Yeah daddy you've been there every years for the last 20 years since you got that dementia diagnosis… Sorry don't remember.

Anyway aged 70 I'll have 28,000 dollars left and I'll go to LA to that cryogenic freezing place and I'll say take me now before the dementia sets in, the last thing I want is to be unfrozen and not remember why I froze myself, that would be awful. And I've got a plan, because conveniently the cryogenic freezing place is in LA, just 4 hours from Vegas, and so I'll be able to go to Vegas one last time, and I can have one last blow out, and because my dementia will be just setting in, it will be like *The Hangover* movies, I can have a night that I will never remember, I'll commit some awful crimes and the next day I'll freeze myself, and then I'll be unfrozen in 100 years' time… and immediately executed.

So in short - of course I wanna know. Because you've got to have a plan. And call me crazy but this is mine.

DAILY NOTES VOL I

May 22nd 2023
Russ - Nasty

Oh don't say you think it's shit. Why? Because its nasty. Yeah sure it is if you say it to someone face unnecessarily – its nasty, you get this in all art but I'd say particularly comedy because people feel they can tell you something is shit as you're doing it, which is unique I think. People don't heckle theatre, they can tell you something is shit as you're doing it and it can become more or often less shit based on the fact that somebody is telling you as you're doing it that's shit, imagine if someone chipped in now and said Nathan this episode is shit, then the episode would then be side-tracked as I dealt with him or her, probably him, entitled self-important man that he'd probably be. Twat.

Anyway, yes telling someone you think something is shit to their face is not great and particularly while they're doing it probably not the best option, but thinking something is rubbish and voicing that opinion online as long as you don't copy in that person, is that such a problem? The world has gone the other way I think, like with Eurovision songs, I mean some come bottom of the leader board for a reason, they are to most people, not to everyone, but to most people not very good, they're bad lyrically, they are performed by someone as stiff as a board, they are to most people not very good and that's why no one votes for them. Is it so wrong to voice an opinion that most people are thinking? As I say not to the person directly, don't heckle, as someone did when I was watching my University panto, to a performer as they were singing the heckle 'don't sing'.

But to say something is not very good, I don't think is nasty it's kind of good in a way because so many kids grow up now on Instagram surrounded by a bubble of mates and then producers whatever going oh you're great you're amazing and you hand it over to public opinion and then its oh no everyone thinks I'm shit. As kids grow up then, there's a benefit in saying na, that's not brilliant, I don't think that's good, you're not gonna encourage a kid that can't run that they can be in the Olympics athletics team, that would be mental, so why are you encouraging someone that can't sing and dance brilliantly to go in for Eurovision. They're eventually going to find out they might be rubbish on a much grander scale, and that my friends will really be nasty.

May 23rd 2023
Boat – Ed Sheeran

So did you see the new 3D images of the wreck of the Titanic this week? It was only discovered of course relatively recently 1985 and now they have the first complete 3D image of the two bits down there, 4000m down, and you can see unopened champagne bottles (that's the real tragedy) and shoes and whatever and people are losing their shit over this saying the scans could offer new insight into what happened to the Titanic on that fateful night in 1912. I mean, what? We've all seen the film, she (we call ships she don't we I don't know why) – she hit an iceberg – why do we need a 3D scan? Yeah but we don't know exactly how she hit the iceberg – oh right typical woman keeping secrets amongst her female friends – no Nathan we just don't know how she hit the iceberg. But, I mean sorry to all the people working on this, and there's many, but why, why are we bothering to do this? It's done – apparently the sea and microbes and whatever are eating away at it and Historians are worried that time is running out to fully understand this disaster.

Let me stop you there – fully understand?! But we understand it don't we – she hit an iceberg, water got in, not enough lifeboats, loads of people died including Leonardo di Caprio and his gran who kept the expensive necklace which she nicked and kept a secret amongst her female friends. Why, to what end are we pumping millions of pounds into this thing to discover more? What more? And even if it's more it's not going to help anyone, I mean it was over 100 years ago I would hope they've learned their lesson and ships aren't as shit now or if they are everyone should open their bottles of champagne in the first few minutes, get those fuckers drunk just in case *she* decides to go down after hitting some water that is a bit too solid, flaky woman. All I'm saying they'll do all that investigation and they'll discover that if it had been a male boat, it wouldn't have capitulated so easily, it would have been a bit stronger, that's all I'm saying, and would have got to New York and there would have been no skeletons and no secrets. That's all I'm saying, so dig all you want, but be prepared to live with the consequences of what you find, sometimes as the saying goes it's better to let sleeping boats lie.

DAILY NOTES VOL I

May 24th 2023
You'll Never Walk Alone – Gerry & The Pacemakers

I'm a Liverpool fan, have I mentioned that? Liverpool Football Club, and one of my most memorable days are taking my kids (not football fans) to Anfield, the ground of Liverpool Football Club for a tour, see the dressing rooms and go to the trophy room, and this song plays out, a well-known anthem for Liverpool they sing it on the main stand there the Kop and its magical. And its unashamedly about nostalgia this city, it's about the present and the past, it's about not clinging on to the past but freezing the past in a statue or a trophy or a piece of memorabilia, you go along to Anfield and you see it, here is the past, when Liverpool won the league in 76, 77, 78, 80, 82, 83, 84, 86, 88, 90 and then not for 30 years. 30 years, success frozen in time, of course there were other trophies, cups, the Champions League twice, but it was the league that they wanted and they got it again in 2020 and that's when I visited with my two kids.

And they enjoyed it, but they didn't get it – 30 years – that's the time isn't it, that's the sweet spot I think, like the Titanic going down, 1912 everyone involved has passed but 30 years you're still surrounded by the people and the things that you had 30 years ago, you understand and appreciate the passage of time, the heartbreak, the effort and I stood next to the Premier League trophy with my kids and we took a photo and you know what, who knows, it could be another 30 years before Liverpool Football Club lift that trophy again, I hope not but it's possible, and that's why nostalgia and the past is so important, because by remembering the past it becomes the present, you can hold the past and it becomes the present, you can hold that trophy and it becomes the present, and it becomes hope for the future.

What this song tells us is that walk on with hope in your heart and you'll never walk alone, don't be scared of digging back into the past, if its full of darkness or light, look back 30 years if you're old enough and see how different things were, things may not change in a day or a week or a month or even a year, but give it 30 years and I promise you things will change. And you can wait 30 years, because we're all in this together, we're all waiting together. Through the storm, you'll never walk alone.

DAILY NOTES VOL I

May 25th 2023
Toughest (Bonus Track) – Ed Sheeran

This track is about a very difficult period in Ed Sheeran's life, and as I say the man for me is lovely, beautiful, and talented and his family and friends are just as great, an amazing guy. And his documentary on Disney Plus is moving and intimate and genuine, an amazing insight. And I'll never hear a bad word against any of them. The end. Oh, there is just one thing I take issue with. Not just in this, but in any similar documentary, you always hear the same thing from people that are famous… 'I work so hard, I knew what I wanted and I went for it.' And sometimes they'll say 'I wrote it down, I wrote down what I wanted, I visualised it and made it happen. I made it happen through hard work. You've got to be the strongest, the toughest.' And I'm sucked in by this as well, I pass these videos on to my son and I say George you've got to work hard, the people that get to the top are the strongest, the toughest, they take the blows and they get back up again. And if you work the hardest and you are the toughest then you will make it.

And elements of that are absolutely true, but it is also of course, bullshit. Because for ever one person that made it through dedication and hard work, there are probably one million people that worked really hard and didn't get what they wanted. I want to see that documentary – that's something that most of us could relate to… 'I worked really, really hard for thirty years and fuck all happened that I really wanted to happen.' And why didn't it happen? Because I didn't have the luck. That's all it is, luck. Same with beating an illness like cancer – friends of mine have survived cancer, friends of mine have died with cancer. So when I hear that someone has bravely fought cancer because they were so tough, I baulk a little bit, I think what are my friends that died with cancer weak? Of course not. Just that life is all about luck, good and bad. You can help to make your own luck of course. Hard work undoubtedly makes you luckier as it gives you more chances to have luck, but everything and I do mean everything is just chance, it's things aligning for you at the exact moment you need them to. And so work hard of course, because the best thing about working hard, then you know that if it doesn't happen for you, when it doesn't happen for you, it's not your fault, you did try your best, you just didn't get the luck. And that's the toughest thing of all. Tough luck.

DAILY NOTES VOL I

May 26th 2023
Human – Cody Johnson

So us humans we're very worried about one thing at the moment aren't we, no not that, AI, we're all very worried about AI and how it's getting out of control and how computers are going to become sentient and take over the world, apocalyptic. Terrible, I mean it's *Terminator* isn't it, it's happening. Nuclear war followed by the rise of the machines, in the film this was in 1997 and more than likely just 30 years later here we are. I mean I get a bit lost with Terminator to be honest, it's 2029 when John Connor defeats Skynet and sends Kyle back to 1984 to protect and fuck his mom, I'm lost – anyway, it's all coming true, apart from time travel, you can't go back in time and fuck your mom – wasn't that the plot of Back to the Future? There's a lot of fucking your mom in time travel stuff isn't there? I mean, thinking about it, if you went back in time to anywhere, would you, it's just a question, would you go back and fuck your mom? You would wouldn't you? As long as you don't get her pregnant that doesn't affect the space time continuum at all. It's a free hit. And imagine the weird vibe when you start to grow up and she's like I recognise you, sure you do, I was the one that rimmed you in that budget hotel mummy.

Anyway, enough of that, you can't go back in time thank goodness, the best you can do is you can freeze yourself and come back to life in the future probably and then I don't know fuck your girlfriend again who is now 30 years older but you're not, it's all problematic. Anyway my point being is that stop worrying about AI taking over because what are humans anyway? We are the things that do this, this podcast I mean, or films about time travel and fucking your mom. Why do you think that we have a right to this planet more than computers? You only think we have priority because you yourself are human and you don't want to die. Well I hate to break it to you, you are going to die, and you won't be able to come back in time and fuck your mom so how do you wanna die? 83 years old in pain in some crappy hospice or over the next couple of years, when computers start to take over, microwave ovens sprout legs and there's a fucking terrifying but very, very exciting few days where you watch everyone get killed and then you die as well. To be honest that sounds awesome. Bring it on.

DAILY NOTES VOL I

May 27th 2023
Ed Sheeran – Life Goes On

Thirty years – that's a long time, but of course the last thirty years was longer ago than it will be to get to thirty years' time. Because that's how time works isn't it? The first thirty years of your life takes much longer then the next thirty years, and the last thirty years if you're lucky enough to get them goes by in the blink of an eye. Everything works differently in the first thirty years – particularly money. Money completely changes value. Do you know what my son gets excites about - £20. Oh someone has given me £20 !! I get it, but if you give me £20 for my birthday, are you taking the piss? My tax bill this year is anything between three and thirty thousand pounds, it's just a number plucked out of the air every year. And you're thinking about giving me £20 – do one.

In thirty years' time, I'll be nearly 80, and finally I will have retired, Daily Notes will have stopped many years ago after a man finally and for the first time ran completely out of things to say, many of you would say that happened mid-way through season 2. I'll probably be sitting in a desert somewhere in Nevada or on a mountain South Island New Zealand. And then of course all we have to live with, our regrets. Do you have a regret of something you did in your first thirty years that's going to live with you forever? Of course you do. And regrets aren't like mortgages sadly – you can never pay them off. Regrets are like a loan shark that comes round your house and says 'I'm going to give you £20… and you don't have to pay me back until next month.' And you think great, and then you're paying it back for the rest of your life.

So what advice can I give you? Well if you're in the first thirty years of your life, try not to make that mistake that you'll regret forever. But it's probably too late for that. If you're in the second thirty years then you're going to have to accept that you'll be paying off that regret forever, so manage those payments carefully, accept that someone has fucked you and learn to accept it, acceptance is the key. And in the last thirty years, that it when great wisdom befalls upon you and you give you grandkids £20 and you see the delight in their faces, and you realise how stupid you were every time someone offered you even the smallest something for nothing and you were ungrateful. It was the greatest gift of all. And you wasted it.

May 28th 2023
Double Fantasy – The Weeknd Featuring Future

So it's a lot of people's fantasies to have sex with two people, but the much more common fantasy is to want to have sex with one person, that's the most common one, sex with one person is amazing, sex with two people not so good, because of the admin involved, the hanging around and quite frankly the mess. Sex is messy, so best to avoid it completely.

My mate was telling me about this thing the other day which sounds brilliant and is the perfect solution if you want the joy of sex with multiple people, without the mess and the STD's, and it's called the cuddle puddle. Google it, it's a thing, the cuddle puddle. Where you go along for non-sexual intimacy, you lie down in a big group and you cuddle someone, sounds great doesn't it? And the first question I asked my mate is what happens if you want to kiss someone, and he says 'no that's outlawed'. Right, so there's someone watching, yeah, and kissing and sexual touching is outlawed, cool, ok, but then he continued… but there are ways around it…

Right – so when she's not watching you could have a bit of a kiss and a bit of a sexual touch. Cool, ok, so basically an orgy but with a kind of lenient police officer, yep exactly. Now, I am totally down with this kind of thing, I do think true intimacy with one person is better than sex with two or three people, all these fantasies doesn't come close to the feeling of intimacy you can create with one person and sex can get in the way. However, the only thing that puts me off these cuddle events is I did a film documentary in 2005 called *My London Party* where I spent a year I tried to invite the whole of London to a party by word of mouth and along the way I met this group who would stand around London offering free hugs to people, which again sounds great, but, oh I don't wanna say it, I really don't, because I'm down with the idea, but, look I'm just gonna say it quickly because it's just my experience and I bet some of it was really good, but…. these people are weirdos, they're stinky weirdos with smelly breath, just meet someone - one two, three, eight people whatever, whatever floats your scrote, everyone is looking for love… just ask around.

You do not have to cuddle the stinky man.

May 29th 2023
Oasis – Stand By Me

What is wrong with people, flaky, not loyal, we only have each other in this world, and as soon as you become flaky and dis-loyal, you've lost everything, you've lost your only bargaining chip that differentiates you from the flies. There's a fly in your kitchen, annoying right, and it's like you can't get rid of it, but you know when it finds the right light, the right window, it's going to fuck off out of your life forever. You think that fly is going to be around forever, of course it's not, there ain't no loyalty from that fly. Don't be the fly. Don't treat your friends like TikTok. Disposable, swipe up, too much choice. Ooh I've maxed out my friends on Facebook, what you've got 5000 friends? No you haven't, but don't announce you're going to have a cull publicly unless you want to come across as the world's biggest cunt, just get rid of almost all of them, you're not loyal to any of them, you've probably slagged off most of them behind their backs and you almost certainly hate ten of them.

The number of kids you can have and still be happy as a couple - zero - the number of friends you can have and trust that they've got your back and you've got their back 100% - three. And even that's pushing it. Two to be comfortable, one if you're really sensible. Any more than that and one of your friends could be going through the hardest time and the best you will do is click 'care' on Facebook. Mm, when you click 'care' do you really care? Or if you really cared wouldn't you text or call the person? How can I make the absolute minimum effort for my friend here when they clearly need friends the most – ooh care, I've pressed the 'care' button. That's enough isn't it? Oh what a fucking effort I've made for my 'friend' here. Clicking care is worse than doing fuck all. What you've done there, you may as well have clicked the button 'I don't care'. 'I don't give a fucking shit'. Clicking 'care' you may as well buzz in through the window, flap around the nearest light for a few minutes and then fuck off again the good you're doing for them. You're worse than the fly. The fly would actually eat this person's shit, you wouldn't go round to see them if it was anything over forty minutes. So I'm announcing a friend cull today. I only have two friends, and if you're thinking ooh have I made the cut, you haven't. Because they're both the flies buzzing around this room right now. I trust them more than I do you, you flaky disloyal fuck.

DAILY NOTES VOL I

May 30th 2023
Ocean Eyes – Billie Eilish

I was in the Whitsunday islands twenty years ago, exactly twenty years ago I had taken three months out to backpack around the world and in the middle of this three months I'm in the Whitsunday islands. It's making me a bit emotional thinking back, my memory works in a strange way I struggle to remember things like it was me doing them, but I know it was me twenty years ago, Whitsundays. Australia. Great Barrier Reef. And I want to go on a boat trip obviously out to the ocean to see the Great Barrier Reef. And there's a few options so I pick the cheapest one. Never pick the cheapest option. Of anything. Second cheapest fine, never the cheapest. So here I was signed into Dodgy Derek's cruises or whatever they were called, with a guy that looked like a cross between Father Christmas and whatever paedophile is most famous in your country. In my country, which has become over the last few years quite the hot child's bed for paedophiles, all paedophiles have white old weird looking faces. So if your local paedo is Michael Jackson it still works. Anyway paedo Phil the fishy man had got my money and out we go on this rickety boat called the Titanic2 or whatever, out into the ocean off Australia with his horrible wife who he argues with and hated because she wasn't a child and that's what he likes. And then in the middle of nowhere he stops and he says this is it. This is what you've been waiting for. And I think no it isn't. This is a con. A con shell. This is a shitty bit of ocean all I can see is admittedly blue water but there's nothing perceptible underneath, you sir are a con man.

Anyway I bite my tongue and I reluctantly jump overboard and this nonce looks at me and barks at me. Use your eyes. Stick your goggles on use your eyes and look down. The first and last time I'm taking instructions from a paedo I thought. Not true, my music teacher Mr Grocock. Anyway, in for a penny in for a pound of disappointment. I stick my goggles on and look down onto the ocean. Oh my God. Easily the most beautiful thing I've ever seen. Beyond words beautiful. I can't describe it. All I'll say is if you can get to the Whitsundays, get your ass on paedo's boat if it hasn't sunk by now, and realise that whatever horrors happen on this world, this world can be beautiful, not everything is awful and there is quite literally out there an ocean full of hope.

DAILY NOTES VOL I

May 31st 2023
Religiously – Bailey Zimmerman

I enjoy religion. I'm not religious but I enjoy religion and religious people. Because they are choosing to believe in something that there is absolutely no evidence for. Millions, billions of people around the world choosing to believe in something, live their life by something that there is absolutely no evidence for. And equally the people who believe there is no God like me there's no actual evidence that there's no God. Well that's arguable isn't it, the pain and suffering in the world and Trump. And Trump is of course the best exponent of our natural tendency to believe in things that there is no evidence for, we don't need evidence, for millions of years we have believed in something with no evidence, we don't need to start now.

And so I was catching up on Depp v Heard, I missed the live stream at the time because I was watching the *Pirates of the Caribbean* films, all of them over and over again. And here we have it played out, people choosing to believe in something without any evidence or with evidence to the contrary, and that's from both sides. And it comes down to this with religion, with matters of abuse, we don't need to see any evidence ever because we make up our minds. And once we have made up our minds, good luck changing them. It's why OJ Simpson was found innocent and it's why Trump could be back in the White House by the time you're reading this book. Because what do we believe any more if we don't care about evidence.

We are in a post-truth age they say, and some people say this as if they're proud of it, as if they want to take us back hundreds of years when people were burnt as witches because they, I don't know, were women. But what about the truth? What about it Nathan, it literally doesn't matter. Don't you want to see the truth? Alright grandad, still banging on about that are you? Time's moved on old man, this isn't the 80's any more. Are you sure that's true? I hope it isn't true.

There's only one thing we believe in…. The absolute truth of our own beliefs and more than anything the fundamental notion that we cannot ever be wrong. And we will take that ludicrous belief to the grave and then only God can judge us. And by the way, when that happens, just tell God any old bullshit, they surely will believe you.

June 1st 2023
Fool Again – Westlife

So I was on a train the other day and I realised I didn't have the correct ticket. It was late though after a gig and I thought oh there will be no one checking tickets at this time… and then what I can only described as a nob came over the tannoy – you know the ones, those awful am-dram children's TV presenter wannabe guards on the trains that delivers the announcements like he's been honing for years in front of an audience of clapping morons - about how he just wants you to be happy and safe but if you're on the wrong train you're fucked as he will be coming round any second to check tickets. He keeps repeating it - I'll be coming through the carriages any second to check tickets. Here I come… I'm coming now… I mean I'm not doing it justice, there's many more words, this is his chance of course, his fifteen minutes of fame, sometimes he'll throw in a joke like 'please take your belongings that's your bags, your coats, your pet dogs, your pet mice'. Ah go fuck yourself Mr Tumble you fucking B-tech clown.

And often he'll be road testing a poem he's been working on for decades, or seconds, I can't decide – I hope you're sitting comfortably, and my name is Billy Womfortably – your name isn't Billy Womfortably – and if it is prove it with a birth certificate Mr Womfortably when you eventually appear but here's the thing - guess what, the cunt NEVER appears! Lying prick. And because I didn't want the social awkwardness of having to explain why I hadn't bought a ticket, the rhyming prick made me buy a ticket online from my seat, when by the way there was absolutely no need to as the train was going to London anyway. Livid.

It was all a con to make you buy a ticket which I fell hook line and sinker for – what a twat. I hope you've bought a ticket, because I'm coming round, but then again I'm not because I'm a lying dipshit. I can't get over this, why would he say repeatedly over the tannoy that he was coming round to check tickets if he wasn't. he was just trying his jokes and poems on us wasn't he? Well this isn't as joke Billy but it is a poem. Next time I hear your voice, and I'm on the train, I'm going to hunt you down, and stick a gun on your brain. I'll pull the trigger, but you still won't care, you're a brainless twat charging me a fucking penalty fare.

DAILY NOTES VOL I

June 2nd 2023
Area Codes – Kali

There's this thing here in the UK called the Postcode Lottery, don't know if you have it where you are. So there's the National Lottery which you're probably more likely to have, where everyone that wants to pays a £1 or £2 and puts that in a big pot in the middle, 35% is taken by the Lottery organisers and then 65% which is millions goes to one person who celebrates with a big cheque in their garden standing next to their wife or husband who they then immediately dump, they go on a drink and drugs rampage for a few years and then they are declared either bankrupt or dead. That's the Lottery. The Postcode Lottery is a little different and it says you are far more likely to get success in this one and the prizes are slightly lower so maybe you won't end up diving with a load of prostitutes down the nearest K-hole. What they do here in the UK is you enter a Lottery and you have to give your postcode and then they choose a postcode out of the bucket and everyone who has entered from that postcode gets to share the spoils and the advert for this has everyone from the one street out having a party together.

And that's where it becomes unrealistic in the UK. Neighbours don't talk to each other. Neighbours hate each other. Neighbours are the ones that play *Return of the Mack* at full blast with their windows open, neighbours are the ones that let their dogs shit on your front lawn, I don't give a fuck whether they have a share of the spoils, the only reason I want to know if these people have also won is have they won enough to fuck off and take their shitting dog with them, which is irrelevant really because I'd only get the next bunch of animals in. In short, the advert for the Postcode Lottery should not be a party, it instead should be a street where people wander around as usual avoiding their neighbours but suddenly there's more gossip, more speculation, do you reckon it's him? He's got a new car, she's got a new lawn mower, who can I beg off? And all the while you know it's you, you've got more money than you've ever had and you want to celebrate with the winners but you can't and you never can because winners make losers even more bitter. Nothing can be celebrated ever, nothing can be enjoyed. Have I just won the postcode lottery? No one will ever know. Because I can never enjoy, I can never spend a single coin. I will take my news to my gold encrusted grave.

DAILY NOTES VOL I

June 3rd 2023
Too Good at Goodbyes

You must think that I'm stupid, you must think that I'm a fool, you must think that I'm new to this, but I have seen this all before. And so Sam Smith begins their fourth song ten minutes or so in to their concert at the Manchester Arena last week which I attended due to a lovely birthday present that I received. And just before this song starts they says 'you know what, I've travelled the world doing shows but I always say, the best place to do shows… Manchester… that's right, all around the world, Rio, New York, Japan, Australia – the best place to do shows… (consults notes as to where they are)… Manchester'. But whatever, cynicism slightly to one side, lets believe them, because they comes across as a nice person, humble. I commented just before they started this their fourth song, you know what, they are humble, they are genuine. And their voice sounded good, we had great seats, everything was set up for a top-notch night of live entertainment. And then they do this song 'Too Good at Goodbyes' when they say that because they have had to do goodbyes so much they are now too good at it, they is too practiced at goodbyes, it's a tragedy but this is one thing they is good at – goodbyes. And this is just after announcing that at the end of tonight's concert there will be a special bonus song and the rumour flying around the crowd is that it will be their new single with none other than Madonna, you know Madonna, that elderly lady from the 80s.

Anyway, excitement, brilliant voice, let's go. This song finishes, and then Sam Smith… just fucks off. They walk off the stage and that's it, the screen goes dead, the arena goes dark. We're sitting in the dark for a few minutes and then an announcement – Sam Smith has cancelled due to vocal issues. Eh? WTF. They literally is too good at goodbyes, they just fuck off, I mean that's the master at goodbyes, they don't even say goodbye. I mean lovely person but Sam, Sam over here mate, its Manchester – it ain't New York or Rio or Japan, all those rainy shit holes you usually play, it's your favourite place, Manchester. At least say goodbye. Sam! Sam, Sam! And everyone was moaning. But you know what. It was good, 4 songs was kind of enough, that was a good night, and the best thing of all, we didn't have to see Madonna. Such relief swelled around the crowd. And so we all just fucked off home and didn't complain too much, which makes us, Manchester, the very best audience in the world.

DAILY NOTES VOL I

June 4th 2023
Harry Styles – Cinema

Cinema will die off soon, like the oceans and Pizza Express. Hey wanna come and pay three times more for a pizza that you can buy an identical one in the shops and eat not surrounded by screaming children? No thanks Pizza Express, no thanks. Dough Balls £6, woah you're spoiling us. Anyway, the next thing to die off is cinema. Every time I go now it's virtually empty, it's only a few years until they're all betting shops. Two reasons, we don't want to leave our houses obviously but main reason is we, I say we, you, are fucking animals that can't control themselves in many situation but particularly situations where we are expected to gather together and shut the fuck up. I mean trains is the obvious one, where no one has headphones and people are snorting like they're trying to suck up the entire train into one nostril. And cinemas will be next.

I mean we've always treated cinemas like dustbins, just crop spraying our popcorn over the floor, savages, but very soon those little messages before the films will be completely ignored – it's time to stop talking, turn off your mobile phones and enjoy the film – I don't think so grandad, this isn't the 80s. I come to the cinema now to scatter popcorn around like I'm Hansel and Gretel trying to remember where I was once civilized, and chat away in comfort on my mobile phone. Can you turn this fucking film down please I'm trying to chat away on my mobile phone, I'm trying to watch someone fall over and jiggling tits. And no it isn't rude, it's called evolution. It honestly is. Things are better now, we can cook our own pizzas and we don't have to pretend any more that watching a film on a bigger screen is a different thing than staying in and watching it on a smaller screen – cinema isn't really going out, it is going out cos-play, pretending to go out but instead doing exactly the same thing you usually do at home but in a different location, it's like going on holiday when there's no sunshine, it's like going to an orgy and just banging your wife, I'm happy we can stop pretending we're doing anything but staying at home under another name. Pizzas are dead, cinemas are dead and orgies are dead, the only thing that matters in this world is your own home and your own phone, everything else can do one. And art galleries, fuck off. Google images mate.

DAILY NOTES VOL I

June 5th 2023
Everything She Ain't – Hailey Whitters

My mom is great, but like many moms she doesn't quite get when the time is to come in with the support and the love. Being loved and supported in the absolutely key moments in life is everything she ain't, and I've never fully understood that until now. I feel supported, I feel loved by her, she would never say 'I love you' of course, that would be preposterous, man up Nathan you don't need to be told that any of your family love you, you have to assume that from the fact that they occasionally cook you dinner, and you have to work it out from the strange ways that she shows me that she loves me – and one of the ways she shows me she loves me is in refusing to believe or hear that there's anything wrong with me ever. When I was 19 I got an ME type thing, I had to drop out of my degree, I went to the doctors back in Birmingham and I was told that my throat was shagged and I may never get better. I went back and told my mom I said, 'mom the doctor has just told me I may never get better.' And she looked at me and said something I will ever forget… 'I need to go back to work'.

She worked in a fuckin sweet shop. She didn't need to go back to work. What about the customers Nathan? Fuck the customers do they really need their gobstoppers I've just been told that my throat may never get better, isn't that the more important gobstopper? So many people think their jobs are essential. They are not essential they aren't event required. Humans were fine in the stone age when no one had a job – no job is actually essentially. What about doctors Nathan? No they just look at you and go that part of you is shagged, go home, you may as well self-diagnose. But unlike the doctors, the thing is with someone that loves you, is that it's very hard for them to admit to themselves that there could be anything wrong with you, because if you love someone that's impossible to bear, so best ignore it mom, best go back to the shop and sell those sweets and those fags, fuck up a few more throats. And of course, it was fine, I did get better in about six months, and so my mom was right to ignore it, and my doctor was wrong, proving beyond doubt that no jobs especially doctors are essential. Apart from comedians, and do you see us going on strike?

Down tools people, and just work hard at love.

June 6th 2023
Riptide – Vance Joy

Dreamers they never see the riptide coming. But then, who can blame them? Better to sail in an ocean of hope than a sea of despair – Earnest Hemmingway, the Old Man and the Sea. And that's what sustains us hope, maybe through doing nearly 1000 episodes of this - that's either actually doing or listening to them, we can find enlightenment, we can find some soul. But then, hope is not always fulfilled, things don't always work out. For the last 20 years of my grandparents' relationship, they just bickered horribly. My earliest memory is my granddad calling my grandma the worst swear word to her face at a family party, I won't go into detail about this incident but if I was to write a book about it, it would be called The Old Man and the C.

But I'm still a dreamer, I dream that as you get older you can grow closer together rather than further apart. And it's hard, you spend over three days with anyone and the cracks start to appear - can you clean that up please, can you not do that please, can you just fuck off and die please. I'm not like that of course, but everyone else is. I'm a dreamer you see, I never see the riptide coming, I know things will end up shit with my partner calling me a cunt in front of the whole family but I'm diving in blind, I'm surfing this wave never expecting it to kill me but knowing deep down that it inevitably will. It's the best way to be. Never see the riptide coming and then when on dry land bury your head in the sand. Who wants to see reality?

Reality is awful. The truth is I can't even surf, I can't even bodyboard, but that won't stop me going into that riptide thinking that everything is going to be okay. Because it will be, you just need to see things differently, say the same words but in a different way, everything is going to be ok, it is - because everything is going to be…okay. Not great, not even good, just okay. And by okay I mean bad but reframe bad as okay and it WILL be okay, I promise you.

What will be will be, que cera cera. Always keep hope, always bury your head in the sand, and never see the riptide coming, sail in that ocean of hope that leads to that destination of okay. It's the only way to travel.

DAILY NOTES VOL I

June 7th 2023
Mathematical Disrespect – Lil Mabu

Did anyone else spend at least two years at school learning sin cos tan? Sin, cosine, tangent. Straight out of school I got a job working out the angles of triangles from the length of the opposite side and the length of the adjacent side – obviously I didn't I got a job in a bank where there were no triangles just squares and cunts, and the square on the hypotenuse was equal to the sum of the cunts on the two adjacent desks.

So much wasted time doing maths at school. I did pure and applied maths, and applied maths was the one that was the true waste of time. If object A is going at 10 m/s around a central point and object B is going in the opposite direction at 5 m/s around that same central point and starts at the same time, at which point will you realise that you are wasting your life? And this will never be required even if you go into mechanical engineering as this scenario is never ever going to happen. I mean maybe one or two lessons on this just in case you set up some kind of race between a fox and a chicken around a post in your garden but surely those 2 years could have been better spent learning anything else – how to make pasta, how to brush your teeth, how to make love. The one thing they never teach you which would change everyone's life for the better – it's a conspiracy.

However - pure maths, do not show pure maths disrespect. I loved pure maths. Because there was a right answer. Do you understand the joy of there being a right and a wrong answer? Oh my God it's so simple, it's so pure, in society now there is no right or wrong answer for anything – is a man allowed to walk around with his cock out in a woman's changing room? I don't know, I don't know anything anymore, there is no right or wrong answer. But with pure maths it was simple, you were right or you were wrong, and in one of exams I got 100%, I completed my maths paper A-level and I just knew I had got it all right, there was no way I hadn't got 100%, a beautiful feeling I don't think I have ever had since - I am right and no one can disagree. I am right and everyone thinks I'm right. I've been searching for this feeling ever since and I'll be searching forever and a day. For infinity, plus one.

DAILY NOTES VOL I

June 8th 2023
Cowgirls – Morgan Wallen Featuring ERNEST

I was on the train from London to Manchester, I get this train regularly. JK Rowling famously came up with the whole idea for all the books of *Harry Potter* on a train from London to Manchester – how the hell did she have the silence required to come up with the whole *Harry Potter* franchise in her head? If I was to write a book about kids on the train from London to Manchester it would be called 'Shut the fuck up.' Shut the fuck up and buy some headphones. Every train journey I'm surrounded by morons who haven't heard about the invention of headphones, snorting twats and kids that haven't been told as I was at their age to shut the fuck up.

Can you pass a message to any kid you know – shut the fuck up. Oh you can't say that any more Nathan – no, one of the best lessons I ever learned I was on a bus at fourteen and as kids do I was shouting my mouth off and some dude turned to me and just said 'shut the fuck up'. I grew up in an instant, it was like a maturity explosion – bang – it's such a simple and effective lesson. You have to be taught it at fourteen, other people exist in this world, shut the fuck up. 'Shut the fuck up' by Nathan Cassidy… how a simple 'shut the fuck up' works like magic on any kid – shut the fuck up.

But I don't have the balls so instead these kids – animals – farmyard animals – like being on a cattle truck surrounded by cow girls and pig boys - just run rampage around me shouting their gobs off and getting ever more lairy. If I was to write a book about them it wouldn't be called Harry Potter it would be called Lairy Fucker. Lairy Fucker and the Gobshite for hire. Kids on a train run riot until one brave individual tells them to shut the fuck up.

That's why Voldemort in my eyes get a bad press, there was a bunch of spoilt brats running around and into walls at train stations thinking they were special and he just wanted to get rid of one of the little cunts. Good on him I say, let's not encourage the kids. You're not special, you're not a wizard, you're a cunt. Voldemort is no more harmful than Philip Schofield. He sees a fifteen-year-old and thinks I wish I'd killed you as a baby, then I might still have a job.

DAILY NOTES VOL I

June 9th 2023
Kali Uchis – Moonlight

JK Rowling wrote *Harry Potter* on a train and because she didn't have a pen, she thought up the entire story in her head. Similarly when I was twenty in the 90s I was laying on the bottom bunk of my bunk beds above my stepdad's sub post office writing mainly aggressive words in the wooden slats above my head, and I too didn't have a pen, but I did have my stepbrothers box cutter knife which he regularly threatened me with and so I would gouge words into the wood. And while JK Rowling wrote Harry Potter I would write words that basically catalogued how I was having a breakdown. Which let's face is how people would have viewed JK Rowling if *Harry Potter* had never been published... what you've been spending your train journeys imagining a school for wizards have you Jo, do you need help?

And that's the problem with a lot of creatives – before they become successful they can be seen as lunatics. Ooh look at me everyone, I've written a song called *Bohemian Rhapsody* which contains the lyric 'scaramouche scaramouche can you do the fandango'... Ah cool, that sounds shit and you sound mental. So there I was laying on the bottom bunk gouging words into to keep me going when I was ill, and two of the main words above my head were these – Nathan Cassidy. Because I wanted to be a comedian and one day I imagined these words would be up in lights, but they weren't in lights they were instead surrounded by a series of negative words, which if I didn't have ME and couldn't move for three months would have probably ended up being tattooed on my face. Words like hide away, shame, hopeless, slitherin. That's right, I thought of *Harry Potter* as well I just couldn't find a fucking pen.

But you don't wanna judge my childhood thoughts on these words gauged into wood, because I wrote them at night mainly, in bed. Don't judge anything from how you feel in the middle of the night. Anyone else wake up in the middle of the night and think, well my life is shit isn't it? All I do is work and shop in Iceland, not the country the shop. And oh fuck, what if the moon explodes? The moon might explode. What is the shittest food in Iceland?

Anyway, if you're struggling, sometimes it takes forever, but know for certain, the night always passes.

June 10th 2023
Energy – Beyoncé

So I was twenty and I got this ME virus thing and I couldn't move out of my bed for a week or two, no energy at all - and my mom would bring me food and stuff, but I wasn't eating enough so one thing my mom got me from the shop, because she was selling them as novelty items for Christmas, was a long straw. A long novelty straw. Now the word 'novelty' is a red flag there obviously, and to give you a clue what the word novelty means, if you got a novelty red flag it would be pink. Because novelty means shit, a novelty item is a shit item. Ooh a novelty item, cool yeah a shit item, one that I'll throw away within hours. Think Christmas cracker motifs, toys in a Kinder Surprise, stuff you buy in a gift shop from a zoo, rings from your first marriage – worthless items.

And my mom and stepdad's shop was full of these novelty items, shitty little presents you'd buy for people and immediately throw away – landfill – you know the kind of thing, big playing cards, oh ha ha ha what a funny novelty item they're playing cards but they're massive – ha ha ha – thanks for those – I will never ever be using these massive playing cards – happy Christmas fuck you. Just give me the cash it's a total waste or time money resources and the planet. Anyway, a long straw from the shop, a novelty item usually – oh ha ha ha, it's a long straw, let's use it once and then throw it away, and it's so long it will never ever biodegrade. But this straw became my lifeline because I was seriously ill, I would struggle to sit up, so I could leave this heavy glass bottle of water on the floor and I'd suck it up supine, it was keeping me alive, and being alive for me at that time had become a novelty item, something that was great for a moment and had now become pointless. Stay in the game, stay in the game, even if the cards are the wrong size, if you still have cards then stay in the game. Don't fold, do not fold. Suck up any life you still have left in you through that long straw and stay in the game. And maybe start by lowering expectations, you were never going to win the game, you were never going to do that well, and what is life anyway, its full of novelty items, pointless things, and maybe being one of those things isn't so bad after all. There are countless pointless things, put into this world to distract us. That's all any of us are, a distraction. Stay a distraction, stay in the game.

DAILY NOTES VOL I

June 11th 2023
Need A Favor – Jelly Roll

There's been a lot in the news in this country over the last week about how the entire commercial television business is run by dicks and twats that don't give a fuck about people and just want to make as much money as possible for themselves and their best mates and be as famous and powerful as possible because they are damaged, narcissistic cunts. Not everyone in the television business of course, there's just one or two bad orchards. And of course all this comes as no surprise to anyone, entertainment is not based on talent in the main, of course you have to be talented no question, but you also have to backstab, walk over shattered glass over your grandma's face and suck the right dick or clit, do the right favours to get up you that greasy ladder covered in the sweat of everyone who is not in the gang's hard work.

That's right the people not in the gang they ain't even climbing the ladder, they sometimes look like they are but they're not, the most those people can do is get a little way up and cover the rung in enough of their hard work sweat to make it slightly more difficult for those in the gang doing favours for each other to get up, but in reality, most don't even touch the rungs, they fly up, lifted up by the hand of nepotism or on the jet pack of corruption. We all know this is how it works, and suddenly in this country, some of these people are coming crashing back to earth, because some of the favours are being uncovered, and they're nasty, underhand, if not illegal then immoral.

And people are finally coming out saying, the system is crumbling. Erm, no, no it isn't. That's one thing that will never happen, bring down the system, exactly the same system will grow in its place, you cannot beat the system – those with privilege, connections and who do the right favours will always rise to the top. So here's what you can do - stop looking at the top of the ladder. Because what is the top of the ladder anyway? It's bland , boring, the same watered down unfiltered old shite. Just redirect your gaze to the bottom of the ladder, then we'd all have to stop this pointless fight for your attention, and the people at the top would wither and die or just look at each other or themselves, which is all they ever wanted to do anyway. It's so simple, and it's not in their hands, it's in yours, so - do me and yourselves a favour, and rise.

DAILY NOTES VOL I

June 12th 2023
ZAYN – Fingers

A few years ago I had come to a temporary conclusion that everyone is a cunt. I realise now that's not true, but you do go through moments in your life don't you where you think can I trust anyone, or are you ultimately going to be let down so are you better off to be alone? That's too big a question to answer here so let's just say I don't like other people's noise, and what other people do around me.

It's mainly on trains when this happens. The worst one I ever had, forget the lack of headphones that's virtually everyone on trains these days - I had someone in the seat behind me stick his fingers around the seat, so my head is bumping into his fat dirty fingers, the worst horror film. And to add insult to injury his moron son was watching TV on his phone without headphones. Which usually would have taken my attention but with his dad's fingers tickling my ears every time I sat back I had bigger fishy fingers to fry. So I banged the sausage fingers with my head, they came back, I then used my metal bottle to bang them, they came back. How can anyone have this level of a lack of self-awareness I thought if they aren't in the government? I thought I'm gonna have to lick these fingers, I'm going to have to put hula hoops on each one of the filthy sausages before he gets the message the unforgiveable cunt. It's people like him that make me want to opt out of the human race and live alone on a mountain in New Zealand.

This lasted more than an hour and I thought what can I do? The train was full and I didn't want to stand and so eventually I snapped, I stood up and I turned to him and I said mate, can you stop sticking your fingers through the seat. And he said I wasn't and I said you were, and he said I wasn't. So obviously I couldn't sit back down again because he would almost certainly hit me or spit on my head, so I had to spend the rest of the journey standing and glaring at him. Or not really at him, more his fingers, I'm still thinking about those fingers, days later, I've got PTSD, which I get most times I get public transport – Post Twat Stress Disorder, so many twats, where are they all going? Coz they're all on public transport – public Twatsport, so here's to you, you twats, here's one big fat fishy middle finger shoved through the seat in front just for you.

June 13th 2023
I Heard – YoungBoy Never Broke Again

Alexei Sayle, he was my hero as a kid, I heard him say he would never do an advert, because he was a pure, credible comedian and he would never do an advert. And I loved him for that, and as a very young boy I knew that was the comedian I wanted to emulate. But then the years passed, and I heard his voice on an advert for Totes Toasties, yes Totes Toasties, the warm sock slipper thing. And it broke my heart, he was the last one, the last pure comedian. And he'd let me down. But of course, he wasn't the last pure comedian, because I had the chance to be that comedian that I once idolised, I could become him. So I worked on and off for over 20 years to develop into that very thing, a hard-working, pure, respected (by some) multi award winning comedian that would never do an advert. And my God it takes work because those that do adverts can maybe earn half a year's wages in literally one or two hours, it's that easy, but you pay the price, because you sell your soul, and that may appear to be a made up thing, but you feel it, that's when you feel the weight of your soul, and you feel something inside you being ripped out, that's your soul, and that's why I would never do it and I could never understand why Alexei Sayle did it, surely he was earning enough money from standup and TV work, why Alexi, why?

And warm slipper socks? You've gone from *The Young Ones*, the rebel to the old man in slipper socks in a matter of hours. Why Alexei? And then you get a bit older, and you have kids, and a mortgage and you need a holiday and you have two gigs cancelled on me like they were tonight because of a thing called sunshine, and then you see it, you see everything so clearly, Alexei was right, and you were wrong, the thing about principles is they're great until they're standing in your way of an easy or a better life. You only have one life, you've got to make it as easy and as beautiful as possible. But what about the soul, what about the trade off, what price your soul? Does your soul really have a price? And you finally realise – yes it does, it's a few hours in a booth doing a little voiceover. Forgive me dear listener, or if you don't, I don't really give a fuck, my feet will be very, very warm, not in slipper socks, but in the warm sunshine of Brazil. Fuck comedy, fuck principles, here comes the sun.

DAILY NOTES VOL I

June 14th 2023
Ed Sheeran – Borderline

There's been a lot of talk due to recent news events of things being borderline okay, a fine dividing line between illegal and unwise and a bit of a pile-on. And what I've noticed out of all this is twofold – number one - this overly stating when something is borderline legal, oh he did it, and it was technically legal but you know what I mean? No I don't know what you mean - was it illegal? No? Well it was legal then. That's what the law is for to decide on what is right and wrong. If you don't agree with the law then petition to change the law, if something is legal then leave them alone but the bigger thing is the piousness of some people…

I mean how could he? Literally how could he do that borderline legal thing? You mean that legal thing? Yes how could he do that legal thing? Because it was legal. But you know what I mean, its borderline legal. Well he probably did it because its legal, he also probably did it because to paraphrase Chris Rock he had the opportunity and you didn't, only if you were in those circumstances and you did something different can you judge, but of course you won't be in those circumstances ever because you just stay in every night watching quiz shows and you go to the football on a weekend and are borderline racist borderline homophobic borderline xenophobic, borderline antisemitic, borderline misogynist but actually you've crossed the border and are just racist homophobic misogynist etc because and this is the main issue, take a look at yourself, because the vast majority of people are either as boring as sin with no opportunities or they've done fucked-up things themselves.

Oh that doesn't count… yes it does count, you masturbated in front of the dog, you made the dog watch as you masturbated. That's legal. Is it? Yes, I guess so. But its borderline wrong isn't it? Its borderline zoophilia, sex with animals. I didn't fuck the dog I just masturbated in front of it. Just?! Well everyone *just* did everything that they did. So leave them alone. If it's unwise but illegal then just let them face the consequences, no need to add to the pile on, because your pious hypocritical stance carries no weight at all, you dog wanker.

June 15th 2023
West life – Swear it Again

I grew up in a time where swear words were not allowed virtually at all on television, even after the 9pm watershed it was kinda frowned upon. Occasionally you got a shit but hardly any fucks and cunts. People were sacked for saying fuck, like a cricket commentator I recall he thought he was off-air and he said 'fuck', you just never saw that poor fuck again, he was gone, it was like some Goodfellas shit, he was gone.

I grew up in a time where 'knackered' was a rude word, you can't say knackered that's a swear word. What the fuck? And now, well of course you can't even watch children's TV without someone throwing in a few cunts and a bastard, and I'm not sure when this transition happened and it's happened quite slowly but I'm kind of pleased that it did, it was always fairly ridiculous to me that you could say country not cunt. I remember there was a German footballer called Stefan Koontz, and it was pronounced kunts as far as I know but of course the commentators didn't want to say kunts as they had the recent memory of the cricket commentator being killed because he swore, so although it was his name it was a dilemma and some pronounced it Koontz and whatever. A pundit called Alan Hansen once said 'I can't see the Germans getting back into this, they've only got Kunts up front'. Funny right?

And it's funny looking back that swear words were ever a problem and its strange to think in about thirty years' time swear words will be used again and again as if it's nothing… Well he we are at the FA Cup Final and I've got to say John, its fucking hot here, I'm sweating like a bakers fuck… I know what you mean John my bollocks are sweating like scallops on the barbecue. And what do we think of the Germans John? They're shit Harry, they've only got cunts up front. He isn't playing John, oh I see what you mean now you actually are saying they're all just cunts. That's right John the German are cunts. Anyway here we go, and we're off. Lump it up to the big twat, and fuck me he's scored, fuck me sideways what a lucky cunt. How do you feel Harry? Like shit mate I had a bet on that lanky cunt's team to lose. I could swear I really could, well go on Harry you can swear now, oh right – fuuuuuuuuck! Cunty fucky Koontz!

June 16th 2023
Royal Blood – Mountains at Midnight

So King Charles has been in the job for a few weeks now, he finally got the promotion, and how do we assess his first month or so in the job? Well, there's one word I can use to sum up what he's done so far. Fuck-all. Hyphen one word – fuck-all. And I think it's a clever calculated move from Charlie, I mean the queen was everywhere wasn't she? She was on stamps, on coins, she loved the sight of her own face on money, she was in the papers all the time, let's face it, she was a fame hungry bitch. But Charlie, he knows the downside of fame, he knows it can kill you, he was married to that of course, he knows where it ends up.

Harry and Meghan you may remember, because they court fame, they had to have, in their words, 'a near catastrophic car chase through New York' the other week. Now of course the other words for near catastrophic are of course 'not catastrophic' and the rumour is they made it up to get in the papers but not Charlie, he hates the papers, it's bad for the environment. Charlie takes after his dad, he doesn't give a fuck, he doesn't want to pander to the press, he thinks they're all idiots and they are, and now he's the fucking King he just wants to lounge about Buckingham Palace apparently in the nude doing Yoga, fucking his misses, getting his dinner cooked for him and watching game-shows.

And he's a clever man Charlie and I'll tell you why, when he took over, the Monarchy were in trouble, Harry and Meghan, the paedophile, etc etc, so what do you do when you're in trouble and everyone's questioning your future? You do what my friend Ryan does when he's in trouble... nothing. You do nothing, you say nothing and even the biggest problems just go away.

Be like the mountains at midnight – you're there, you're regal, you're huge, you are the story, but no one can see you so it's like you're not there. God Save the King, and God Save the eternal power of doing fuck all.

DAILY NOTES VOL I

June 17th 2023
It's Crazy – J Hus

It's crazy isn't it to think that women at one stage not paid the same as men in tennis, isn't that just crazy, now that's all sorted out of course and for example the men and women at Roland Garros in the French open both earn 2.3 million euros for winning and that's fair. Because they both play the same number of matches. Of course yeah sure, but? What? No, I just mean that the women's matches are significantly shorter, like Iga Swiatek beat an opponent in fifty-three minutes in the French open 6-0 6-0. What you saying? Nothing. You are... Well it's just that undoubtedly the women in general play much shorter matches than the men so... what? No nothing they should be paid exactly the same, for less work.

For years men were paid more for the same work, so now it's redressing the balance isn't it – women now get paid the same for less work. I guess it makes up for all that lost time. What are you saying Nathan? All I'm saying is that... look ok I'll say it.... less people are interested in women's tennis...

Now Nathan you're just making that up. I am, I admit it, I'm just guessing but I'm probably prepared to die on that hill. Well you will die on that hill Nathan because everyone agrees that women tennis players should be paid the same as men. Even if they work a lot less? Yes even if they work a lot less. Ok, everyone agrees that do they? Yes everyone. Even though I was having this conversation with a few women today and they said... I don't want to hear what anyone said Nathan because everyone believes that women tennis players deserve to be paid the same as men - shall we just say that everyone agrees the agreed narrative for every single issue when it comes to gender and gender equality – yes. Let's say that. It's easier isn't it?

It is but also crazy. What? Nothing. Nothing at all, I just need to keep my mouth shut don't I? Yes you do Nathan. Ok, fine, I'll just... you know ? Man up. What?

June 18th 2023
The Weeknd – Sacrifice

So I saw The Weeknd at The Weeknd gig at the weekend. If you get me. It was at The Weeknd, a weekend or so back at the weekend and anyway I took someone for their birthday and you have to celebrate with the special people in your lives on their birthday don't you, because it's the anniversary of their birth and that's an important day to recognise isn't it even though you're in your 40's. Anyway, the birthday just happened to be on the same day as the Champions League football final, Man City v Inter Milan, and I'm not a fan of either club but it's the Champions League final and any football fan is desperate to watch. Not me though because someone special in my life had her birthday and she doesn't like football and that's fine because it's her special day and although she's in her 40s she needs to celebrate that very special day. So instead we went to see The Weeknd at the weekend a weekend or so ago, and it was great and everything, but I tried not to think about the greatest game of football I was missing. However by a cruel twist of fate The Weeknd were playing the concert at the ground of Manchester City, the Etihad Stadium in Manchester, so I was forced to look out on to the pitch throughout the whole concert, now to make it clear they weren't playing the football game too at the stadium, that was elsewhere, but still it was fairly triggering having to look at a football pitch for the duration of a concert where you wanted to be watching the football.

And as I looked around, everyone has their phones out obviously, but they weren't filming the concert, of course not, these were mainly local people, they were Manchester City fans who had made a mistake and long back bought a ticket for the same day as the Champions League final or worse still had to treat the very special person in their lives because it was her birthday and the anniversary of the day you were born four decades ago is a very special thing. No it isn't, grow up, you're not a child. No, it's very special and I wasn't allowed to watch the game I had to watch The Weeknd and just get a sense from the cheers in the crowd what the score was and what could have been, sitting at home on my own, and having the weekend of my life. And I'm sorry if this episode wasn't great, I'm just depressed looking back at the weekend at the weekend, and so forgive me if this hasn't been funny or interesting, and forgive me that the episode has a particular week end.

DAILY NOTES VOL I

June 19th 2023
It Was A Good Day – Ice Cube

I was joking yesterday when I was jokingly moaning that I spent the evening watching The Weeknd rather than the Champions League football that I actually wanted to watch, obviously that was a joke and had no basis in truth at all, I promise you, you have to believe me it's true. Anyway, I am joking really because as the years pass, I do stop to mark it in my mind - that was a good day. When you're younger you never mark that do you? You think that was an amazing moment, on to the next. Now, its gratitude isn't it that whole day was good. So what marks a good day for me? Good question. Well I wake up and I give my daughter a big kiss before she leaves for school. I'm still in bed, I ain't getting up for that shit, its 8am. My son has left by then for school, no kiss for him and I go downstairs and make my smoothie and I sit in a comfortable chair. I'm not getting old or anything I do just fucking love a comfortable chair.

I then go up to my laptop and I sit there for 8 hours in my pants slogging out shit like this and award winning shows and ground breaking comedy ideas for you idiots who hardly ever truly appreciate what I'm doing here and then my kids get back and they says daddy have a shower so that reminds me I'm actually a person in society, and I wash, make them dinner and then I go out to work in the evening. And I'm never happy obviously, have you spotted anything there that would make a person happy? Of course not, but I am contented, and I'm healthy, and I'm grateful for that. And this is every day, every single day, apart from the very odd occasion because I'm so in demand that I get the evening off, and that's when I'm truly happy, because I plan it way in advance I think on this day I'm gonna be by myself, on my own, doing what I want to do, doing what makes me happy, and watching the Champions League final but oh no we have to celebrate your birthday, Jesus, like you're. a child, yes sorry it is still about that. I can't get over it and I never ever will. You're not 7, just let me watch the football.

Anyway, that's today's episode about a really bad day in my life. Why is it called good day? Because I'm going now, back to work, good day.

DAILY NOTES VOL I

June 20th 2023
Nicki Minaj and Ariana Grande – Side to Side

This song is about soreness after sex, not mental soreness that's the most common type of soreness after sex... Oh no! Why did I do that? But in this case the actual physical soreness you feel after sex in your genitals or asshole that's what this song is about, some songs you'll find are about rainbows, this one's about the soreness you feel in your genital or asshole or mouth after sex. And the worst soreness I had after sex was a few years ago now, I'd had sex with someone and I was a bit sore... in my ears, not really, just keeping it light – I was a bit sore on the tip of my penis and had a little something that could have been a STD so I went to a sexual health clinic and I waited with the other legends and I went in to see the nurse, and he sits me down and he starts the small talk, he asks me how I am. And I say fine but it's a strange feeling that you don't get in any other scenario unless you're clubbing in Ibiza – you think, well I've only just met you, but in less than three minutes you're going to be handling my dick. I mean I'm sure he wouldn't put it like that, but there was the usual questions, when's the last time you've had sex, how many sexual partners have you had, what are you doing next Tuesday night, do you want to go for a drink? But that's all preamble obviously, he just wants to see my penis and see what it is – this is his job, looking at penis's and he knows his penis stuff by now, just show me the penis...

But this is the interesting bit, I'm sitting next to him and he could quite easily say ok now's the time big boy let's have a butchers at this red raw magnificence, but he says go over there, like a metre over there, I'll draw a curtain, get your penis out, then I'll undraw the curtain and have a look then. Ridiculous. Why? Why this ridiculous charade. In this situation, in fact I'd say in all situations where seeing your penis is on the cards, let's get it over and done with straight away – so many things stand and fall on what the penis looks like – most dates and certainly the STD clinic. So he has a look and I was worried about nothing - I didn't have an STD my penis was just red raw because and I think I'm remembering this correctly he said 'I must be a legend'. He notes down the word 'legend' with a red felt tip and I was out of there. And that's it, what do you want - stories about rainbows? Stop with this ridiculous preamble, let's have a look at the legend.

June 21st 2023
Go Hard – Lil Baby

I've seen a lot of stand-up over the last 13 years, sitting at the back of the room waiting to go on, and I'd say the biggest misrepresentation of our human race and that's what stand-up essentially is, a misrepresentation of the human race - oh men are like this, women are like this, kids are like this, cats are like this - no they're not you're generalising - that's the heckle you need when you next see stand-up – stop generalising. Stop generalising goddammit! Anyway the biggest generalisation that you see from standups is about foreplay and it's from female stand-ups saying that their boyfriends foreplay is terrible. Well, let's start from the beginning shall we – sex education is terrible in this country and I assume around the world, apart from France no doubt – I bet it's amazing there – anyway we don't learn about sex properly and we certainly don't learn about pleasure, so unfortunately it's up to women to teach men if that's the kinda relationship you're in – tell me where everything is and what feels good, it's up to you to teach the kids, in President Macron's case literally as he was having sex with his 40 year old teacher at 15 - that's how good the sex education is there – it's magnifique.

So what I'm saying is don't blame the man, blame the women that the man slept with when he was learning sex as a teenager, blame the women, and I say that with a barely disguised sense of irony that I hope you spotted. Anyway, this isn't about that, this is more about addressing the balance from the things I've heard on stage, women, yes women I'm talking to you, you ain't brilliant at foreplay either sometimes, you just expect us to get hard, and stay hard no matter what you do. Well not always, in the main but not always – if you're yanking it like a gear stick on a clapped out 1970 Austin Allegro, if you're sucking it like a Pret coffee with a shit plastic lid then maybe it won't get hard, maybe it won't stay hard for long. As the bible said those who do bad foreplay cast the first stone. I'm just saying let's get equality here, everyone's a bit shit sometimes, the only difference is that when women are shit, the men still get the blame. So, you know, what I'm saying is - it's time to stop being so lenient on stand-ups. Remember the heckle – stop generalising! Don't be soft on stand-ups. My advice – get hard.

DAILY NOTES VOL I

June 22nd 2023
The Bare Necessities – Phil Harris/Bruce Reitherman (Jungle Book)

What a song. Jazz. We need music in our lives don't we? That is one of the bare necessities – imagine life without music, well imagine no more and just listen to any music radio station – oh Pam's been on and she says she's enjoying the sunshine in her garden – oh great on you Pam, and David's been on and he's a rent boy in Newcastle and he says all the tunes are getting him through a hard day of sucking dick behind the bins round the back of the station – what tunes! No – what tunes? You ain't playing any tunes love you're just gobbing on - I don't give a fuck how many dicks David's gobbed off or how many dead ends Pam has whipped off which sounds ruder to be honest, play a fucking track goddammit.

So, yeah music, one of the bare necessities, so what are the other? Some people say food, well not really, there are very good liquid based diets now, get all your nutrients from a single shot, that's what I'm planning, fuck cooking and eating right, so boring, oh what's for tea daddy, can we have sausage gnocchi – no we can't have sausage gnocchi I've been making that shit now for fifteen years and you still don't tidy your rooms. I'll tell you what's for tea, see those little sachets of milkshake, open your own one, fill the glass with tepid water and get it down you, you don't need food and you don't need drink, you just need that gloopy nutrient shake.

You don't need sex that's over-rated, you don't need exercise if you're not eating, so what do you need apart from music? Well isn't it obvious, we need comedy, we need to have a laugh, have you ever met anyone with no sense of humour, fuck me that's a tough five-minute chat at a wedding isn't it? Well Nathan I actually do give them more than six months… Oh cheer up you humourless cunt – you need comedy, its essential, life is awful without a laugh. So we come to our conclusions, in life we just need two things, music and comedy. So here's my question, why the fuck do the downloads go down on my podcast around this week every year, I'll tell you why, because of the sunshine in Europe. Fuck the sunshine, we don't need that, that will kill you, along with food drink and sex, they all kill more than anything on this planet. Stay in, and listen to my podcast, there's 1000 episodes and more to come, truly the bare necessities of life.

DAILY NOTES VOL I

June 23rd 2023
Hits Different – Taylor Swift

It's only a small step from hits to shit isn't it, you ask any band, they have their hits and then they have their shit, and they keep sticking their shit out for years until they realise they can't do hits any more so they stop doing shit and instead release a Greatest Hits album with no shit just hits and they tour that for a bit and at the concerts they do one of their shit songs to give everyone the chance to go to the toilet.

Anyway, the interesting thing about hits and shit and what makes them especially close and different sides of the same coin is of course shit and hits are anagrams of each other. Funny right? Who knew? But I'm serious, look closely, the letters in hits are the same as the letters used to make the word shit. It's true I promise you. It's like those clickbait Instagram videos – once you see it… I know right, have you seen it, fuck me. Yeah something you may not know about me, I've genuinely really liked anagrams since I was a kid, I am one of these strange people that find anagrams clever and even amusing. So this episode has given me the chance to share with you something I've been dying to share with you for nearly 1000 episodes now, some amusing anagrams.

So for example. Admirer becomes married, and such is life. A decimal point – I'm a dot in place. Alec Guinness – genuine class. Conversation – voices rant on, Clint Eastwood – old west action – Debit card bad credit. Desperation – a rope ends it. Election results, lies lets recount. It is amusing isn't it, you thought it wouldn't be but it actually is amusing, this is my favourite ever episode – listen – silent. Heavy rain – hire a navy. Funeral – real fun. Mother-in-law – woman Hitler. And that's the thing, with some of these you think, is that a really a coincidence ? Slot machines – cash lost in 'em. The eyes – they see. The morse code – here comes dots. I mean no one says 'the' morse code but it is funny isn't it, it's amusing, I like anagrams.

Anagram of Nathan Cassidy – satanic shandy. There are no coincidences, or maybe there is, and this is all stuff sent to distract us, because we go searching for hits but in fact they are just shit in disguise. There is no point, there is no meaning – perhaps the 'meaning of life' is in fact - the 'fine game of nil'.

148

June 24th 2023
Ed Sheeran – Colourblind

I went to school in Aston in Birmingham and I now live in Hackney in London and what links both these areas? Erm, they're both shit holes? Nathan, yes true up to a point, because they are places in the UK, but that's not what I was getting it, I meant they are both ethnically diverse. I have grown up and lived in very ethnically diverse shit holes and so now I operate on that very annoying phrase of 'I don't see colour' – but I genuinely don't, I don't see colour, I look at everyone the same, all I see in other people usually is that they are assholes, it really doesn't matter what colour someone's skin is, they are all assholes.

But there is no bigger asshole than the racist, and growing up and living where I did I have to constantly remind myself of the very sad and inescapable fact – oh yeah, a lot of people are just racist, and so when I see people talking about racism online my first thought is usually - is it that bad? Is racism really as prevalent as you suggest? And I have to remember oh yeah, it is because people are assholes, I don't see colour I see assholes. And you're reminded of it in football, when fans, sometimes fans of the actual team they're abusing, shout racist stuff at footballers for the world to see and normalize this asshole behaviour, and it gets better and then it gets worse and it gets better and footballers take the knee and then it gets worse, and so it would be easy to give up, and they say it will never be eradicated, and of course they are right, nothing can ever be eradicated, but its incumbent on as all to try to at least make it much better.

And the first way to make that happen, do not like me be colourblind, recognise that we are all different and we all have different experiences but what we all share is we are surrounded by assholes, and these assholes will display different ways of being assholes. And call them out on it if you can. I've started standing up to assholes now, 'stop being an asshole', and if I ever saw racism happening, I know I would stand up and call it out. I don't give a fuck any more. I think it's my age. I don't give a fuck. I'm blind to danger. I'm danger blind. If there's an asshole, spread the word - Nathan Cassidy will sniff out that asshole and lick it into touch.

DAILY NOTES VOL I

June 25th 2023
War Bout It – Lil Durk Featuring 21 Savage

There's a war on. I'm not sure whether you've heard, maybe you were watching *Succession*. But yeah there's a war on, Russia has invaded Ukraine or is trying to protect itself from Ukraine depending on who you believe and whether or not you're insane. And it's easy to get war fatigue and forget about it. When the war first started a lot of people cared about it more didn't they, particularly comedians, straight out of the traps with their benefit gigs - how can we make this war about me, and my comedy? Oh no the awful war, another chance to celebrate my awful comedy which in truth is worse than most aspects of the war. And here we are a year and a half later, not even the faintest whiff of a benefit gig, it's not like we don't care but people need to be reminded now don't they – oh the war, war about it?

What do you want me to do about it now, after a year and a half, what you want me to still care? Yes! Your caring has a limit, I get that, but it's just to be honest about that and a worthwhile reminder that you essentially are not a good person, and you essentially don't care about anyone but yourself and your own family and to a lesser extent friends. So next time you're passing judgement on someone you don't know, remember that it's fine to do that but know that you yourself are nothing incredibly special and you genuinely care more about Netflix and your food being warm than the poor people of Ukraine, or the poor people of Russia depending on your perspective and whether you're insane, and maybe you are insane, because you have the insane ability to forget about the biggest tragedy facing the world in a generation and moan to someone that your food isn't warm enough at a restaurant.

It's not that I saw someone do it, sure send it back whatever, it's the attitude, the entitled - this is the worst thing to ever happen in the world - attitude of almost everyone in society, almost everyone that hears there is a war on and thinks war about it? I'll tell you what about it, some of those people have no food, and their homes are floating down the street as their lives are smashed to pieces. But still, sorry that cold chicken has ruined yet another day for you and me in paradise.

DAILY NOTES VOL I

June 26th 2023
One More Time – Daft Punk

So this is almost certainly completely off your radar, even if you live in the UK, but a comedian called Viggo Venn has won Britain's Got Talent, the prestigious talent competition that has been won at least twice in the last 15 years by a dog. So this guy is more of a clown than a comedian if you don't know him, lovely guy very funny and I won't do the act justice but one of the main things he does is dances around the stage to the tune of this track 'One More Time' taking off a layer of clothing every time to reveal another high vis top, you know those bright yellow thin tops you wear to stand out if you're, I don't know, riding a bike or you're a builder. So yeah that's the act and he won, its brilliant, I know this guy I've gigged with him and anyway while he won, he angered a lot of people online for winning as all he does is dance around and take off high vis jackets, conveniently forgetting that this is a competition won twice over the last fifteen years by an actual dog, twice in the last fifteen years a dog has been the most talented person in the country. A dog. You're attacking the wrong person – at least this guy is human. A dog. FFS a dog!

But Viggo Venn winning is where we are in the world right now, the TikTok generation need something simple to laugh at, the world is a horrible place sometimes we need simple stuff, and that's not to denigrate it, it takes lots of work, I realise that, to dance around and take off high vis jackets and let's face it most pieces of art seems ludicrous before they become successful – Harry Potter, a load of school wizards that sounds shit, Bohemian Rhapsody scaramouche scaramouche are you seriously ok babe? Who's to say in ten years' time we won't all be dancing around taking off high vis jackets. It's better than forcing your fucking dog to walk up and down a seesaw and jump through hoops. A competition previously won by a dog has now been won by a human – that in my book represents incredible progress, and I for one hope that next year a human wins it again. And who knows, the way the world is going I think we're only a few years away from the competition being won by a plate of vomit being eaten, I'm not joking, a plate of vomit being eaten and vomited up again and again and again to the backing of dance music, one more time.

June 27th 2023
Reality – David Bowie

I saw the film *Reality* last night and it's a really great movie that is very different to anything I've ever seen, it tells the story of FBI agents swarming into some young girl's property who, while working for the Government, may or may not have done something she wasn't allowed to do. And what makes it different is it's about a single incident, it's about a moment in time, it's about something that is relatively trivial and yet fundamental and the way it's shot and the way its acted and particularly the pace of the film really gets under your skin, and what it becomes is a movie about what we're being told, what is the truth, and whether or not you can beat or indeed affect the system.

So what is the system? Well not just in this film, but generally, it's the people in power, the rich the privileged, in whatever walk of like these people are in charge, and can't you beat them – no, that is the reality. They don't tell you the truth, things are ultimately for self-interest rather than the greater good, and people spend their lives fighting against their system like the rocks trying to hold back the tides, eventually they are going to break you down, eventually they are going to win. People spend their lives protesting, posting on twitter, trying to mobilize people to bring these systems down – and I respect these people of course I do but essentially they are just people wearing bin bags and glueing themselves to lampposts and very quickly they are going to be hoovered up and dumped on the nutter pile.

Only a handful of people throughout history have ever succeeded in beating the system in this way, and then as I say almost always another one only pops up in its place. Reality. So what can you do? Well you can only ever do what is in your control to do, and in this case it is to create a new system yourself, if not for everyone then just for the people you know, the people you can affect, that's something we can do, and by doing that without standing in the street or shouting into the blackhole on social media, you're making a difference.

And if everyone did that then together we could truly make a new reality.

DAILY NOTES VOL I

June 28th 2023
Stoned – Ed Sheeran

What was the worst day of your life? Any takers for today? Let's not think about that now its comedy, but for me it was undoubtedly during Edinburgh Fringe 2017, a month of shows and at the end of one of the shows in the middle of the run I'm taking the acclaim of the crowd and I slip off the stage and I have full on spasm in front of the audience – I hobble outside and think well I can't move, I order an Uber and that takes me to A and E where I wait for 6 hours unable to move and then I'm seen by a nurse who doesn't do an X-ray, she just moves me around for a bit and then says well 'you've shagged your back', it's Scotland that's how the nurses talk. Thanks for that mate. She says I'm gonna give you a diazepam take that that will take the pain away and hopefully you'll be able to stretch it out and it should be a lot better after 24 hours.

So I take the diazepam and I get into another uber and I pass out. The moral of this story is diazepam is fucking great. I was in agony and I wake up back at my flat and I can climb the stairs like I'm on *Strictly Come Dancing* – I'm only doing it because I'm on drugs, and my marriage is about to fail. It's a miracle, I could hardly get into the cab and I climb the stairs and think oh I'll go to sleep now and in the morning I'll be fine. That's one of the world's biggest myths isn't it – that things will be better after a good night's sleep. If your life is shit, after a good night sleep, it's equally shit, or worse. I have a good sleep and then I wake up I can't move, I can't get out of bed. Every time I try to move I'm in agony. What the fuck do you do – who do you call? An ambulance? They'd laugh at me.

I'd call my mom, now my mom is lovely but she's like an Orangutan, in that I think she shares 97% of human DNA. She's almost human, you know what I mean, she says and does things that aren't quite human, and in this situation I know she won't be able to help because she'd tell me oh well I'm sure it will be ok later and hang up. So I call my drugs friend, we all have a drugs friend, particularly me I'm a comedian at the Edinburgh Fringe. So I was living alone during this Fringe and I would usually stay with a mate but this particular year I'd chosen to live alone because I had come to a temporary conclusion that everyone is a cunt. I call my mate - Please get me a diazepam – she laughed and said easy I'm at the

Edinburgh Fringe the biggest drugs festival in the world I'll be there in 30 mins. This girl comes round she give me a diazepam and she says shall I put on a film for you? And I say yes – so this was 2017 remember when everyone still watched DVDs and I was at this rented flat in Edinburgh and they'd left behind 4 films, one of which was *Life Of Pi*, so I thought yeah Life of Pi, I'll be passed out in a few minutes anyway. So this girl put on Life of Pi and I was just waiting for the diazepam to kick in and watching the first part of this film, *Life of Pi*, and just as it kicked with the tiger and the hyena and the zebra I think I started tripping, I stopped crying in pain and started tripping, and it was magical, animals flying everywhere - I've never done drugs but now I know why people get stoned – the *Life of Pi*, and now I would be living the life of high – more on this tomorrow.

DAILY NOTES VOL I

June 29th 2023
Oasis – Stop Crying Your Heart Out

So I'm carrying on my story from yesterday, remember at the start of the year I did stories in these episodes which lasted half a month each – go back and listen to them, they are very good, one is about travelling about the world on Christmas Eve looking at porn or something, I just couldn't keep them going. Back breaking work. And a reminder I'm at the Edinburgh Fringe 2017, I've slipped off a stage the night before I'm in agony the next morning unable to move and my drugs friend comes round and gives me some diazepam and I stop crying and I start tripping, which is made even better because I'm watching the film *Life of Pi* on a DVD.

If you haven't seen it it's a young boy on a boat with a tiger, a hyena, an Orangutan and a zebra. Now as I said yesterday I've always thought of my mom like an Orangutan because she shares around 97% of human DNA so my mom was the Orangutan, so it's floating above me, an Orangutan with the face of my mom, and she was there watching over me, caring for me from a distance, but also judging me, and thinking it was my fault for having a bad back because and I quote her directly now 'if you don't do anything in life Nathan you will never get injured'. 97% human DNA. Then there was the hyena, the aggressive little fucker that just wanted to kill everyone - that represented most comedians and the comedy industry, horrible little fuckers that want to kill you and feed on your flesh. There was the zebra - that represented the few nice comedians out there, who are doing it for the art and not the fame, it's a zebra and the black and white doesn't represent the comedy industry's bizarre approach to diversity it merely represents a simple choice between good and bad, right and wrong, and it doesn't matter whether the zebra is black or white because the zebra is good and right. Anyway the zebra gets easily ripped apart by the hyena because the hyena went to Public School and the zebra's limbs are everywhere but unlike the hyena they never had any connections. And finally there is me Nathan Cassidy, the tiger, who kills off the comedy industry and survives. That was one hell of a trip, and I came round and I was better, not completely, but I could carry on, because I had stopped crying and now learned I had the heart of a tiger, and could never be beaten. Is that true? Isn't the truth that I just carried on crying my heart out? And so it goes with God.

DAILY NOTES VOL I

June 30th 2023
5 Leaf Clover – Luke Combs

I spent many an hour when I was a kid looking for a four-leaf clover because it was said to bring good luck, little did I know the odds of finding one are about 10,000 to one, and anyone that is looking through 9,999 three leaf clovers to find an abnormal one is themselves abnormal. Yes, little did I know as a kid that to create luck for myself I should have perhaps learned a musical instrument or a language instead of looking through the dirt for a deformed plant. But no matter, I searched, in the patches of grass and greenery around my house to no avail, all that I did is stung my hands on the nettles which give not a shit how many leaves they have their job is just to sting you. And every time I was stung I would rub my fingers with a dock leaf because as we all know dock leaves alleviate the pain of stringing nettles. And now, later in life, I learn this is bullshit, there is no scientific evidence that dock leaves reduce the sting of nettles at all, it's just a placebo effect, and it's working right now on millions of kids around the world – I know right, it blows your mind, your whole childhood was a lie, everything they told you was a lie just to get you out of the house and appear to be doing something.

And the ambition was slight anyway, because we were never told, there's a five-leaf clover as well, there is - that's a million to one shot, no one ever told me to look for the five-leaf clover, even in my childhood fantasies there was a glass ceiling for no reason. We're just told what we need to hear aren't we to keep going, to maintain hope, it's the placebo effect isn't it, we've all been stung by life and here is the dock leaf that I'm giving you to make it feel better, even though it does fuck all. But if you stay in the game , who knows you might find the jackpot, the best thing ever, the four-leaf clover. That's the best one, and they never tell you about the five-leaf clover, they keep that to themselves.

I did none of this shit with my kids, I told them how life is – hunt not for the four-leaf clover but for the nettles – achieve the achievable, and keep achieving, keep being stung and carry on, and if you carry on and don't give up, who knows, there could be a six leaf clover waiting just for you.

DAILY NOTES VOL I

July 1st 2023
A Fool in Love – Ike & Tina Turner

Tina Turner an amazing artist and inspirational woman, suffered abuse by Ike Turner, beaten but not beaten and Ike Turner admitted to punching her but not beating her which is a surreal distinction to make and if it was today we would have probably had a Depp v Heard style trial, and the truth would have been lost because people don't care about the truth they only care about what they believe. And I was in a relationship once where I was abused physically and emotionally. But perhaps like Tina Turner, I don't know her state of mind, but what do you do when you come out of that? Because your initial emotion is anger but anger usually gets you nowhere apart from into trouble, so what Tina did was to say fuck you in terms of what she did next, building an incredibly successful career she didn't even need to call him out on it, she did do that later on and people then went one way or the other in terms of believing, but she did the fuck you bit first so the second bit didn't matter, she did the fuck you bit first.

Anyone in love is a fool because most times it doesn't work out, you'd have to be a fool to keep going back again and again, but the bigger fool is someone that thinks the world owes them anything, that people will believe you when what you're saying is true, the biggest fool thinks that they can never find the love of one person but the whole world of people will love them, the whole world will believe them. The only thing we can control is the fuck you bit, fuck you, this is what I can control, fuck you and watch me rise, watch me rise and you know what you did, so I don't need to call you out, because every time you see what I've done you'll be called out, fuck you.

Ultimately no one cares about you, even when everyone appears to care, no one believes in you, even when everyone says they believe, so just do the fuck you bit first and then you are someone that we can believe in, that we can love, that can be loved by one. And if you think there's not one person in the world that will love and believe in you, then you really are a fool. Don't look back just look forward, the past will be taken care of by the future. And whatever you do, don't beat yourself up, that's crazy - we are all just like you, we are all just fools in love.

July 2nd 2023
Scotty McCreery – It Matters To Her

Divorce eh? What a funny old thing. Divorce. No it isn't funny is it? Why the fuck does anyone get married – its mental, literally mental. 50% end in failure, the other half end in unhappiness. What the fuck have we all been doing, surely this will change soon and we'll all look back and say what the fuck were we thinking? Why did we sign that bit of paper, what benefit was it to us when it always ends here in financial settlements and courts and lawyers and acrimony. A few of my friends are going through what I've gone through without acrimony, and this is the big benefit of marrying someone as I did that grew up with no money at all like I did, they don't see money as important as people with privilege. The arguments people get into over money around divorce totally show people at their worst, I am not religious but I believe a sin will come back to bite you, and greed is a terrible sin with consequences. If you're going through a divorce and something looks reasonable to outsiders and lawyers, then please take that option, even if you think you can get more. Ask yourself why you want more, and people will say because it matters, it matters to me, it matters that my sacrifices as a parent are being honoured, it matters that I can bring up my children in the way I want, it matters that I can go on that holiday and not have to work, yeah we getting closer, say it for what it is – it matters to me because I'm greedy. I'm greedy, forgive yourself, greed is the devil's work and it's not necessarily your fault if you've been brought up in a particular way, but at least recognise why you're doing this, its greed, its nothing else but greed. And once you recognise it, then you can walk away and down a different path, because the pathway leading from greed is a very lonely road.

Unless you have nothing like I did and I often still have, you don't realise the pure joy of it, the pure joy of being happy with nothing, it makes life so beautiful, so freeing, you're not yearning for anything and you don't have that greed that will eventually rot you from the inside, these material things ultimately do not matter, you can't take it with you when you go and more than that if you're greedy you will never be happy, it will never be enough. I'm all for sinning, I love a good sin, but recognise why you're sinning, because when you're sinning, usually you're not winning. And winning is what you want right, because ultimately that's all that matters to us all.

July 3rd 2023
Ed Sheeran – Curtains

There's a pair of curtains in my bedroom and many times when you open the curtains the curtain rail falls down. And I go fucking hell and I spend at least 5 minutes standing precariously on a desk pushing the curtain rail vaguely back into the slots that it has long since fallen out with and I know that the whole thing will inevitably come crashing down again, but do I look to fix the problem which would maybe take an hour? No, I choose instead to spend 5 minutes on this every few days for the rest of my life, maybe 20 minutes a week, 1000 minutes a year, 30,000 more minutes in my lifetime I will spend on this rather than spending 60 minutes fixing the problem.

And that's of course mental but I'm not alone. Who wants to spend an hour on anything when you can spend 5 minutes and forget all about it? For a few days before it comes crashing down again. But ultimately, who cares, because this is the very spirit for me of living for today, I don't care that this will inevitable come crashing down tomorrow because I have more time today and today is all I actually care about, what kind of loser spends an hour fixing something for tomorrow? Jesus, what kind of dweeb fixes something so they don't have to spend the equivalent of weeks and months botching a curtain rail back up there for the rest of their lives?

This separates the rock and roll from the squares, fix something forever you are a square, and me standing on that desk four times a week, that is rock and roll. At least when those curtains come crashing down it lets a bit of light in, you have no light in your life because you fixed the curtain rail like a square, like an idiot, like a cunt, and so light is permanently excluded. You may have working curtains, but your life is over, my life is rock and roll and your life is over, your whole life is curtains.

Oh fuck they've just fallen down again. This is how Jimi Hendrix died didn't he, fixing a pair of curtains. Pull yourselves together. This is rock and roll.

July 4th 2023
Rihanna – We Found Love (feat. Calvin Harris)

One more thing on what I've been talking about the last week or so, the diazepam trip I had at the 2017 Edinburgh Fringe when I had a bad back and was watching *Life of Pi* thinking I was the tiger. The interesting thing about diazepam, when I started tripping out on diazepam, my skin started to turn slightly yellow when it was kicking in and this is one of the side effects of diazepam along with the hallucinations, I was this yellow/orange beast, I was the tiger, and I've never done drugs but this gave me the taste for them it was magical. I'd found love in a hopeless place, that's what drugs are aren't they, they give you those feelings of love and happiness when in many cases your life is in a bad place, and the worst place your life is in, the harder the drugs often need to be and the bigger the trips and the hallucinations you need.

And I was in a bad place that day and my God that hallucination was the best. So the question of course is, why don't I do it again, why don't we all do it again tonight, why don't we find love in a hopeless place with a dodgy batch of diazepam? Well it's the side effects isn't it – do we all want yellow/orange skin, do we all want to see or hear things that are not there, do we all want to start having delusions, thinking things are true when they're not true – and by the way hang on doesn't this explain Donald Trump? Seeing things that aren't there, delusions, orange skin, he's off his face on diazepam – and say what you like about Donald Trump he's having a great time, maybe we should all do it too. But there has to be a safer way, a way to experience this trip without drugs, without a dodgy batch of diazepam, and of course there is – and the secret is in nothingness – I studied this in Psychology - it's called the Ganzfeld affect. It's when nothing happens and your brain creates hallucinations to fill in the gaps in the nothingness – in simple terms you know when you're watching a comedian on TV and you start imagining anything else – it's that. But we can do it now – put your head back, close your eyes, put your hands over your eyes, and you see flashes of light don't you, and now they're yellow aren't they, we can come together, see the tiger, we're all together as one, we are the tiger, and together we can find magic out of the darkness. Or maybe just take a diazepam, it's much much much much better.

July 5th 2023
Moving – Ed Sheeran

The goal posts are moving in the world and in sport particularly – all around the world we are seeing teams going for it, just go for it, attack attack attack, whether that's France, Argentina, Brazil - Manchester City in football or if you follow cricket the new way England are going about cricket at the moment – attack attack attack. And it's been very successful for these sides, and of course sometimes it fails – sometimes you lose a goal, lose a wicket. And what I've seen a hell of a lot of recently from commentators and journalists is scathing criticism when this approach goes wrong. The England cricket team last week got criticism for attacking Australian bowlers. My goodness the press about the England cricket team 'Brainless batting' … taking a few risks to score runs quickly like they've done so much recently to develop a mainly winning formula. The batsmen 'took leave of their senses'. No they took risks to win. And have fun. And it's mainly, not always, working for them.

Why can't we be positive about anything? Here are some sportsmen taking risks and mainly winning and being really entertaining. That's the truth. Everything else is awful over the top negativity written by people who always did things the same way and mainly lost. What they're really saying is 'why can't they lose like me?' And that's the thing – you take the negative approach in life, news flash, you also lose sometimes, and losing in a negative manner never gets the criticisms, oh they were trying not to lose but poor them they still lost. When they try to win by attacking and lose what the commentators and press, mainly older people, are actually saying - 'Why can't they fail like I've always done.' 'I hate my life' … 'I wish I was them - taking risks and being young and having fun.' 'But I'm not young and taking risks and having fun so they are cunts'.

I've got an idea – and it may seem crazy but I'm just gonna throw it out there - try to enjoy anything. Please God try to enjoy anything. There is only one life, and life is hard sometimes, when someone comes along, sportsmen and whatever, taking risks and having fun, try to enjoy it with them. Take a risk, take a chance on enjoying life, move to a different place in your thinking, you never know where it may lead. You might just win.

DAILY NOTES VOL I

July 6th 2023
Oasis – Slide Away

So when Oasis stopped playing together what was it twenty years ago or something now, the brothers said they hated each other and still do, constantly slagging each other off, and that's how it should be, rock and roll, don't slide away with no one noticing, go down in flames, fuck dignity, who remembers dignity? No one. Oh they had such incredible dignity, even in defeat, oh bore off – we remember winners and people who lost having a screaming hissy fit.

Have you seen that clip on the US programme *Claim to Fame*, what seems like an amazing gameshow where everyone has a famous family member and they have to guess who the others famous family members are and if they are guessed right they have to leave the programme. Well there's this clip of some twenty year old being the first to be voted off because she was correctly guessed as being related to Tom Hanks, I mean yeah what the fuck is this programme? I mean at least there's some honesty here – you're related to a famous person so you need to be famous too, but when she's voted off, you know most people on these shows are disappointed they cry and there's a big hug – she basically loses her shit. You've got to see this if you haven't - she screams, she starts shouting shit about her uncle's films – *Forrest Gump* this, *Toy Story* fuck you, and whatever it's the ultimate car crash that I will never ever forget.

Don't slide away, don't leave with dignity, be Zinedine Zidane, leave with a head-butt to the chest that we'll always remember. That was me, I did my thing and now fuck you, fuck the lot of you, I can't wait for the last episode of this, maybe it will be episode 1000, who knows but if it is you gotta tune in for that. All I'll say is I'm gonna be going out in a blaze of glory in that one, I'll probably tell you that me and all of you have masturbated in front of our own pets, like a cross between Louis CK and David Attenborough. And don't tell me David Attenborough hasn't masturbated in front of an animal. Oh yeah I will be bringing some famous people down in that one, that pervert Attenborough and especially my great uncle Tom Hanks, fuck him, fuck that *Turner and Hooch* cunt.

DAILY NOTES VOL I

July 7th 2023
Never Imagined – Lil Durk Featuring Future

The Titanic submarine thing was obviously very tragic and more so for my friend's daughter Chloe as she was a student at Strathclyde University with one of the guys that died. And I was chatting with them the other day and I said to Chloe I mean what a tragedy right, him and his dad, what must the mom think. And Chloe said yeah, Christine I know her, she came to visit Suleman her son at the University. And I was like yeah its unimaginable isn't it, I mean of all the ways to die, you think you've considered everything but no one would have considered your son and husband dying in an imploding submarine, that's the last thing she would have thought. And she's a bit pedantic is Chloe, a bit of a, well like a typical University student a bit of a pedant – so she kind of did this… well… and I said what? And she said…well it's just that you said submarine – it's actually not a submarine, it's a submersive. And I said what's the difference and she said a submarine has the engines to get to shore and back a submersive basically just drops and comes back up again. Erm, sorry to be pedantic, but not in this case.

And at that moment do you know what I feared, not that I would kill Chloe, I feared that Christine, grieving mother and widow would visit Strathclyde university to thank his friends for all their support and she'd go up to a crying Chloe and say oh my God Chloe, I'd have never imagined in a billion years that my son would die on a trip to the Titanic on a submarine. And Chloe would be like… well this is awkward but it was a submersive not a submarine. And all I'm saying is if you found out I'd died on a submersive on the sea bed next to the Titanic you'd be surprised because I don't get on submersives, you surely must be less surprised that people that get on them might…. Anyway, condolences.

And Christine would be like thank you, I guess at moments like this thinking about my husband and son you've just got to have prospective. And Chloe would be like – prospective – do you mean perspective? Not prospective, prospective means prospects the future and one thing your son and husband don't have is future. And Christine would be like WTF Chloe, why are you this much of a pedant, and she'd be like well it's not me, actually it's the comedian Nathan Cassidy, who is stringing this bit out far too long. It's sinking and it's about to implode. Insensitive. And Christine would be like who's Nathan Cassidy? And Chloe would say 'he's a friend of my mom, he's one of these subversive comedians'. 'Subversive did you say?' Yeah, and Christine would say 'I haven't heard of him'. And Chloe would say 'well-being pedantic that doesn't mean anything about how good he is or isn't the fact you haven't heard of him'. And Christine would say 'well he's not Mark Maron is he?' And she'd say, 'who? I've never heard of him'. And Christine would say 'Nathan Cassidy is no Marc Maron', and Chloe would say 'well no he's not Marc Maron, they're different people'. And Christine would get angry and she'd say 'look all I'm saying is Nathan Cassidy is not as good as Marc Maron, he's a sub-standard Mark Maron'. And Chloe would be like, 'well being a pedant, there's just a much quicker way to say that someone is not as good as Mark Maron'. And Christine would say 'how?' And she'd say 'well you're not gonna like it, but the quick expression is sub-Maron'.

July 8th 2023
Tina Turner – We Don't Need Another Hero (Thunderdome)

So the world is becoming this *Mad Max* dystopia, and I'm not talking about the wars I'm talking about the way things are, in every street, in every town and city in the world, we are on the brink everywhere of losing our shit. And it spilled over recently of course in France after a boy was shot and killed by police, which was awful of course, but the way that people often choose to show their anger in these situations is to yes riot and set cars on fire etc which I guess is what rioters do, but what they also do you notice, and it happened everywhere in this kind of situation too, is to ram their cars into shops and loot them. It's always called looting during a riot, if there's no riot it's not looting it's just stealing, but if you steal during a riot it's a different thing isn't it it's a loot, which sounds more romantic, more pirate, but it is in fact just stealing.

And it doesn't make natural sense really does it? I'm angry about this boy losing his life, I'm angry about the police, I know what I'm going to do to show my anger, I'm going to ram my car into the local supermarket and steal some avocados, and the really ripe expensive ones as well, because that's how angry I am. When of course the truth is yes we're angry, but the looting is a separate issue, because we all know in these situations the shops aren't the problem, the shops aren't the police, but when we're angry about anything, we also remember we're skint, and cheese is £5.50 when last year it was £2. So that volcano that's been simmering for years - oh fuck we're skint, those with privilege have everything and we have nothing, cheese is £5.50 – suddenly bursts out and we think yeah I'm gonna get myself some free cheese, this is what I'm really angry about, I want a fucking cheese sandwich and not have to feel it's a fucking luxury.

All around the world we are on the brink of riots like this, we are living in a *Max Max* film, welcome to the Thunderdome, and we may not need another hero, but what we do need is another cheese sandwich. Stick some of that lovely ripe avocado in as well. What boy in France? Mm… delicious.

July 9th 2023
Hannah Laing & Roro – Good Love

There's good love and there's bad love, but the love of your kids is always good love right? Well not always of course, kids can be idiots, kids can be cunts, and what do you do when they become people that lie to you, that disrespect you? It's odd isn't it, because it's like being in an abusive relationship with someone but this time you're legally unable to get out of it. Can you legally divorce from your kids because you don't like them? I doubt it, and I would never want to do that of course but there comes a time when you feel that enough is enough, the lies have to stop. It's gaslighting isn't it? They're gaslighting me – my kids are gaslighting me - I didn't say that, I didn't do that, when I know you did. Is there anything we can do about this bad love?

Things were easier in the 70s when you were allowed to slap their arses. That must have been great, because that's how you feel sometimes , I just want to give you a good slap and the law won't allow me any more, damn. So what can we do? Well we could fight fire with fire – where's dinner dad? It's on the table. No it isn't. Yes it is I cooked it. It isn't there? Well I swear I cooked it and put it on the table… Yeah see how you like the bullshit you little cock.

We could give them more slack. No that just encourages the abusive relationship to continue. So what can we do? Well it's what I advise in all situations where someone is an asshole – let it ride, just let it go, because in almost all cases where someone's an asshole they're gonna be an asshole whether you shout about it or not, assholes are gonna be assholes, even your own kids, and no amount of shouting or slapping them on the bottoms is gonna change that.

And in my experience assholes are only assholes while you care about it, as soon as you stop caring they disappear out of your life, in this case probably to university and ten years later they'll come back to you nice as pie and pretend that none of it happened and can they have some money. And of course they can have some money, I put some in your bank earlier today…

No you didn't. I did, I swear.

July 10th 2023
Against All odds (Take a Look At Me Now) – Phil Collins

Fans of me and there are several, and fans of this podcast will know that I love the 80s, I love Phil Collins and his music. I guess when I think about it, I want to love anything that's unpopular, like myself, I want to love anything that the majority of people don't love, because what do the majority of people love? Shite. Pure unfiltered shite, served up to them on their phones - easy, unfiltered shite. I want to love the things that no one else does - the ones that have succeeded, against all odds. It's very hard to love someone that has succeeded where things were handed to them on a plate, give me Phil Collins any day, no nepo baby here - his dad was an insurance agent and his mom worked in a toy shop and later as a booking agent at a Stage School… hang on – his mom was a theatrical agent and Phil Collins started in theatre didn't he playing the Artful Dodger? No, not Phil as well. FFS. Is there no artist on earth that has succeeded against all odds?

Well of course there is, my other great love from the 80s – Wham! And there is a Netflix documentary out at the moment about how they started - there is a proper against all odds story, just two kids in a senior school on the outskirts of London doing demo tapes in their lounge that weren't brilliant, but one of their moms knew a head of a record label down the road – oh fuck it was their mom again, that's how they got their break, FFS! Mom, dad, why did you not know anyone? Jesus – my mom worked in a sweet shop just like Phil Collins' mom but unlike her mom she did not start working as a booking agent so my mom's only contact was Hancock's Cash and Carry – half price gob stoppers. Fucking hell.

Moms, dads everywhere, if you're thinking of having a kid sure go to your classes and learn about different birthing techniques but for goodness sake, get yourself some contacts in showbiz, because if you have a kid and you don't have contacts in showbiz they're gonna struggle, and they'll be like me, pushing fifty and never once handed anything, and I've got basically nothing. Apart from one thing – the love of people that love success against all odds. And I'm one of those people. So I love myself, and that, according to the 80s, is the greatest love of all.

DAILY NOTES VOL I

July 11th 2023
Tina Turner – GoldenEye

So there was a 99-year-old War Veteran Captain Tom, Sir Captain Tom who has now sadly died (100 is no age, gone too soon) – who raised hundreds of millions of pounds for the National Health Service in this country, which virtually everyone contributed to so it was like a very clever way of taxing everyone double – genius. Anyway, of course brilliant effort he walked up and down his garden a few times, that's what's regarded as effort these days and he raised hundreds of millions. And off the back of this Captain Tom's daughter Hannah started the "Captain Tom Foundation" a charity to carry on raising money after the pandemic. What good people!

Well, mmm, so to start with I don't want to generalise, but these people are posh. How do I know? Because his daughter Hannah has a double-barrelled surname – her name is Hanna Ingram-Moore. So yeah Hannah I-grab Moore decided to pay herself from this Charitable Foundation £85,000 a year from the charity, she did actually ask for 100,000 but the charity commission called her and I quote a 'cheeky fuck'. Anyway a year or so down the line she's used funding for the "Captain Tom Building", a spa pool, which was "for private use by occupiers" ie Hannah Igrab-Moore and her hubby and the local authority granted permission for the spa to be built on the tennis courts at their Grade II-listed home. I personally think this is absolutely fine, as is their "Captain Tom" BMW, the "Captain Tom" golden bog roll and two Golden Eyes for the selfless Hannah-IgrabMoore. Cheeky fuck indeed.

I'd imagine Captain Tom will be turning in his grave, and let's hope he's not, because Hannah Igrab Moore will then try to monetise that movement - he's turning, please give me one million dollars for every turn, I need to take the whole Foundation on a "Captain Tom memorial trip to Vegas" and snort some "Captain Tom Cocaine" off some "Captain Tom" hookers' arseholes. I'm raising money for the "Captain Tom memorial dildo" for myself, nothing feels better than when it's shuffling up and down my garden.

Oh I've taken it too far have I? No, Hannah, you took it too far love. You should be "Captain Tom fucking ashamed" of yourself.

DAILY NOTES VOL I

July 12th 2023
Ne-Yo – So Sick

I've been ill the past couple of days, it came on very quickly, tiredness, headaches, fever, nausea, I hit the cold wind and I shook uncontrollably, like a flu but not a flu because I still move around, so the one thing I don't do in this situation is go anywhere near a doctor. I'm not sure how the health service is in your country but they wouldn't give a shit about that kind of thing in this country even though flu is probably one of the biggest killers, anyway last time I had symptoms like this I figured I had a urinary tract infection so I handed in a urine sample into the doctors and she called me up and said have you been having sex recently and I said I'm Nathan Cassidy does that answer your question? And she said you haven't really got an infection but I have seen trace bacteria and I can't remember the name of it but it was something like bacteria pooey pooey penis up the bum bum, so in short I didn't want to go back to the doctor, embarrassing.

So I kind of self-diagnosed a urinary tract infection, and was happy with that - as with virtually everything mental or physical, give it three days and you'll be better or you'll have something much worse to worry about. Anyway the days went on and I had similar symptoms but no problems downstairs if you know what I mean, I could piss in the kitchen easily that's what that means, so I thought it's not really a UTI is it and I mentioned it to my doctor friend and he said you know what it sounds like – Covid. Of course, fucking Covid – how easily we forget. 'Covid – that's a blast from the past'. And he said we're seeing lots more Covid recently but no one gives a shit about that any more, the news agenda has moved on. So I did a test, negative, and my friend said I tell you what it is - hay fever. What, even though it has none of the symptoms of hay fever? And then another friend genuinely said, because of that shaking you could have early onset Parkinson's and I was like shut the fuck up everyone, I just need a good sleep, I'm knackered – and I've had a good sleep and I'm better today. I had none of those things I just needed a good long sleep. All things can be cured by a good long sleep, I promise you, even death – a good long sleep even sees death off. So on that note, sleep well my friends, you haven't got Covid you've just got amateur doctor friends who know absolutely fuck all.

July 13th 2023
Oasis – Champagne Supernova

28 years ago – it seems like a long time but anyone my age will know that it goes by in the blink of an eye. And I was out the other night and I looked around at a lot of 21, 22-year-olds and I realised I haven't done this for so long, just go around bar to bar, a group of friends, no responsibilities. Fuck I'm really going to sound old now but if you're 21, 22 cherish every moment, get out every night, wander around, suck it up, talk to people, hold people, love people, cherish these days, hold on to these days, and I appreciated what I had of course in my early 20's but I'm not sure I appreciated it enough. So many people are still living with their parents at this age, I had my own swanky flat with a balcony looking over Limehouse Basin in London, I had it all. Fuck.

Anyway, at this time I didn't have masses of money but any bit I had spare instead of going out even more than I did I used to buy bottles of Lanson black label champagne and stick it in the wooden bottle holder in the lounge, I'm really not sure why I did this but if I'm being honest I'm not flash but there was something about that flat, swanky, looking out on to Limehouse basin in London, and then there would be a full bottle holder thing of champagne and people would go wow, and I did this for years, and I hardly ever drunk the champagne because I wanted to keep the thing full of champagne and one time somebody came round and said you do release that champagne isn't like wine, it only lasts maybe 3 years, and I thought what?

I opened one of the bottles and it was awful, it had gone bad undrinkable. And that's when I knew – never try to hold on to anything, keep anything for too long, because over time you'll see it go bad, you'll see it rot. If you have something wonderful, the brightest star, then see, hold it, cherish it and move on, the only thing you should hold on to is the feeling when you first saw it, hold on to that feeling when you were 21/22, don't let it rot in your mind - cherish it, freeze it in time, and then at any time you can close your eyes and picture it, and let it shine upon you, a supernova, exploding in a brilliant burst of light radiating enough energy to last for lifetimes.

DAILY NOTES VOL I

July 14th 2023
0800 Heaven – Dawe/Corry/Henderson

It's not really a thing any more with OnlyFans and porn at your fingertips 24/7, and that's my favourite porn as well, fingertip porn, just the tip of the finger, that's right, loosen it up, and then fuck me, fuck me. You see I'm giving you that for free (unless you subscribe to my £5 Patreon at patreon.com/nathancassidy which you don't). Back in the day you used to have to phone a number from the landline for your pornography – that's right kids, you don't know how easy you've got it, with your easy access p and vg, any time of the day you just get p and vg. Back in my day, when I was 20 you had to phone an 0800 number and some old sort would heavy breathe down the phone to you – 'hey thanks for calling, I'm very hot today, I've been doing DIY, I'm feeling my nipples now' – and in reality no they weren't feeling their nipples they were hot because they were doing the ironing and earning an extra £12 an hour listening to you masturbate as they watch Saturday night telly.

The lengths we had to go to masturbate back in my day, to masturbate I had to go to great lengths, enormous lengths. If you know what I mean, but I didn't of course, the thought of calling one of these 0800 chat lines was ludicrous, it was all about getting you to stay on the line like an 80's cop show where they were trying to trace the call, another thing that has been sadly lost in the mists of time, when you had to trick people to stay on the line. How was your day? Have you ever been tobogganing? He hung up, shit we didn't get the trace. Now it's boring isn't it - oh he's calling from that exact location and we can just follow him around and pick him up at any time. Wait until he stops masturbating – cool yeah will do. I once lived with a guy and we got the phone bill and it was £250 more than a normal month, and I said to him, this must be a mistake, unless you've been … and he just said …don't worry, I'll pay the bill. And it was never mentioned again. I couldn't believe it at the time. Why would he fall for such a scam? I'm angry looking back at the stupidity. I'm getting hot with anger. I'm getting so hot I'm gonna have to take off my clothes and feel my nipples and my enormous long cock – stay on the line, have we got a trace yet, oh no sorry I'm doing this, stay on the line, even when the episode ends listen to the next one, then join my Patreon for just 5 or 10 pounds per month you can listen to me doing this, fudding myself 24/7, do it, do it…

DAILY NOTES VOL I

July 15th 2023
Nick Jonas – Jealous

Do I want to earn a lot of money? Well maybe a bit more but not a lot more, because as soon as you're a super-rich celebrity then you're opening the door to nutters aren't you. The BBC I'm sure you know, best broadcasters in the world , the BBC stands for integrity and excellence all the way around the world, they publicised their best-paid presenters list this week, at number one is Gary Lineker, and Gary Lineker gets so much shit, daily reminders of how he pooed on the pitch in the World Cup, and then there's Zoe Ball who gets paid a million pounds a year from the corporation for hosting a radio breakfast show where she plays records for a few hours, a million pounds!! A million pounds, Jesus, I mean Christ you can see where some of the nutters might get jealous, a million pounds have I read that right? And in third place it's Alan Shearer who is paid nearly half a million pounds to comment once a week when the football's on and he'll say one of two things – 'shocking defending' or 'power, pace'. That was great, have half a million pounds Al. You can call me Al the jammy twat.

I mean FFS, really, a monkey could do that, or a turtle, fucking hell. The only one that deserves his money is Huw Edwards, have you heard of Huw Edwards? He's a newsreader, they choose him for all the state occasions Royal weddings and whatever, he announced the death of the Queen, he's basically the voice of the nation, the voice of the BBC, Huw Edwards, heard of him? Anyway he came fourth. And I for one, love to watch him coming forth, there's nothing I love more, my kids love it too, watching Huw Edwards coming forth. The whole Nation love to see Huw Edwards coming forth and we're not jealous of him one bit, not one bit. None of us would want to swap places with Huw Edwards in a million years.

Alan Shearer though – Jesus, fucking hell, the world has gone mad. Alan Shearer half a million pounds – that's of our money – my money – did you see this week an unnamed BBC presenter has been accused of paying for nude photos from a teen, if it's you Alan I'll send you some shots of me in the bath as a kid, that can't be any more scandalous than you earning half a million quid for saying that was a shit pass. Of all the shocking things about the BBC that's the most shocking of them all.

July 16th 2023
Ed Sheeran – The Hills of Aberfeldy

Never been to the hills of Aberfeldy, never been anywhere in Scotland apart from Edinburgh for work, and it's ridiculous really my favourite place on the planet is New Zealand and much of Scotland is like South Island New Zealand – mountainous, nothing but sheep. You've got the Cairngorms, Ben Nevis, mountains, lakes, National Parks, they're all on my doorstep but I don't know about you and where you live, if its right there in front of you, do you wanna go see it? Na fuck that. I've had periods of my life when I've been obsessed with travelling and have travelled the world and now I'm planning maybe going to Brazil and back to America, but how can I afford everything, cost of living, what happens if I can't get away, what can you do?

Well I live in London, a city that the majority of the world would like to come to and explore – have I explored London? Have I fuck – London – shit hole, I mean some bits are nice but I don't want to explore them, boring, I'd rather spend a fortune going to Istanbul that I have no real idea whether it's beautiful of interesting it's just not the place that you live. And that's the key isn't it, getting away, the holiday is an escape for the mind, an escape from the monotony of life. Why would I want to go to a place where people look like me and talk like me and moan like me, and worse still recognise me?

Take me somewhere where nobody knows my name and I can't understand them and they can't understand me and I end up ordering duck's face. I could climb the beautiful Hills of Aberfeldy and I'd get back to the guest house and they'd say did you have a nice walk and I'd say yes thanks and they say would you like a drink and I'd say yes please – and they'd say tea or coffee and I'd go don't bother and they'd say how about some food, we have some scotch broth on tonight and I'd say what like I had all the time as a kid, stop talking to me in my language, stop offering me drinks I've been offered all my life, I need an escape, life is so fucking monotonous I need an escape give me anything different, please, surprise me. And that is how I feel when I listen to Ed Sheeran's latest album. That's a joke obviously, but you know what I'm saying, occasionally in this life we need a glass of Sangria, some patatas bravas and a Bangkok ping-pong show. We all need a proper holiday.

DAILY NOTES VOL I

July 17th 2023
What's Love Got to Do with it – Tina Turner

It was the Wimbledon final yesterday and I do like the tennis and I'd watch it if it wasn't for one thing – over the last few years they've introduced a thing called Hawkeye – a computerised system which tells you whether the ball is out or not. Now how it works nobody knows. Do we have complete trust in it? Yes. If it says that the balls is a millimetre out then it's a millimetre out because we trust Hawkeye more than a stupid old human who is sitting near the line and thinks it's definitely in – no its not in because I trust Hawkeye over you any day, I'd put my life on the line with Hawkeye because he makes your eyes look like shitty bits of jelly from a rancid trifle. You know nothing and Hawkeye knows everything.

Anyway, Hawkeye is used when the players challenge a call and there's always a little delay as Hawkeye who is better than you comes to his decision, and in fact his decision-making process is played out on the big screen as the ball sails towards the line and we all find out whether the ball is in or out? All sounds reasonable up to this point, but it's not, because this beautiful piece of technology is ruined every time – for as the ball sails towards the line the audience collectively decide they have to clap maniacally. And my question is why? Why are you doing that? Oh it's just what we do, we all clap when Hawkeye is deciding. Yeah but why – no reason – no why? There is no reason! So why do you do it then? No reason, it just fills the gap doesn't it? Exactly – no reason, when you ask the doctor have you got cancer and there's a little pause do you start clapping? No you don't. Will you marry me? Clap clap clap. There is no reason, just have a pause, have a gap! Na I think we'll clap thanks.

I mean thank God the machines are taking over from humans, we are utter morons. Oh there's a slight gap so I have to clap like a cunt. Leave the gap! We don't need the clap leave the gap! This is what it comes down to, people are terrified of nothing, particularly in tennis, they don't want nothing. In tennis they don't want nothing so much that they don't call it nothing, they call it love. But it isn't love, love has nothing to do with it, it's nothing.

Learn to love nothing – it's unquestionably the secret of happiness.

DAILY NOTES VOL I

July 18th 2023
I Can See You (Taylor's Version)

It's odd the world we live in, isn't it, odd, well it is in this country. Privacy laws in this country mean you can't name anyone in the press if they're under suspicion of doing something wrong, like I don't know paying an underage person for explicit photos and sending pics of themselves naked to teenagers and whatever. And quite right too, if someone is under suspicion then of course don't name them, name them when they've definitely done something wrong. If the press were to print just rumours rather than substantiated fact then, well, that's the tabloid press isn't it?

My only interaction with the tabloid press in this country was when I was doing a musical at University and it involved male semi-nudity it was like *The Full Monty* (they copied us) and the Sun newspaper phoned me up and talked to me under a pseudonym that I'd chosen to ascertain whether they were stupid, the pseudonym I genuinely chose was Chris Packet, yeah Chris Packet, they did spot it and just went oh ha ha ha Chris Packet that's a funny name it sounds like crisp packet - I don't think they really cared whether it was made up or not to be honest, because this journalist then said, 'right, do you mind if we just make up the whole story?' And I was like, fine, that's what we all thought you did thanks for confirming it, thanks for substantiating the fact you just print utter bullshit.

Anyway, the press has all been full of rumour about an unnamed TV presenter in this country, but, if you go online on Twitter, his name and the naked photos he's allegedly been sending are everywhere, so then we have this ridiculous dance of people on TV saying the unnamed celebrity, the mystery figure, and everyone is thinking, well it's not much of a mystery, his arse is all over twitter, I mean yes it could be fake but it looks pretty real to me, it looks as real as that Prince Andrew snap. Let's stop pretending that what we can see isn't real, it is real, we've all seen it and everything else may be made up but what we see is real right? The moon landings, real. Hasn't the time come to ditch all of this online bullshit, life was better before it, we used to see each other, we used to look into each other's eyes, or asses, and know what was true. Now we have no idea. A very depressing future where we never know what is the truth and what is a lie – I can see you.

DAILY NOTES VOL I

July 19th 2023
Let's Stay Together – Tina Turner

Episode 200 of season 3. My oh my. Shall we stop now. No, let's stay together. Me and you - the audience. Just like most partnerships – let's just stay together out of habit. It's not really going anywhere is it, nowhere positive anyway, like most couples let's just stay together until death. You could cheat on me, like most couples, you could go off and listen to someone popular like one of those comedians talking about being a parent, wanging on a podcast about being a parent or what's your favourite food…

What's your favourite food?
What's your favourite food?
What's it like being a parent?
And you get the excitement from that because you find out, I don't know, David Tennant for example likes crisps.

But however exciting that undoubtedly is, you keep on sloping back to old Daily Notes because it's there isn't it, its dependable, it pays your mortgage, it doesn't pay your mortgage, it certainly doesn't pay mine, but it's there. A constant in your life and you know in your heart of hearts you would be lost without it. But you do have a choice, just like you in any relationship, to ditch it, completely and go off permanently with someone else, or even more dramatic, leave me and be on your own, with no podcasts, and maybe just read a book and masturbate for the rest of your life.

Yes you could do that for sure, but pay attention to history, and what happens when you do that, history is littered with relationships like ours that break down, you go off for a year, or twenty years, and then eventually you think – oh I wonder what they're doing now, so you look me up again and then we get back together, and you're forced to do the catch up chat, can you imagine if you leave this podcast for 20 years and then you're forced to catch up on 20 years of this bullshit. So just stick with it, stick with your relationships, put in the bare minimum of effort, 5 minutes a day and we can all hurtle towards the end together. There is no other way.

Roll on episode 201, don't go anywhere, just turn another page - you wouldn't want to see me jealous.

July 20th 2023
Labyrinth – Jealous

Scrolling through TikTok or Instagram – it's addictive right, but why? Well there are two emotions you go through, only two, the main one is ha ha ha you're a loser, you're banging into something, you're falling over, you're shit at trombone, you're fat and on a water slide. That's the first emotion – amusement, thank God I'm not them. And then they mix that up with – I wish I was them, they're amazing, they're good at trombone, they are thin and on a waterslide. Amusement, feeling good about yourself, and then jealousy, feeling bad about yourself, they're the two emotions and that's why TikTok and Instagram work, because in both cases we're feeling something. Often we go through life feeling nothing.

We go to these social media platforms to feel something, and often the balance is tipped towards jealousy and feeling bad about yourself so we go to these platforms to feel worse about ourselves, and we know its gonna happen and we keep going back, it's an abusive relationship, and we can't get enough. And these are the feelings we get when we look up an ex, bump into an ex, this is what this song is about, I'm jealous that you seem to be doing well without me, but of course that's just social media mainly, people always look like they're doing well without you, but in reality, you know the score, they're probably not doing great. And if you're into them doing really shit without you they're probably not doing really shit either, if you're playing the odds you'd have to say they're just doing ok, they're fine, not too good not too bad, because that's pretty much everyone, no one's that great, no one's that shit, they're just a normal person on a waterslide.

There's no TikTok viral excitement for them, the truth is they were ok with you and now they're ok without you. But the last thing we want to imagine is our ex being just ok and boring and fine – I've just doom scrolled photos of my ex and she's saying her life is ok, and that she feels fine. FFS! Why does the new guy get that? With me she was a fucking nutcase.

July 21st 2023
Hell N Back – Bakar

So I was ill and then I got better and whenever I'm ill, like a bad illness a flu or a UTI or when my back was bad, particularly when my back was bad, I lay there thinking two things – the main thing was I wanted to die, if you had offered me death at that moment I would have taken it, but the other thing that flies through my head in this moments is what I'd be prepared to do to get better, and it's in these moments that you tend to hear the exact same phrase – I would suck the devil's dick.

It's an easy thing to say isn't it because you're never gonna find yourself in that position, probably. And even if you do, the enormity of having to suck the devil's dick won't seem quite so bad after the, I'd imagine, significant disappointment of dying and finding yourself in hell and then seeing the devil. By then you'd probably imagine… ah man I'm gonna have to suck that dick at some point, you'd be resigned to it by then. Who's to say you might actually be looking forward to it, like now I'm here, when in Rome and all that, I may as well get the whole hell experience now I'm here.

Anyway so you'd be down there sucking the devil's dick and you'd start to think, well he's enjoying it isn't he, I'm bringing a smile to the devil's face, which is a difficult thing to do, he's a notoriously grumpy man, and then he'd cum and contrary to popular belief he wouldn't cum fire would he, there wouldn't be fire cumming out of his dick and into your mouth, you'd die, and he doesn't want you to die, he wants you to suck his dick. If fire came out of his dick when he came he wouldn't want to cum would he, he'd be like na I'm good thanks. So the devil would cum semen and you'd swallow it all down, and in those moments you can't help yourself can you, having kinda feelings for the devil. Come on you've just shared a super intimate moment. And you'd be like this isn't so bad after all, excuse me Mr D would you like to suck my dick now? Sorry it's not as gargantuan and impressive and red as yours Mr Beelzebub. And he'd say but Nathan, I can send you back now, to where you were, you've done the trade, you've sucked the devil's dick and now you're back will be better. And you'd say 'but devil, it might get worse again', and he'd give you a cheeky wink and say 'Nathan, honey, I'm counting on it'.

DAILY NOTES VOL I

July 22nd 2023
Ed Sheeran – Life Goes On

Global warming is terrifying, isn't it? That's undeniable. But the inconvenient truth is that the 70's and 80's were much better because we put a positive spin on this catastrophe, and everyone went about their days all happy. When we had record temperatures in this country in the 1976 the Sun printed the headline 'Phew! What a Scorcher' – 'Hotter than Honolulu as we hit the Roaring Nineties'. There was no global warming back then, well there was, but we decided instead to have a good old laugh and celebrate it and go down the beach and have an ice cream. Better days.

Now the sun is dangerous, in the 70's and 80's we were encouraged to 'bask' in it – no one 'basks' any more. When I was a kid I used factor 2 oil so the sun could cook my skin even better, my parents used to cover me in oil to keep me safe. A heatwave in Europe would have been celebrated in this nation as much as a Royal Wedding, as we all would be right now planning our £99 holiday to a sun-trap destination to cook our skin even more. 40 degrees in Europe? We would have been wild with happiness, hunting out the hottest places to go to on sex holidays on the Thomson big yellow banana plane, the one where they play a fanfare when it lands because they are so surprised. We'd be watching Judith Chalmers on *Wish You Were Here* basking in her bikini in the 'gorgeous' sunshine. That's right, the sunshine used to be 'gorgeous'. Poor sunshine. It's been #metoo'd. Sunshine used to do exactly the same thing in the 70's and everyone loved it, now apparently it's a bad boy.

I wish we could go back, yes I know it's apparently dangerous now but I wish we could go back to when it definitely wasn't. Same as smoking, that used to be fun too in the 50's. My advice is anything you enjoy now, enjoy it while you can because in a few years' time they'll be telling you it's bad for you – like staring at your phone for 7 hours a day or air-fryers. Everything is bad for us eventually. But there was nothing like the childhood innocence of the 70's and 80's, because nothing was bad for you back then, nothing. Not even Jimmy Saville. Take me back, and let me bask in happiness and innocence for just one more beautiful sun-kissed day.

DAILY NOTES VOL I

July 23rd 2023
Alison Moyet – Invisible

I saw a magician comedian last night, an American based in Barcelona check him out he's @funnybadgy.me on Instagram and he did a few things and one of them was producing like umbrellas, 4 foot canes out of basically thin air and the crowd were like yeah whatever and I was at the back thinking no hang on guys he's just produced big umbrellas out of thin air, this guy is incredible, what's wrong with everyone? On your feet, standing O, an umbrella, you try it, you try producing an umbrella, not a small pocket umbrella, a full-size umbrella out of thin air twice, I was a few feet away from him and I couldn't see how he did it, mind blowing.

But our minds aren't blown any more are they, because we've become cynical as a world haven't we? In the 80s we were impressed by magic, when David Copperfield made the Statue of Liberty disappear our mouths hit the floor, when he flew we believed anything was possible, and now if a magician flies we all say as one, 'it's invisible wires, it's obviously invisible wires'. Take me back to that age of innocence and wonder, it was only 40 years ago, why did we collectively choose to move away from it. It's because we like being clever isn't it. We want to know everything, we want to act like we know how everything is done, but the truth is over the last 20 years certainly, the world has got more stupid because of social media, all we do is sit open mouthed dribbling at someone falling over or jiggling their tits, it's totally within our grasp to recapture that innocence we had because we are dumb now, we are far more stupid than the 80s.

So I see a resurgence of magic, its TikTok but live, little funny things that we see and we are in disbelief – how could he do that, but instead of someone falling over and hitting their head we can sit in wonder at someone producing umbrellas out of thin air. The door back to a magical world is there for us all if we choose to step through it – a world where people can fly and women can get sawn in half – good, honest and wholesome entertainment where women get sawn in half and smile as the horrific live operation is being carried out. The magical door is there - the trouble is we choose not to see it, because we can't see it, its invisible. It's magic. She wasn't really sawn in half, that would be horrific. You'd have to go to Instagram for that.

180

July 24th 2023
Rihanna – Work (feat. Drake)

Ah fucking work tomorrow isn't it, work work work work work that's all we all ever do isn't it, going to work in that piece of shit job. I don't want to wake up tomorrow. If I was to give you a million pounds would you give up work? Yes instantly, fucking hate my job. I hear you, you're probably being bullied by a woman called Pauline - I was when I worked in Banking, bullied by a woman called Pauline, it's always Pauline isn't it - an unhappy, loveless woman called Pauline. Obviously if you offered me a million pounds I'd give up work instantly.

But how about if I offered you 10 million pounds and the only proviso is you couldn't wake up tomorrow and go into work? You couldn't wake up at all. Well obviously, I'd choose to go into work tomorrow. So your work is worth more than 10 million pounds? No I didn't say that – yes you did in effect – you'd rather get up and go into work than die – yeah? Well there you go then… no that's a pretty low bar isn't it, work is better than death. It is better than death, so every day when you go into work and you feel life couldn't get any worse, know that it could and you could be dead.

And here's something to keep you going, maybe the only thing that will keep you going if your work is shit, if you hang on in there and survive, and do the work, there will come a day, maybe in one, ten or twenty years where they let you go, or you retire or get another piece of shit job, but the day will come I guarantee you when you'll be free of the shackles and you will be able to go up to Pauline and call her a cunt. And you know the best news of all, that day is today. Go up to your boss Pauline, the one that bullies you, and say Pauline you are a cunt, and she'll say oh you're in trouble now, and say what for, and she'll say you just called me a cunt. And you'll say no I didn't, you're making it up, that's the weirdest thing anyone has ever done. I think I might report you. And her head will instantly be scrambled, you are in control now, you are the captain.

And that's why you're alive, and that's why calling your boss a cunt is worth far more than all the money on Earth.

DAILY NOTES VOL I

July 25th 2023
Never Been Better – Olly Murs

I've never been better right now, I mean obviously I have been better, 35 years ago I was better when I was a kid, when you never got tired and things seemed possible, I was definitely better then. But right now, I've never been better. A few weeks ago I was very ill with a UTI and in previous years I've had a bad back or whatever and as I said the other day you'll do anything to get better and I don't know whether you do this, I vow whenever I'm feeling really bad that when I get better there's going to be a new me, a more appreciative me, all that matters is your health. And when you get better of course, no fuck that, health is a given, I'm not going to be appreciative of health. Appreciating your health is for losers.

I mean I could try really, but when you've got your health you can't be truly appreciative of it can you? It's like water, those without water in the world know of the value of water and they say to themselves if I ever had a ready supply of water then I'd be grateful every day and it would be the only thing that mattered. Guaranteed when those guys get water it would be like… 'Water? I'm not being grateful for water, water is not something to be thankful for, yes yesterday I was dying of thirst but today there's a tap, it's not a miracle is it, it's a tap full of water, now I want something more.'

And that's what you want when you have the minimum, health food and water – that doesn't really make you happy, it makes you happy for five minutes if you haven't had it for a while, and the transition is almost invisible – when you're ill, when I had a bad back, I would suck the devil's dick for a good back - when I get better I tell myself I'm going to live a different life, you will see a new me, and within seconds of the pain going – ah life is shit because I have to wait 10 minutes for a train. Why is life so shit there are no fucking Ubers?! Fuck my life it's raining this is the worst day ever.

It's not the worst day ever because you are healthy with food and water. It's the best day ever, it's the best day you could have ever hoped for. Will you ever really appreciate the small stuff? Will you fuck.

DAILY NOTES VOL I

July 26th 2023
Olivia Rodrigo – Vampire

I saw the new *Mission Impossible* film the other day and it's hard to think that Tom Cruise has done anything but hit blockbuster films, I mean of course he's had his detractors, but many a time I think people have been out to get him. All he did was jump up and down on the Oprah Winfrey sofa in celebration of being in a relationship with Katie Holmes and everyone smelt a rat but their marriage lasted 5 years which is the time that all marriages last. Yes he doesn't see the kid Suri but, you know what I mean, he has other kids - you can't love all your kids. And everyone bangs on about scientology whilst conveniently thinking that all other religions are ok and sane when all of them clearly aren't they're mental, why are you believing that?

And then we come down to perhaps his most controversial film project *Interview With the Vampire* in which he starred opposite Brad Pitt and Christian Slater who took over from River Phoenix , the filming was apparently a disaster and the writer of the book and the screenplay Anne Rice never wanted Tom Cruise in the part as it was a blonde European part and she treated him badly and made him feel unwelcome. But here's the thing, apparently she looks back at it now and thinks… you know what that was ok, that was interesting. Look back on anything and it wasn't as bad as you think - Tom Cruise jumping up and down, he was just happy and trying to be entertaining on a talk show, when he was ranting about Covid in that famous clip he was just under pressure and trying to make sure the filming went ahead in trying circumstances. What I'm saying is everything looks different after a few years, let's face it everything looks different after 3 sleeps, often after one sleep. Don't rush to snap judgements.

Tom Cruise is I'm sure amazing, even though my mate who was an extra on one of his films said he was an all ends up cunt. You can't please everyone. You actually can't please anyone. Trying to please anyone these days it's Mission Impossible. Don't let them bleed you dry Tom, there will always be people baying for blood. You're no bigger lunatic than any of us, you're just the one that everyone can see, you're the only one amongst us all that casts any shadow.

July 27th 2023
Oasis – The Importance of Being Idle

You know what everyone says to me, how are you so brilliant Nathan? You know the other thing people say to me, take a day off Nathan, you need to rest more, for God's sake stop doing standup comedy, get off the stage. They're being kind of course in the main when they say that, they just have my best interests at heart because they think I'll burn out, I work so much, it's nearing episode 1000 of this podcast, all my shows, books, other work, it's too much. But here's the thing, I can't understand people that do nothing, or just watch television, they think they're doing something but they're doing nothing. I mean most television, there is television that moves you, that changes you, but that's not most television, the only television that I think is truly great is the Netflix series *Is it Cake?* I mean is it cake or is it a toilet? We don't know until he smashes the toilet to bits and shits into the cake and tries to flush it only to realise he's produced a nightmare concoction of shit and cake. But is it shit or is it cake – no sadly it's shit, but I guess that could be argued is edible so it's a type of cake. But it's not cake in the traditional sense...

Anyway, you get my point. Most TV is mindless nothingness and I don't want to spend my very limited time on this planet doing nothing, I can't do it, as soon as I stop I fall asleep, as soon as I start to watch a film or TV I fall asleep, I'm not tired when I'm working why would I want to waste more time than necessary sleeping? And people say ooh I love sleeping, but not if you don't have to. We've all been given this tremendous ticket to the show called life, do you want to miss the show being asleep, no this is the show I want to see, because it's life, it's not cake it's life. I mean some of life is cake but that's not the most important part of life, although some cake is really delicious and kinda makes my day.

Anyway what I'm saying is I'm not stopping, I'll stop when I'm dead, and as you can schedule Instagram posts up to 18 months after you die and podcasts indefinitely even death will not stop me. You wait for my funeral, it's gonna be only the start of the entertainment... you wait until you see my body at my funeral. But will it be my body – or could it be, is it... is it cake?

DAILY NOTES VOL I

July 28th 2023
Nevermind – Dennis Lloyd

So your life hasn't turned out how you wanted it to? Well as the saying goes, never mind. No that's not skating over the issue, never mind. Of course your life hasn't turned out like you wanted to, no one's has, even Brad Pitt is unhappy. Oh I'm not in that film, I miss that person, we're all unhappy because we are never satisfied with what we've got, and that is the secret of happiness which we all miss every day. You're in the game, you should be happy - you were never gonna win the game, you were maybe never gonna do well, look at all of us - and what is life anyway, its full of novelty items, pointless things, and maybe being one of those things isn't so bad after all.

There are countless pointless things, don't get down thinking you're another one of those pointless things and stay in the game. It's great being pointless. Kylie Minogue is essentially pointless, she doesn't have a point, but has made a very successful career out of it. There's no point to Kylie Minogue , Ellie Goulding, Nigel Farage, Andy Murray's mom, that's unfair – Andy Murray's wife, Piers Morgan, that guy from JLS, Michael Gove, Ant from Ant and Dec – there's no point to any of these people but stay in the game – what I'm saying is we're all pointless, but stay in the game and you never know you might have some fun and/or present Saturday night television quiz show that comes down to… do you know this song? How about this song? Do you know this song? Pointless.

There's even a gameshow in this country called *Pointless*, they're fucking with us, *Pointless Celebrities* where comedians pretend they are not only celebrities but professional comedians who don't live with their parents. It all doesn't matter, it's all pointless, we're just having fun. So really, if you're having a bad day, never mind, you're just probably looking at the day totally the wrong way, the day's going badly because you're not winning, but you were never meant to win, you are pointless, so you're doing exactly what you should be doing. So you are winning, you're here, you're in the game, and when the game goes wrong, know that it was always going to, really - never mind.

DAILY NOTES VOL I

July 29th 2023
Elton John – Rocket Man (Live at Glastonbury)

Oh my goodness if only I could play like Elton John, I've seen him live twice this year at the O2 - once with my son and he played Rocket Man just like he did at Glastonbury to close the show there and it's the magical virtuoso piano performance that send shivers down the spine, it's so beautiful and emotional and I was captivated and I turn to my son who's a pianist and he's captivated and he gets home and he's immediately inspired to practice and try to recreate it and then just uses it as inspiration for his own piano riffs and you can see the whole experience propelling him, rocket man, burning out his fuse up here alone. And it could happen for him, I can see it happening for him I really can. I was with a comedian friend last night Ashley Haden who is a joyously nihilistic person who says the best thing you can do for children is abort them because bringing children into this world shows them no love at all, as he says you wouldn't willingly take someone into a burning building. And yes the world is burning in so many ways, its inhabitable, so many things make it inhabitable – Earth ain't the place to raise your kids, in fact it's cold as hell. If only it was, we've almost destroyed the planet. But there is still hope that out of despair comes joy, out of the darkness comes a shining star, and why not that be your own kid, why not that be my child?

Well I'll tell you why not, because that would be a bit convenient wouldn't it, you're looking for a saviour, someone to unite the world in music and joy, like a cross between Elton John and Martin Luther King, and what it's going to be your son is it? Just like your own kid could be a model and all other kids are ugly buck teeth freaks. Oh your own kid is the special one are they? Grow up! How many kids have you had Nathan? Two? And one of them is going to change the world? That's lucky isn't it? Maybe you'd need to have tens, hundreds, thousands more kids before the odds were in your favour, it ain't gonna happen. Or if it is, I think its gonna take a long long time, a long time of you fucking various brilliant people in the hope of producing a champion, like an awful Grand National Kentucky Derby breeding programme. I'm up for that. You're not up for that Nathan you're pushing fifty. You don't know me, why do you think they call me the Rocket Man? I'm not sure, because you should retire?

July 30th 2023
Commodores – Easy

Easy like a Sunday morning. Sunday mornings haven't always been easy because when I was a six-year-old kid my parents sent me to Sunday School at Church, to get in with the local youth club and in my first meeting there the church person told all the little boys and girls that if we lied I'd get a black spot on my heart. Which is singularly the most ridiculous thing anyone has ever said to any group of children ever. I instantly knew this was ridiculous, even at six years old. Don't forget at that age I believed in everything, absolutely everything I'd been told, but I knew this was crazy, Disney shit. And in an instant, I was put off religion for life and I never went to Sunday school again.

And now, like virtually the whole world, we don't worry about religion on a Sunday morning, because Sunday mornings are about doing nothing. The only person working on a Sunday morning is the guy telling 6-year-old kids that if they lie they get a black spot on their heart, and to be honest they don't deserve a lie in. Everyone else, we do nothing don't we, Sunday morning is about lounging around, realising that the rest of your working week is awful and treating yourself to a massive breakfast. The rest of the week grab a banana and go – oh no really all I need is a banana, that will keep me going til lunch… Sundays, I know what I want, I want to go to the Toby Inn, mainly associated with carveries in this country but they've started doing breakfasts – breakfast buffet all you can eat – I wanna go there with everyone else and load my plate with eggs, toast, beans, mushrooms, hashbrowns, black pudding, sausages , bacon, more sausages and… you guessed it – the breakfast Yorkshire pudding – which isn't a thing – it's like saying the breakfast pizza, the breakfast vodka and tonic, they are using up the Yorkshire puddings from the carvery the night before. Awful and completely delicious.

Anyway, so this is what we all do on a Sunday morning now, this is our church, Toby is our God, and I know it sounds ridiculous but it's true - with all those sausages, bacon, fried potatoes and breakfast Yorkshire puddings, the one thing we're all gonna get on a Sunday morning… is a black spot on our heart.

July 31st 2023
Oasis – Morning Glory

Morning Glory right, we all know what that means, morning glory, well maybe you don't - look up Morning Glory on google and it's a plant, it's a flower, every return on google it's a plant, it's a flower – no it isn't – yes it is according to Google it's a plant that's earned its name from the fact that it's beautiful, fragile flowers unfurl in the morning. But beauty is fleeting. The flowers last only a day and begin fading about two hours before the sun dips below the horizon. Great but that isn't morning glory is it as we know it, what's wrong with you Google, what's the point in having the internet if it isn't going to show you pornography and pictures of penises because morning glory is obviously the erection that a man wakes up, we all know this.

My son asked me once – daddy why do I always wake up with an erection? Well son, it's because in the middle of the night, the tooth fairy comes and she checks under your pillow for teeth and if there isn't any well that's her chance to earn some money, how do you think she pays for all those pound coins for all the boys and girls' teeth in the world, so she whispers into your ear, would you like to be wanked off? And if she doesn't hear a 'no' she takes that as consent and she wanks you off either until you cum – yes that's a wet dream – or until you at least wake up with morning glory. What the flower? No not the flower morning glory is not the flower.

Ok daddy, will I always wake up with an erect penis? No son, when you get to my age it will hardly ever happen, in fact you'll be lucky to get an erect penis even when the tooth fairy appears in front of you and shows you her tits. Why's that daddy? Well let me check Google - why does morning glory fade? The beautiful, fragile erection unfurls in the morning. But beauty is fleeting. The erection lasts only a fleeting moment and begins fading before the sun dips below the horizon. Everything fades my son, even morning glory. What the flower? No the erection. Everything fades, so use it while you can little boy, but not now because you're 15, go back to bed, you never know the tooth fairy may come and make you cum. Aren't you the tooth fairy daddy? Erm, now I've said all that… I do hope not. Sleep nice.

DAILY NOTES VOL I

Aug 1st 2023
Moving On Up – M People

I'm Moving On Up to Edinburgh later today for the Fringe and obviously you have the nerves, the trepidation, what's going to happen – not about the shows obviously, they're gonna be great, but about the train journey – now this is my favourite subject obviously for avid listeners of this podcast you'll know that I have a little issue with people on trains so I thought I'd run down my top ten cunts on trains.

10 – the things on the other seat cunt – oh I'll just put down my coat on the seat next to me rather than above my head because I am a cunt – yes we all don't want people sitting next to us but we don't all have to be cunts.
9 – sitting on the outside seat cunt – next person I see doing this I'm gonna climb across them and stick my balls in their face.
8. grazing cunt – yeah sure you need a sandwich and a drink, grab a meal deal, sure, you don't need a picnic, this isn't a park, and clean up your shit when you get off, who's cleaning this away your slave? Oh I paid good money so that means, that means what? You can be a cunt – NO!
7. The whistling and humming cunt – don't do it on a train or anywhere. The only place for whistling is when you're trying to direct sheepdogs.
6. the loud cunt – yes you're not in the quiet carriage but you're not in the loud cunt carriage – I'd like there to be a loud cunt carriage.
5. having an actual business meeting on zoom cunt. Your business is not gonna fall apart if you don't attend this meeting Carol – you sell yoghurt.
4. No headphones Instagram cunt – yeah we've all seen the prick faceplanting into wet concrete we don't need to hear it over and over again you cunt.
3. No headphones film cunt – he's got no headphones and he – yes he it's always a man – is watching an entire film. Entitled cunt.
2. The ticket inspector. Stop being such a cunt you're not a police officer and let me off, the train is going there anyway.
1. And number one – the obvious one – the biggest cunt of all – me. I should always drive – I have a car – why am I getting the train full of cunts?
This makes me, undoubtedly, the biggest cunt of all.

Aug 2nd 2023
Ed Sheeran – Sycamore

Day before my Edinburgh shows start, I have a month-long slog up here in Edinburgh, of course it's not a slog it's the best job in the world, and everyone is very stressed about how their shows are gonna go, and I'm not stressed because I'm dead inside and also I've been doing comedy long enough to know it's gonna be ok. I'm the sycamore tree of comedy – I used to love the sycamore tree, it was my favourite tree, it had things on it that I now know are fruits called samaras, and you may know them, they fall from the tree and spin like helicopters, I love them. And what I loved about trees was the fact that you can count their age in rings, the dark rings are the age, and sycamore trees can live up to 400 years, 400 dark rings and from a very early age I knew what this meant for me – it meant I was insignificant, standing next to this tree I was nothing, it was there before me and would be there long after me, I wanted to be someone but I would always be insignificant next to this tree.

I am ambitious, I work hard, but I will never be as good as the tree, so there is no need to stress – I may be dead inside but you can count my age from my dark rings of truth in my standup material, oh my God that guy is the truth, and he's dark, he must be in his mid to late 40s – spot on. I loved that tree, and I wanted to be it so bad, and now I am as close as I will ever be to that tree, I'm old, I have dark rings, I have a tough bark that no one can penetrate, maybe just the odd kid writing 'penis' on me, and I never forget or betray my roots.

But I tell you what I also have, I have little surprises up my sleeve, I have little fruits that I occasionally drop, and they spin, they spin with a magical wonder. I inspire, just like that tree in that Birmingham park inspired me as a child. And I don't just inspire, I give life. I give life to the entire world. Even people that have never heard my jokes about crisps and my son's morning erection, they don't know it but just because they can't see it or hear it, indirectly my comedy is like oxygen – it's keeping them alive. I am the tree.

As kids today would say I am sick, but I'm more than sick though, I'm sick and more.

Aug 3rd 2023
Simply The Best – Tina Turner

It's the first day of the Edinburgh Fringe shows for me today and I'm doing two shows Amnesia and Fifty and they are to coin a phrase, simply the best. Or the best to give the song its correct title. Jointly the best. That's not the title of the song – jointly the best. You're jointly the best, better than all the rest, apart from one other, who you're equal to – you're jointly the best. But how can you judge whether you are the best? Well it's impossible in most situations isn't it – one person's best is another person's worst. I mean I love Phil Collins, some people say Phil Collins is the worst singer in the world, no he isn't is he, he's not worse than me. It's impossible for everyone to agree who is the best or worst at anything. I mean I can't think of anything where it's clear – I mean like the best runner – Usain Bolt obviously. Erm really, what about women? Sorry, I thought you meant best male runner, no I didn't – you said best runner, so that's Usain Bolt, best female runner Flo-Jo, Florence Griffith Joiner. But she's not as good as Usain Bolt is she – isn't she? She set the world record in 1988 and its never been beaten – but she's not as quick as Usain Bolt so he's the better runner, does quicker equal better oh for fucks sake you can't win!

Ben Johnson was the best runner if he's been allowed to take all the drugs he wanted he'd be the best runner, no the best runner not on drugs – you didn't say that, you said the best runner , the best runner not on drugs – ok but you mentioned Florence Griffith Joiner she was on drugs wasn't she – no, yeah she was, it was never proven. Alright then Usain Bolt, definitely not on drugs – what are you saying? Well how do you get that quick if you're not on drugs? Alright for fucks sake Phil Collins he's the best runner, no he isn't he can't even walk. Yes he is he's the best at everything.

Anyway, this is my point, you can't really judge if anything is the best can you, not everyone agrees, but that's the funny thing, there is an exception, my two standup shows, everyone agrees that they are the best. Who have you asked the opinion of? Just myself? Just myself – don't talk to anyone else. Everyone else is a cock. Good point Nathan you're the best, I know that. Lots of love Nathan, this book is great. Aw Nathan, fank you.

Aug 4th 2023
No Way Out (Theme from Brother Bear) – Phil Collins

So I was somewhere in the world, I really can't remember what country I was in, was it Australia, maybe New Zealand – it was called something like Stuart Gainsborough's Puzzling World, it wasn't that but something like that and it was a theme park of sorts but with just puzzling things like mirrors that made you look short or massive, you know hilarious things like that, and then there was this maze, where you started in the middle and you had to make it to all four corners – and I just couldn't do it, the person I was with I could hear shouting at me – like where are you?! And I was still basically in the middle. And that's when I thought – I'm missing a trick here – cheat – if you're struggling, cheat, lie – it always works.

Don't listen to anyone, kids, that tells you not to cheat and lie, the most successful people in the world all cheat and lie – it's like people who struggle for the whole day on a crossword clue – you know all crossword clues are instantly Googleable – type in the question and the answer pops up – why the struggle? The way out is easy if you just cheat. Anyway so there I was in the middle of this maze and I noticed that you could crawl or roll under the hedges – so that's what I started doing, rolling under the hedges listening to my friend's voice and rolling closer to it, and I was shouting 'coming, I think I'm finding the way out, coming!' Little did I know that when you got to the corner you climbed up on a little turret and you could watch what people were doing – so she was just with another woman she'd just met laughing at me cheating and saying it was disgusting – no it isn't. You're the losers, the reality is I've just got exactly where you are but I cheated which is better because it's quicker (if I'd thought about cheating instantly) and it shows courage, and it's just cool isn't it? Cheating is cool.

Oh I'm the square that is gonna work out how to get out of a maze without cheating or I'm gonna spend all day on a crossword – you're a mug is what you are, you're pathetic. That's why Chat GPT is writing these now, so much easier. Cheat. Every time - cheat. Cheats always prosper.

DAILY NOTES VOL I

Aug 5th 2023
Ed Sheeran – Wildflowers

Remember that lesson, don't know whether you had it, where you had to go out of the school into the local park, and pick wildflowers and then press them into a book, flower pressing it's called obviously. And this was a great lesson because any lesson which got you out of the classroom was incredible, that amazing moment where the teacher said let's do the lesson outside – fuck yeah, get in, best day of the year. Pressing flowers was obviously boring and pointless but only looking back do you realise how much more exciting they could have made it, because the teacher didn't get over the wonder of what it was, in the same way that they'd teach history in such a boring way without bringing it alive and making it clear how history shapes our present and future, I was never told when pressing flowers that they could last preserved for hundreds of years.

There are pressed flowers in the Natural History museum from the early 1700s, and now I'm a bit older you love looking back at something 30 years don't you, a photo you'd forgotten, a thing you wrote, something you found, everything gains value with the passing of time, just like any antique. What was just a flower picked and pressed as part of a boring lesson at school, becomes a frozen moment in time , where you were and who you were with comes back looking at it. If you're having a boring day today, nothing much going on, imagine how much value this day will have in 30 years' time, as you look back on your much younger self and probably shed a tear of how you used to do what you're doing today, even if it's nothing.

Because even if it's nothing, I guarantee you will look back at the precious wild flower you once were, you will still remember the sights and smells and sounds, and you will see the beauty that you can't perhaps see now. The only difference is that now you will be dry, and depressed and flat, and everyone will think you're boring. But you aren't, and you weren't. You weren't who you thought you were.

Yes, if you can capture any moment in time, one day in the future you will see it as the beautiful flower it always was.

Aug 6th 2023
America – Razorlight

I have a big birthday next year, it's got a zero in it, all I'll tell you is I'm not sixty and I'm not zero. And the plan is America. Apart from New Zealand my favourite place, I want to go New York and LA, I wanna do Vegas, America, that's my dream right there. But as I was falling asleep last night, it's worth questioning isn't it, why is it my dream, my fantasy. Well I've been there before, I love America, I love Vegas, I love the deserts of Nevada, the casinos, the scale, the Hoover Dam, Red Rock Canyon, I love the food, the service, I love everything, that's why you travel isn't it, all those things. But then I started to think about Life of Pi, the book Life of Pi, and how this kid who has to go through hell sets up a fantasy for himself involving a tiger and a hyena, and a zebra just to mask reality. Is this what I'm doing? I'm setting up a fantasy for myself so I don't have to deal with the reality of aging. I can have all this in place, I can talk about it, I can live it as if its real but it's just a fantasy to mask the hellish reality of aging, and something I don't want to face up to.

Because just think of the things I just mentioned – America – sounds amazing – I said the deserts of Nevada – do I love them really? There's nothing there and its fucking hot, and I still can't change a tyre on my car if I get stuck. The casinos, they will just take my money, and they're gaudy, brash, everything I'm not. I said I love the scale - that's meaningless, the Hoover Dam – I don't love a big concrete structure really – the food, the service, I can live without all of this, so why is it my fantasy? It isn't my fantasy, my fantasy is one that can never come true, my fantasy is really that I do not age, I do not grow older and instead I'm held, I'm in love, someone loves me for eternity without exception and makes me feel special and wanted and desired not just because there's a zero in my birthday, not just because I'm fifty. But I can't say any of that can I, and so I continue to plan a week in America. Because that's the one that's easier to sum up and invite people to – it's my birthday – let's do this. That's the story that's easier isn't it. Which story do you prefer? The one about a trip to America, or the one about being scared, needing to be held. The first right, the one about America. And that's why I chose to tell that one. And so it goes with God.

Aug 7th 2023
Rema – Calm Down

Everybody calm down, everybody, running around like little ants, gotta do this gotta do that, aaargh that makes me so angry, I can't believe they did that – calm down everyone and learn from our early ancestors that had the antidote to this crazy lifestyle, the way around a harsh winter, and just an all-round beautiful way to pass the time and indeed hold back ageing – there is really good evidence that our ancestors hibernated – yes, we hibernated, what we thought was just the domain of the mice and the birds, we learned to hibernate, we learned to slow down our metabolism and sleep for months. And I for one, am all up for bringing this back. Because it is possible, mammals do so this – bushbabies and lemurs hibernate so why not us? Let's face it, who doesn't want to give this a go?

If we weren't going to age very much, I'd gladly take a winter or two off to hibernate – sign me up. I reckon we could do this, it's just we've stopped trying because oh we've got to do this , got to do that. No, once we get to about thirty and realise that contrary to what we thought when were twenty, ambition leads nowhere, we have a choice just to lie back, not give up, just lie back and recharge and hibernate. Now to be scientific for a moment, it is said that we cannot lower our core temperature enough to hibernate, but nevertheless we can enter a deep sleep called a torpor which could go on for months, maybe six months. Who's up for a six-month sleep? Yes please, Nov-April, every year, sign me up. We just need to make the effort, so everyone November the 1st, get a comfortable bed where you won't be woken up, do it with your partner or dump your partner - you don't wanna be disturbed - and seriously just keep your eyes closed, see what happens. I reckon it's just lack of effort, I do think this is possible. We know it is, we could just lie there. Would you need to drink or eat? No, you wouldn't be doing anything. There are no downsides, I looked up why is hibernation bad and google just said the most common argument against using hibernation has been the wear and tear of the mechanical hard disk due to frequent shutdown and start-up. Humans don't have a hard disk, we'll be fine. Seriously, let's do this, I can't wait for winter now, fuck Christmas, fuck Valentines, it's all depressing, see you in April for my birthday, the Masters golf and the world snooker. I am literally in dreamland.

DAILY NOTES VOL I

Aug 8th 2023
Lewis Capaldi – Wish You The Best

I wish you the best for the next thirty years, because the next thirty years are going to define I think whether we will survive as a species, and I don't mean the big things like nuclear war and global warming, I think those things are going to be ok, Vladimir Putin is shit at war and I think it's actually quite nice being a little bit warmer, you know what I mean, cheers people up. So the biggest threat to the species is surely how dumb we will all become over the next thirty years. We've seen the shift in the last ten years from people reading books on trains to now just scrolling through videos of people jumping over things, from choosing a film with your own free will to the Netflix *surprise me* feature, surprise me! And now we have the launch of the Apple Glasses, a snip at 3000 dollars to augment your reality so you can just lie back and imagine you're doing something when you're not.

This is where we've been heading for years of course, first it was TV, then video, DVD, Netflix, every invention has been taking us down this road of sitting down, doing nothing, and imagining we're doing something, and these glasses I think represent the final nail in the coffin of activity for the human race, as we can be totally shut off from reality, lie back and play a permanent game of let's pretend. I'm told that on the outside of the glasses there will be a visual representation of your own eyes so when people are talking to you it's as if you're looking at them, but you won't be, you'll be looking at whatever you choose to look at, and if TikTok is anything to go by that will be old men face planting into wet concrete and jiggling tits.

So with that in mind, good luck, I wish you all the very best with the next thirty years, and I'll see you then, well of course I won't see you then, it will appear I'm looking at you but I won't be, I'll be laying back and dribbling, being fed through a long novelty straw and I'll be watching an augmented reality montage of life before this all happened, I'll be looking at today, when we knew we were heading on this path of destruction and had a choice to jump off but we didn't. But in reality, there was never a choice. Reality was never an option.

DAILY NOTES VOL I

Aug 9th 2023
Oasis – Some Might Say

When you die people are going to say stuff about you at your funeral or if you're very, very famous like me, on the TV and radio in the hours after your death. And I get to wondering what some might say about me. I started thinking about this when a newsreader George Alagiah sadly died of cancer in his 60s a few weeks ago and there was an outpouring of beautiful words about someone who was clearly a really loved and respected journalist and man. They said he was so giving and warm and generous and loving and selfless, they said he really helped others who were starting in their careers, supportive, brave. All these things I am.

I know right, I know I'm saying this myself, it's not your own thoughts about yourself that are played out on the radio or at your funeral are they, disappointingly, but I would hope some people would step up and say that I was warm and generous and loving and selfless, I'd hope all the people who I helped at the start of their careers would speak up, and they would say I was supportive, and just like George Alagiah dodging bullets in a war zone, when I was dodging heckles in a comedy club I was brave. But I do have a slight fear that the handful, and I do mean the handful of times I've been a cock in my life is going to overshadow the good things I have done.

I think I've been unlucky, I've said like a handful of cocky things in my life and I do think I'm gonna be remembered for these. And that's the thing with mistakes sometimes – they are debts that can ever be paid off – they aren't mortgages, they're £20 loans from a loan shark that says you just have to give me £2 a week but you read the small print and it's £2 a week for life. Someone is going to stand up at my funeral and say oh yes Nathan he's the person I told oh it's my dad's 50th next week – and Nathan said – what the 50th time he's fucked a dog? What even does that mean? These things haunt me and they will haunt me as I lay there dead and someone steps forward and says oh what an amazing warm kind loving supportive generous person he was, and everyone else thinks – really, Nathan Cassidy? We all think he was a complete and utter cunt

DAILY NOTES VOL I

Aug 10th 2023
Oasis – Whatever

I'm free to be whatever I, whatever I choose. That's the feeling I had as an 18-year-old. Back in the eighties when you were 18 or 21 you were given a massive key, representing a key to the door as a symbol of the limitless doors you could now open in your life. Now of course if you've got to 18 or 21 and you're not already successful online you may as well be given a massive chain round your neck and weighed down in the middle of a field covered in dog food. The best you can hope for is to be fucked by a passing dog. Seriously if you're not already a success at 18 forget about it, go and sit in a field and spread dog food on your ass and stick it in the air. You only have one other option if you're not already a TikTok success at 18 - join the army. Where you'll be doing the same thing – sitting in a field and waiting to be fucked.

In the 80s there was a song called 19 which argued that war was a bad thing because the average age of soldiers was 19. That song wouldn't work now would it because now we'd all think 19 – that's so old ... if you're not already successful on TikTok when you're 19 you should be forced to go to TikTok's headquarters in China, and there you will do an interview on whether you should live or die. Have you done a dance to *Cuff It*? No. Have you done the blackout challenge? What's that? Oh it's just when social media users are encouraged to hold their breath until they pass out due to lack of oxygen. Already killed seventy-two people. No I haven't done that. What have you done on social media Nathan? Well, I once tipped some cold water over my head. The Ice Bucket Challenge grandad. That was 2014 you decrepit old cunt, that was nearly 10 years ago. So I'd fail The TikTok interview, the Chinese people in charge would then shackle my legs just like they do with bears to stop them taking them over and then I'd be forced to walk to Vietnam where they will cover me in shit and make me sit in a field, in my case in a bucket full of ice, which like TikTok fame melts away in 3 minutes. But that's not gonna happen is it, so I hate to break it you 18-year-olds, if you have already got a million followers on TikTok or Instagram you may as well give up and like my son whenever I say you need to work really hard now to make something of yourself in this world he just says – yeah sure dad, whatever. Get that paté ready sunshine, here comes the dogs.

Aug 11th 2023
Kylie Minogue – Padam Padam

I'm still up in Edinburgh of course at the Fringe. Week 2 of the Edinburgh Fringe and my heart is beating fast its giddy with excitement being here for the 78th time, I really feel it's going to be my year. But what was my year – well in reality it was 1987, I was 13 and my whole life was ahead of me, and that's really the last time my heart went padam padam because everything was in front of me, and at that age I remember very clearly realising – oh wow, I can do anything, I've got my whole life ahead of me and I can do anything, and the first thing I want to do – have sex with Kylie Minogue – yes she was an adult and I was a child, but I still held out hope, little did I know that in the 80s lots of celebrities were having sex with children so I did actually have a realistic chance. Kylie meant everything to a boy like me then and she still holds a very special place in my heart, which is meaningless, but it doesn't matter, because Kylie embodies meaningless, in a good way. Let me explain.

I should be so lucky, lucky lucky lucky… it was meaningless, it didn't mean anything, my love for her, meaningless, she doesn't know who I am, all her songs, and I mean this in the nicest possible way, meaningless, they're not going to move you, inspire you, make you cry, it's just meaningless fun isn't it, and that's what we all need, that's when my heart went padam padam because things were meaningless back then, I had my whole life ahead of me and all I could picture was meaningless fun, there was never gonna be stress, worries and nothing but success and happiness and probable sex with celebrities even if they were adults and I was a child. I didn't need meaning, I never did.

And now all we want is meaning – what does Padam Padam mean? – it means being gay and having a great time one fan explained on Instagram – and you know what, that's utter bullshit but at the same time completely true, its meaningless and that's its beauty, it means everything and nothing and Kylie always takes you right back to being 13, where nothing had meaning, and so much made your heart go Padam Padam. I don't think my heart has done that in 35 years, but don't worry, I don't worry, because nothing means anything, it's all just meaningless. I should be so lucky. Padam Padam.

DAILY NOTES VOL I

Aug 12th 2023
Arctic Monkeys – Fluorescent Adolescent

My mom and stepdad have always had an incredibly bright light in the kitchen, they are fan of the big fluorescent tube light over the dinner table like it's an operating theatre or a snooker club, so as an adolescent I remember if I ever wanted a good look at my face I would take the mirror down to the kitchen as that was the only light room in the house, but it was too light, in the other mirrors my face looked good, in this mirror it was like oh my god what's that, what on earth is that, how has that appeared? Do I literally need to drain that? Do I need hospital treatment for that? This happens when you're an adolescent of course. And today, as the years drift away, there are no real surprises with your face apart from every six months or so see a new line and think fuck, I didn't know how lucky I was to be young.

You've seen your face thousands of times, in good times and bad, in good lighting and bad. You know that good lighting in a hotel or bar mirror – you're like fucking hell, I mean this isn't me but it is me, that's the lighting any self-conscious adolescent needs in their bathrooms or kitchens growing up, every day would be like oh my God I am a fit ten-year-old, I'm beautiful, let's have a selfie, oh go on then. Anyway, when I was reading something on a small screen for a while like a book or an article the words were very slightly blurry so I thought I'd go to the opticians and they prescribed some very light touch glasses to sharpen things up a bit, and I put them on and they made all the difference, I thought my eyesight was fine but this made things crystal clear – and then I made the huge mistake of going into the bathroom and looking my face with my glasses on, what, what the fuck, that doesn't look like that, what, oh fuck, no.

Now, I'm alive, so I'm beautiful, if you're listening to this and don't like your face, believe me, you're alive so you are beautiful. But oh my goodness – if I could give you one line of advice that will improve your life like nothing else - take the glasses off, take out that fluorescent tube, and stick in that hotel bathroom lighting everywhere. Or better still, be like the happiest person I know, and throw all the mirrors away. Sometimes, we're all better off in the dark.

DAILY NOTES VOL I

Aug 13th 2023
Tattoo – Loreen

I don't like drawing on my hand, a lot of stand-ups write their set lists on their hands, but I have never done that because as we all know pen takes ages to wash off, and I don't want my set list on my hands for 24 hours. I don't want written on my hands – tits, cock, cock and balls, cock and tits, mental health, tits, cost of living crisis, end song, tits. It's embarrassing. So I kind of want a tattoo but I would have to be so sure, I would have to think about it for months, before I committed something to my skin that couldn't be washed away. And surely everyone is like me right? No of course they're not, because the world is littered with the remnants of shit tattoos.

Oh my goodness, there are some shit tattoos. A guy I knew had Mickey Mouse on his arm and I said why have you got Mickey Mouse on your arm and he said I just got drunk. That isn't an answer is it? We've all been drunk, but only you have Mickey Mouse tattooed on your arm. Being drunk is not an excuse, that terrible decision is down to you, it was inside you all along and now its outside you, permanently.

But the biggest risk you can take is tattooing your face. As soon as you tattoo your face, you have instantly dropped out of mainstream society. No one in government, police, lawyer, teacher, no one with any mainstream job has a tattooed face, and I'm not saying it can't look cool and you can't get a job, but you make it much more difficult for yourself, because when you have a tattoo on your face we think you're either a drug addict criminal, or Mike Tyson, who also had a boxing career.

Don't do this – learn from an old friend of mine who had the word therapist tattooed on his face but the tattoo artist left a little gap between the e and the r and so what he actually had tattooed on his face was the rapist, and when I saw it I thought, man, now you are exactly like Mike Tyson. Please think twice before you tattoo your face or any part of you, and if you're a tattoo artist welcoming in drunk clientele that pass out as you scar them for life with Disney characters, then you are worse than the worst things Mike Tyson has ever done, and that includes all of his terrible tattoos.

DAILY NOTES VOL I

Aug 14th 2023
Half the World Away – Oasis

Where will we be in 28 years' time? What will have changed? Well the obvious thing to say is that our phones will be implanted in our heads, I mean we've already got these apple glasses we will definitely have chips in our heads in 25 years' time that pump the information direct to our eyeballs. The world is getting fatter and lazier and the surprise me feature on Netflix isn't needed any more because we'll have phones implanted in our heads just scrolling through people falling into wet concrete and jiggling tits.

The content won't change that's the interesting thing. 28 years ago we weren't looking at videos of people face planting into wet concrete, falling off a cliff and jiggling tits, but TikTok have definitely found the sweet spot and I swear it's not going to change – they know what we like now – videos of people falling off swings, bashing their heads, being shot and bleeding out, that's big on my timeline right now, I wonder is there a setting where I don't see people being shot and bleeding out, probably not. Anyway, this will now never change, apart from the falls will have to be bigger and the tits and the shooting more deadly.

So that's us pretty much in 28 years' time, sitting at home all with iPhones implanted in our heads just consuming a scrolling mess of concrete, bullets and tits. Sounds brilliant. But of course we'll still have to go out, so what will standup comedy be? Well I look back 28 years, and thankfully, it was pretty much the same, standup comedy will be the same too, live obviously I'm talking about live. Standup comedy on TV, there will be no TV of course, standup comedy on a screen that shows YouTube and TikTok and whatever replaces them will go something like this I believe in 28 years' time – someone will dance on, there will be music and dry ice and they will say something like 'wooooh ooooh ahhhhhh ooooh ahhhhh eggy eggy wooh wooh' – and then canned laughter – and then possibly 'woooh ooooh ooooh woo-woo panty poooooo'.

So I'm getting ahead of the game right now and here's a joke that I definitely think will stand the test of time. Aaaah oooh eeeeeh wooooh poocy pooo wooo wooooo. The future of comedy.

DAILY NOTES VOL I

Aug 15th 2023
Ice Spice & Nicki Minaj – Barbie World (with Aqua)

Did you see that news about a month ago – the value of original Barbie dolls, in the boxes obviously, an original 1959 barbie doll - $27,000. They were $3 dollars at the time. So if you find a box of 100 anywhere that's basically a million dollars, the only more expensive Barbie is the limited edition diamond encrusted one released for the 40 year anniversary of De Beers, shall I get De Beers in? Well if you did again you're sitting on a fortune, but to be fair that one cost $85,000 to buy and is now worth an estimated $85,000, and to be honest if you own one of these things you're probably a multi-millionaire anyway – I mean imagine being down to your last $85,000 and thinking I know what I should buy now, darling I've invested our money. I mean to be honest it's not a bad investment. As long as you keep it in the sealed box, fuck me, you've got to keep it in the box, are you taking that Barbie out of the box? You're a fucking idiot, yeah I know you wanna play with it, you're four and whatever, but I want a fucking retirement you selfish little shit.

So I was watching the *40 Year Old Virgin* with my son the other day, and the main character Andy the virgin keeps all his toys in their boxes and my son asked me why does he keep them in the boxes and I said so they maintain or grow in value, and he said why are they more valuable, the toys, if they're in their original boxes? And I said well then they're in their best condition and he said how about if they're in their best condition but not in the box, maybe in cellophane, and I said no they have to be in the box, and he said why, and I said because it's a made up thing, it's made up that some things have more value, it's made up that original Barbie is valuable, it's made up that diamonds are valuable, that's a made up thing too, everything is made up when it comes to money, nothing is real, so best to just avoid money and just get out there and don't be like Andy. And he said what don't be a virgin? And I said well you're fifteen so no but yes, live your life, try not to worry about collecting too much money, just play, have fun, because one day, well, playtime's over. 'Do you mean I'll be dead?' said my son. And I said 'yes, and if you die before me don't worry, I won't bury you I won't cremate you, I'll shove you back inside mummy's vagina because you'll have more value when you're in original box.'

DAILY NOTES VOL 1

Aug 16th 2023
Metro Boomin, A$AP Rocky & Roisee – Am I Dreaming

I'm still here at the Edinburgh Fringe obviously I've been here 72 years now and I watched a video the other day about the Edinburgh Fringe and I thought – oh my God – is this real – am I dreaming? The corruption, the difference between those with money and those without is frankly flabbergasting, I won't even tell you what this video is because I'm here in the middle of it and it's going really well and I realise I'm in a more fortunate position than some but oh my God, and of course it's not just the Edinburgh Fringe, it's everywhere, the corruption and the greed of people, the Old Boys' network, the way that connections and privilege shapes our entire lives, we know it's happening but when you see it in front of your own eyes played out it's almost funny if it wasn't so scary, and if people saw it, I mean really saw it in their own lives there would be riots that are now not allowed.

So it's time to drop out of society I think, and if you think no it isn't, almost certainly you already have dropped out of society - society is those with massive family wealth or the few that created their own, going about in society parties and affording branded cereal, the rest of us aren't in society any more. I went to the supermarket the other day – the shelves were virtually empty, cheese that was £2 a year ago is now £5.50, there were no staff on the checkouts, the only affordable cereal was called Malties and it was dark, ghoulish, and an 85 year old lady approached me and said 'where is everyone? Where is all the food?' And I said to her that now exists in another world of which we are not inside, that is society and you and I have dropped out of society, and very soon it will be apocalyptic and you and I will be fighting over live rats amongst the bins, not even proper rats as well, Malties rats that are actually just dirty snails covered in carpet fluff. We'll be fighting over snails old lady and I will show no mercy. But you know what I said to her, even though that sounds grim, it's still a millionth as grim as being handed everything on a plate, never having to work, never having to graft, can you imagine how empty that would be? And the old lady said I just want to die. And I said, no, the only people that die are the privileged, we don't have enough money to die, we will never die, because we are the ones with spirit. And spirit never dies.

204

DAILY NOTES VOL I

Aug 17th 2023
Westlife – Flying Without Wings

Ah man I've been listening to a lot of Westlife recently it's like a sausage factory – banger after banger after banger. And this is perhaps their most famous song – Flying Without Wings, which I've always found problematic as it's supposed to be a very uplifting song, but it's literally the opposite isn't it because if you're flying without wings, you're dead, unless you're in a helicopter, but you're not, you're on a plane aren't you and if you're flying without wings you're fucked.

And this was always my fear, flying, I was a nervous flyer when I first started flying because I didn't get my first flight until I was eighteen and I still remember that feeling on take-off of what the fuck's this? If you leave flying to when you're an adult it doesn't seem right, so ever since then I've wanted to be by the window looking at the wings, so I can be the first one to spot if there's a problem. The wings are where there's gonna be a problem, engine explosion wings falling off, so I'd spend my early flights constantly looking out of the window thinking well if I spot a problem like the wings falling off I can flag that up to the air stewards I'd say 'excuse me the wings have just fallen off' and they'd say 'oh cool, please return to your seat sir to prepare for death'.

Anyway I spent years doing this, being nervous, looking out through the window and I thought this has got to stop, so I did one of these fear of flying courses and it was good and whatever to be in a room of like-minded people and then the guy running it said 'how many of us are worried the wings are going to fall off?' and I raised my hand thinking others would, and they didn't and he said 'Nathan why do you think the wings are going to fall off?' And I said because they've been screwed on and shit happens and he said ah but when you're thinking they're gonna fall off, which way do you think they'll fall? And I said 'downwards obviously' and he said ha wrong, actually if wings ever fall off your plane they'll fall upwards, and I thought… that doesn't fuckin help me, and ever since then I've been just as scared but now I'm waiting for the wings to fall off upwards.

But I guess that would be ok in the end, because I'd be flying without wings, and that, according to this bullshit song, is brilliant.

Aug 18th 2023
Old Dominion – Memory Lane

I've been looking back at the last thirty years for my new show I'm writing and obviously the things that stick out are the most memorable moments, the moments of joy and love and also pain, the most memorable dramatic parts of the journey down memory lane. So as we embark on the next thirty years together, we have an amazing opportunity, to build memory lane, to construct it, this lane will be the last road you ever travel down, so you may as well make it as interesting, as joyous, as memorable as possible, this is the lane you will be thinking about when you move from this world, it's this lane, this memory lane that we start to build together now that is the most important lane ever.

So will there be twists and turns in the lane? You bet there will, will there be a speed limit? No. You see this immediately sounds dangerous to me – a lane, so a single road of traffic with loads of twists and turns and no speed limit – that sounds like a fucking death trap. But of course it is a death trap, this lane will inevitably end in your death, but that's what is so cool about it, death on this lane is not to be feared, it is inevitable, it's the only downside to this lane we all must travel down. I say the only downside, there will inevitable be some cocks along the way, hell-bent on ruining your journey by being dicks, but ignore them and keep on driving, without fear.

I mentioned a newsreader that died on this a few weeks ago and he died of cancer and he was asked in an interview are you scared of death? And he said I do not have the time to waste to be scared of death, it is as futile as it is unnecessary. Instead, he said 'I choose to spend whatever days I have remaining loving my friends and family, it's all we really have along this road'.

I don't believe in hell, but hell must be getting to the end of the road and thinking – I don't want to remember the journey. The journey could be long or short, but make this journey the most exciting, the most exhilarating journey of your lives. This journey is your life, and there is no other. And if there is, I'll be seriously annoyed. What prick told me to cut this one short driving like a prick down a thin road? Don't listen to me, don't listen to anyone, just drive!

DAILY NOTES VOL I

Aug 19th 2023
Rick Astley – Never Gonna Give You Up (live at Glastonbury)

Week three, final week of the Edinburgh Fringe and here I am in an arts festival surrounded of course by people, the majority of whom are younger than me, it feels like Glastonbury, and I see a much younger person in front of me and I think, oh no, why is that much younger person being seen more than me? Why is that much younger person more visible than me? And then I suddenly realise, it's because they're on somebody's shoulders, someone is literally carrying them, they're there waving their arms around being basically incoherent and drunk and everyone's looking at them, they're on TV, and there's someone literally carrying them, and this person is never shown – he's the guy with the money of course, and he's in pain, why do I have to carry this useless fuckface? It's because I inverted commas love her, and now she just is able to live off the fact I'm carrying her and everyone loves her and she's on TV all the time – fuck, fucks sake.

Anyway, that's how I feel at any arts festival sometimes. But did you see Rick Astley at Glasto? Rick Astley if you don't know him was a big star in the 80s with his hit single *Never Gonna Give you Up* and one or two others and then he hasn't been seen a lot since because he was over 25 and therefore shit, but here he is 35 years later and he did two sets at Glasto, one on his own and one with a band doing Smiths covers, and everyone was like oh my God, Rick Astley, he's actually really good, he's got a great voice, he's a great singer and performer and I thought well fuck me what a surprise, just because you're over 50 you're actually good at something?! You're better aren't you, because the more you do anything the better you get, and fuck me what a surprise Elton John was actually good as well, he was the best, and he's in his 70s.

Dicks on other peoples' shoulders at Glastonbury should be ashamed of yourselves, you don't realise it but everyone behind you hates you because you're blocking their view, you're blocking their pathway to the stage, get down off the shoulders and all I'm saying is make this a fair fight, you'll be older very soon too, and people will start to give you up, let you down. I'm just saying that should never happen, never.

Aug 20th 2023
Kylie Minogue – Can't Get You Out of My Head

So I did Rick Astley, I did *Never Gonna Give You Up*, and there's a song like no other that you can't get out of your head, a bit like this one, and it's always seen as a bad thing isn't it when you can't get a song out of your head, oh this damn song I can't get this song out of my head – but be careful what you wish for, because what is the alternative to having a song in your head, it's silence isn't it? It's nothingness. Have you tried having nothing in your head?

It is awful.

Because it doesn't stay nothing for very long. Like a mosquito loves blood or a wasp loves lemonade, there is nothing bad thoughts love more than an empty head. You're not allowed are you to have nothing in your head, I'm not sure why that is, meditation is the closest you get from ridding everything from your head but that's because you have a nice voice telling you that you're relaxed and a bit of music that you can't get out of your head, no one meditates in complete silence do they because if they did they'd been trying to relax but as the saying goes an empty vessel will soon be full of shit - as the empty head inevitably and very quickly gets filled up with a massive deluge of the worst thoughts imaginable…

Nathan do you remember that thing that happened?
Do you remember that show?
Do you remember when you shit yourself?
Do you remember that other time you shit yourself?

No, no, get these thoughts out of my head, play anything, anything in, what even Rick Astley? Of course, play that on a loop, anything, Kylie Minogue, yeah any of her shit. Yes anything, Westlife, yes definitely Westlife…. What about Ellie Goulding? Erm, what? No actually, that's fine. But I thought you said… Doesn't matter what I said, I'm fine with my thoughts thanks. What even thoughts about death and the worst moments of my life? Yes absolutely anything cheers, anything but Ellie Goulding – don't do this to me, please, please God no!

Aug 21st 2023
I Wonder – Kanye West

I wonder, as I'm sure we all are wondering, what is Kanye West up to at the moment? I wondered this at the end of last month and was pleased I did because Kanye West is someone to me that I wouldn't be aware of anything he's up to because I don't keep in touch with celebrity in that way, but he's always up to some bat shit crazy stuff. If he's not announcing he's running for President then he's as he was at the end of last month, dressing his daughter North West (yeah that's her name North West) in a white hoody with a pointed hood that covers the face and small eye holes that look like a KKK outfit.

This is an unreleased piece from his Yeezy collection, what's that you might ask. Well this is the thing, if you don't keep up with the Kardashians or North by North West or whatever their latest reality cluster fuck is this year then you'd have no idea, these things would totally pass you by, everything would pass you by unless you see it, it's like a tree falling in the woods, if you had a camera on every tree in every wood then you'd be obsessed with falling trees in the woods and every time one fell you'd go oh my God a tree has fallen in the woods and you'd tell your friends and they'd say what was the tree wearing and you'd say it was wearing like a green foliage top from the Treesy collection and they'd say oh wow show me this Treesy top and they'd say they disagree with that Treesy top and you'd say why and you'd suddenly be talking about something that you'd have never noticed if you hadn't set up the cameras to watch, it would have literally made no sound, because no one can hear.

Kanye West and the Kardashians' whole careers are built upon the fact that people are watching, and to keep them watching they have to make what would be a boring forest fucked up – they have to dress the trees in KKK hoods else no one would look, don't fall like that tree, into their trap, they are making no sound until you listen and watch.

Cover your eyes, cover your ears, but preferably not in a Yeezy 2023 collection KKK hoodie.

DAILY NOTES VOL I

Aug 22nd 2023
Noah Kahan – Dial Drunk

My mate has just has a kid and called him Noah which is a lovely name and he's a Muslim and somebody commented that Noah was an interesting name for a Muslim father to give and he tells me that Noah is actually a figure in Islam too and I said what did he do and he said exactly the same as the Noah I would know and I said what the guy with the Ark and two of every animal and he said yeah. This obviously blew my mind and I had to look it up and yeah he's right, Noah – in Islam – a messenger of God, who was tasked with telling people they should worship God, but some refused so he did what anyone would do in this situation he built an Ark and everyone on it was saved from the great flood.

I'm not sure whether the animals went in 2 by 2 – Huzzah! Huzzah! But yeah basically the same story, which is cool right, different religions coming together and admitting what we all know – Noah is the best one, isn't he, the best religious figure. If you can't be God, you wanna be Noah, maybe with Moses a close third with the parting of the seas shit – but ideally you wanna be Noah, for so many reasons. All those animals on an ark it's cool isn't it, two of absolutely everything, on a boat, an admin nightmare and don't forget he had to build this ship from scratch. Have you seen the film *Evan Almighty*? Well if you have you will know what a not fun and completely humourless task that is, but the main thing that makes him the best one is unlike God who people can attack and moan at – why did you let him die, why is my house so shit or whatever, Noah has got that priceless commodity of smugness where he can say I was right, I told you that the flood was coming if you didn't believe in God and here it is and now you're drowning to death and me and all these animals are absolutely fine so fuck you.

The biggest 'I told you so' in history gets played out as Noah sails through the flood happy as Larry, if Larry is happy being surrounded by a million shitting animals. Noah my friend, if you did exist, I hope you built yourself a soundproof room. You're a cool guy though my man, you're cool, I love you – no I'm not dialling drunk - if religion is a real thing, which of course it isn't, I wanna be you man, I wanna be 2 by 2 be you.

Aug 23rd 2023
George Michael – Father Figure

A few more days of my two shows up here at the Edinburgh Fringe and I've made myself proud but more than that I've made you proud but more than that I've made my mother proud but more than that I've made my father proud. I mean making your mother proud is easy isn't it, your mother would be proud of you whatever you did, as long as you can wipe your own arse a mother would be proud of her kid. Oh you'll never believe what Nathan is doing at the moment, yes he's wiping his own arse, I'm so proud of him, is your son wiping his own arse? No, well my son is better than yours. But my son is 18 months old. Doesn't matter, Nathan is in his 40s and he's better than your son because he's wiping his own arse.

Anyway, a father is the harder nut to crack by far, he's not gonna be proud of anything easily. So you're wiping your own arse, so you should be, tell me when your wiping Kylie Minogue's arse. Well that isn't gonna happen unless I work in an Australian care home in 40 years' time and you'll be dead. Well I ain't proud of you then. But as luck would have it, while he tried to push me into studying Law when I was a kid, the thing I became, a stand-up comedian, makes him the proudest of all. He never encouraged me to do this, he never helped me to do this but I did it, and it makes him very, very proud.

I've really bonded with my father over the last year or two, after he wasn't around much as a kid. I asked him recently I said 'Where were you when I was a kid?' and he said 'It's a hard thing to admit Nathan but for the first ten years of your life I was down the pub watching sport.' And I said, 'What?!' And he said, 'football.' Not what sport?!

And I said to him recently I asked him why does it make you so proud that I'm a comedian and he said well its basically down to me isn't it. What? Yes I've read, he said, that all comedians have had no love from their fathers and that's why they seek the love of others. I guess, I said. So it's down to me he said, every bit of success you have is down to my neglect. And you can't argue with that can you, well you can, but he'd be watching the football and he wouldn't even hear. Makes me so damn proud.

Aug 24th 2023
Don't Mess With My Man – Lucy Pearl

Don't mess with my man and don't mess with my nan, my grandma, a formidable lady that I've taken so much from, and I've been talking about her for a month in my show 'Fifty' up here at the Edinburgh Fringe (now available on Amazon Prime) and I mention briefly in the last show that for the last 20 years of their relationship they just bickered my grandma and grandad but really in truth my grandma and grandad had the relationship that I've subsequently found out many people of that generation had, they just stayed together because there was no choice back then, you stayed together, there was no divorce. Once you were married that was it and if you didn't get on you had to work a way around it, and that's what they did and that's what many couples of their generation did, they ended up sleeping in separate rooms, for the last 20, 30 years of their lives together.

I remember them blaming it on my grandad's snoring but in reality they had reached the point that nowadays couples would get divorced – you know that point that all couples reach it's like – get out, get out of my bed, why are you here, sleeping next to me? Smelling, farting, breathing, stop breathing like that it's so annoying, you're popping is what you're doing, yes popping, making a weird popping noise from your nose, stop it get out of this bed. So off my grandad went to the spare room where he slept in a single bed for the last 20/30 years of their relationship. But you know what, to my knowledge, he was happy, he was like me, just leave me alone and I'm happy, let me sit in the corner, reading the paper and watching the cricket, that is heaven for me as it was heaven for him.

He was an artist and a musician just like me – my cousin said at his funeral that when I walked in it was like she had seen a ghost because I looked just like him, and I had his mannerisms. Well I do but more than anything else I have his spirit. His spirit lives on inside me, as does the spirit of every man that says it without saying it – yes, you've won, I give in, I'll be there in the corner forever now, as long as you leave me alone, don't hassle me any more, leave me be, and let me pop away forever in peace.

DAILY NOTES VOL I

Aug 25th 2023
Alison Moyet – All Cried Out

Sometimes you need a good cry right, its cathartic, I need to get that out, that's really helped me, it's part of the healing process, I can move on now. The trouble is in art and indeed comedy you want to go back to some of the most traumatic moments of your life because there's unfortunately or fortunately a lot of comedy in those moments. Comedy – tragedy plus time. But I always say to people, from past experience, make sure you've fully processed the trauma yourself before you put it on to a stage and try and get comedy out of it, otherwise you're using the audience for a therapy session that neither of you want - they don't want it because its traumatic and you don't want it because you're essentially saying the same thing over and over again to your therapist and they're just laughing at you, if you're lucky, but more often they're just looking perplexed at why you're playing out your trauma like this in a comedy show, tell us a fucking joke mate.

And I do agree with that to a certain extent, but there are some things that happen in your life that are so awful, so traumatic that you can never truly deal with them - does that mean they can never enter the stage, does that mean they can never be talked about in comedy? I hope not, because comedy = tragedy plus time, which must mean in terms of mathematical equations – great comedy, truly great comedy = truly great tragedy plus truly great time. And I'm always looking for great comedy, so I do need to go looking for that great tragedy? And of course I don't need to go looking, it's there, it's just how to talk about it without scaring the audience away who are there for jokes about how busy and expensive trains are.

Damn what a beautiful dilemma, the truly great comedy lies in that paper thin line before you completely haunt the audience forever, or maybe you completely traumatise them but they don't realise they've been traumatised. That's the secret isn't it, it's called traumedy, or it should be – it's great comedy because they're actually being traumatised by the tragedy – they just haven't realised. Yes, I think I've had the idea for next year's Edinburgh show. It's going to be absolutely horrific and hilarious, the perfect combination.

DAILY NOTES VOL I

Aug 26th 2023
Relax My Eyes – ANOTR & Abel Balder

That's the Edinburgh Fringe done for this year and it was obviously amazing and now it's time to Relax my Eyes, take a break, have a holiday, do some meditation, put some cucumber on my eyes, have a facial, go for a walk – I can't do it, I can't do it, I've been so busy here this month and everyone else would be craving for a holiday and I am but I just know that eight minutes into that holiday I'll be thinking this is boring I need to get back to work. The thing is of course I don't think I'm getting high from it but without it I get low, it's a drug, my work is a drug and there's no weaning myself off it.

When I get too old to work I'm going to be a fucking nightmare – I'll be ninety and still think I need to be entertaining people, but of course everything that comes out of my mouth then will be racist, there's no way of avoiding it. I know it's a ridiculous thing to say that all ninety year olds are racist, but it's also a ridiculous thing to deny that really technically they are, they don't mean to be most of them, but you're just inevitably behind the times of what the accepted word is to use, how things are described now. So there'll I'll be, ninety years old in my care home organising nightly gigs so I can try out my new five minutes of half-baked racist ideas, and my family will be embarrassed, my kids and my grandkids who are forced to come and visit – but the trouble is in front of the other residents I'm kind of storming it every night, they're kind of my perfect audience, they are all a little bit racist too and they don't remember how shit I was yesterday.

And I'll look out to the crowd and I'll see her, my partner and she'll have that look on her face that she often has – take a day off Nathan please, meditate, relax your eyes, you're going to kill yourself working so hard. But that's not true is it? The people that die are the ones that retire, that stop, you hear it all the time – oh as soon as he stopped, he dropped down dead.

That's never gonna happen to me – I'm never gonna stop, so I'm never gonna die.

DAILY NOTES VOL I

Aug 27th 2023
Nik Kershaw – I Won't Let The Sun Go Down On Me

I said yesterday that I was never gonna die, I won't let the sun go down on me. But of course that's not true, and in these moments of tiredness, exhaustion after a run of shows like I've just had, I am starting to recognise things don't go on forever. My eyesight's going, and the terrible irony is I can't find my glasses. That's how bad my eyesight is. I've got the antidote but I can't find it, I'm like Superman when he couldn't find the antidote to Kryptonite. I forget what that was, wasn't it just trying doubly hard to get over it. Get over it Superman, it's only Kryptonite, who's allergic to that shit? What you talking about? That's actual Kryptonite, my Kryptonite is actual Kryptonite. Don't be so stupid that's just an expression, 'my Kryptonite'. It's not a literal thing. That's like saying your Achilles heel is your Achilles heel. Well that could be the case if you hurt your Achilles heel. Anyway, they're all dead now Superman forget about it.

My eyesight isn't bad, it's just a little bit off, and that's what's happening to my whole body, everything is now just a little bit off compared with 10 years ago, my body aches that little bit more, I'm that little bit more tired, my hair is that little bit less thick, my clarity of mind, the way I form my words is that little bit less sharp and it's that inevitable and slow descent isn't it, of the sun beyond the horizon. Na fuck that, this isn't happening, its stopping right now – the sun is not gonna go down on me – I'll tell you what I am, I'm fucking Norway, yeah you heard, I'm Norway, north Norway, or wherever the sun doesn't go down on them, I'm that. Your eyes starts to go, your body starts to ache and you think oh there's nothing I can do to reverse this - yeah there is, you can reverse it in an instant, and here's the secret the world has been waiting for, just don't tell anyone, virtually all of aging is imperceptible to the onlooker, it's pretty much mostly down to you telling people you're aging – oh my eyesight's going, oh I ache, oh that fucking Kryptonite is giving me a headache, oh my back. What about your thinning hair? Wear a hat. What about your slightly less muscly body? Cover it with a leather jacket. Oh a mid-life crisis, it's not though is it, I'm past my mid-life, but no one knows I am because I don't bang on about it, I never mention it, I'm north fucking Norway baby, and the sun never goes down on me! I am Superman!!

DAILY NOTES VOL I

Aug 28th 2023
In Da Club – 50 Cent

I'm back home from the Edinburgh Fringe now and as you take stock of the whirlwind month and how unbelievably successful it's been its still easy isn't it to focus on the negative – we all do it don't we – I never get on to the stage thinking its gonna go amazingly well, even though it always does. And even after a month of success it easy to dwell on the one or two things that have gone wrong, or the one or two things that have made you less happy. So I won't do that this year, my focus is purely on the positive… however I will say if you come to my show as some American lady did this year and tell me on the way out that you really enjoyed it but sorry you don't have any money on you – I take card by the way - and then proceed to give me 50 cents – then I will remember you forever. You don't have any money? What are you talking about – you're visiting Edinburgh from America – you have lots of money, I absolutely cannot believe you're down to your last 50 cents – I mean if you are what an amazing gesture which I will take to my grave but as that is bullshit - why, why did you do that to me?

I mean just leave without saying anything or giving anything, if you say that you've really enjoyed it then in that split second I'm expecting ten or twenty dollars, don't then give me 50 cents – why? Just give me nothing – you said you had nothing, so give me nothing. Giving me 50 cents is like telling me you enjoyed the show, telling me that you've got nothing and then spitting in my face. You may as well have spat in my face the way that makes me feel – this was a show I poured my heart and soul into, for a year, it was emotional about my grandma, a woman who really had nothing, she had nothing, and I tell you what made her such a nice lady – she didn't go to a comedy show and really enjoyed it and then spat in the performers face on the way out.

Anyway, some really good things happened too this month, someone brought along a date who was drunk and chipped in to the entire show, and on the way out he gave me fifty pounds. Made my Fringe. Fifty pounds. Not cents, pounds. But I'm surprised I can remember that because right now, I can't see anything but that stingy bloody woman - my eyes are completely covered in stingy twat's spit.

Aug 29th 2023
New Order – World in Motion

So we go again, at least for a few more episodes. I think I'm going to take a pause at episode 1000 which is in 29 episodes time. It's hard to take a pause sometimes but sometimes you've got to look up and see the supermoon. There's a supermoon this week, and I'm told this is great and sometimes I think no it isn't, it just means the moon is slightly bigger, what's great about that? What's great is what I'm doing as a comedian and with my kids and partner, that's what's great. But if you look up at the supermoon and take a pause, you get things in a new order don't you, the world is in motion, spinning through the galaxy, and we are just grains of sand, it's all irrelevant isn't it, it means nothing.

But of course it does mean something, and travelling on a train today three hour journey an old lady was texting on her phone, in landscape, which immediately annoyed me, and every time she pressed a letter, I think she had one of those old-style phones where you had to press the buttons a number of times before you got the letter you wanted like an old Nokia, and every time she pressed a button, a little beep went off, a little fucking beep, and I thought what do I do, it's 3 hours. Yes she's an old lady but this is fucking annoying, I have to say something, I started staring at her, imploring her to look up and when she did I'd be forced to ask her as kindly as possible whether she had a silent mode on her fucking phone, but of course she didn't look up, not once, for the whole journey, as the beeps kept coming and coming for the entire three hours.

And that's when I realised there is no supermoon, there is no world in motion, there is no kids, no partner, it's just you isn't it, and this fucking beep, this is my whole life now, this is the only thing that matters in my life. This will never pass. I need to stop making excuses because you're old. I'm going to be old soon, and it doesn't mean I can turn into a cunt. I mean I will for sure, what's being old about apart from getting away consistently with being an old cunt, but it isn't an excuse. There is no excuse for this noise that will never, ever stop. Fuck me, it will never stop.

And then of course it does. And it's beautiful. And that's why the most beautiful thing will always be a pause.

Aug 30th 2023
Gunna – Fukumean

Sometimes you have to stand back and say – fuck you mean? What the fuck do you mean? What is wrong with people? Why are people looking for beef the whole time, trying to get at you, what the fuck do you mean? Is no one like me? Seriously? Does no one understand the beauty of a quiet life with no beef? If my dad taught me anything it's this – the beauty of a quiet life – I just want to watch the snooker. That's what my dad taught me, and my grandad before him, I just want to watch the football, just sit me in a corner with the football and I'm happy. Sure I'll talk with you, I'd love to talk with you, but if you're gonna start any beef or have a go at me, seriously I'm happy until the end of time sitting in the corner and watching the snooker.

I love the snooker. I don't talk, and they don't talk. They don't talk to each other; they just play the game. They don't give each other any shit and as they're playing, they too are sitting in the corner and watching the snooker. Because that is what any sane person wants to do – say nothing and just in the corner watching the snooker.

I never start beef with anyone, even if they really annoy me, because ultimately where does it get you? I struggled enough to change my own children's behaviour at five, six years old when they were pliable, malleable, you can't change an adult's behaviour or attitudes, so why are you getting angry with them, chatting shit to them, what the fuck do you mean, it's the biggest waste of time in history telling another adult that they should do something differently. Sure they might listen and pretend to say oh yes that's what I'll do, they'll do it for a few weeks, a few months but then they'll go right back to how they've always done it because adults do not change.

Five, six years old it's set in stone, you are who you are, everyone is how everyone is and I am how I am – it's this – sit me in a corner with my laptop writing, with my piano, with the snooker on and I'm happy, and if you want to come into my corner and be happy and loving and generous and kind and fun then please be my guest, and if you wanna start beef with me, get angry and talk shit at me, then seriously, what the fuck you mean?

Aug 31st 2023
HARDY – Truck Bed

My mate who lives down near Brighton on the south coast of England tells me about these divorced men who are forced out of the family home and live on a road of trucks and vans because they can't afford accommodation any more because divorce in this country is so costly when you have kids. The man usually loses over half his wages, half his pension, the house, as the mom needs to keep all that because she is, erm, I'm not sure. That's right, it's 'all the women independent', until it comes to divorce and then it's let's bleed the man dry and live off what he has earned for the rest of his life while he has to sleep on a truck bed. Throw your hands up at me.

And that's all you can do as a man – throw your hands up and admit defeat. I can't say this strongly enough – never get married, never get married. Please listen to me. As we get to the end of this book and you're taking or leaving everything I say, stop now and listen. Take this advice. Never ever get married. As you look into those eyes of the person you love and the Celebrant says does anyone know of any just impediment why these two should not be married, and there's that little giggle from the congregation, I'll tell you what that giggle really is, it's the nervousness of everyone coming out knowing how ridiculous it is what you're about to do, and that's the very moment where you as a man can say, yes I know of a just cause or impediment why me two should not be married, because in five, ten, fifteen years' time she's gonna chuck me out after finding a new man and after all those years dancing around to Beyonce she's gonna say I know by the law I can have half, and half of future earnings, and all the house, and half the pension, oh yes please, half forever, even if we're only married a few years, half forever.

Yes please, half, forever. Because yes greed is a sin, but I'll tell you what's worse than greed, it's sleeping on a fucking truck bed for the rest of my life.

All the divorced women independent throw your hands up at me. Oh I can't see a single hand. Funny that.

DAILY NOTES VOL I

Sep 1st 2023
I Know? – Travis Scott

It's 5am can we still fuck? We can but, you know, it's only gonna go one way if we do anything at 5am apart from sleep, unless you work nights – nothing good is achieved at 5am. Maybe as a one off, but in the long run if you find yourself doing stuff at 5am then somethings going slightly awry. 5am is for sleeping. It's like Mark Wahlberg gets up at 5am doesn't he to go to the gym, and we all go ooh the dedication. No it's insanity, and it's gonna catch up with him real soon. In a couple of years' time he's gonna age like Imhotep, he'll be barking like a dog because at 5am he should be asleep. Rest, pause, take 5am off. 5am is nothing to do with you, wake me up horny at 5am once and it's sexy, do it for a second time and I'm worried about your state of mind, let me sleep for fucks sake you nutcase.

What about staying up til 5am partying? Nothing good is gonna happen in the last hour, 4am is the cut off, stay up til 5am and you're tempting fate aren't you, it's like you want something crazy to go down. She's not the love of your life you've both just gone crazy because you've stayed up past 4am, oh but we watched the sun rise and something came over us, yeah crazy came over you, 4am is the cut off, I mean really 2am is the cut off, even at twenty I wasn't up past 2am because I realised even back then this was the cut off for crazy, the only things you should hear after 2am are foxes fucking, and can you hear the sound of those foxes, they are crazy, that's a crazy noise right there – ooooorghh!

Did you hear those foxes baby? Yes I did. I'm horny baby. Really… it's 5am. Baby, I'm horny, why can the foxes fuck and not us? Because we are human love, not rabid animals and the only people fucking at 5am are the crazy animals that have spent the last 3 hours going through the bins so they're now so tanked up on bits of KFC remnants they're drugged up howling barking nutcases that seem exciting until you spend more than a few weeks with them. How do I know? Believe me, I know. Its fucking good, and then, you'll know. Just like I know. I know.

DAILY NOTES VOL I

Sep 2nd 2023
Standing Room Only – Tim McGraw

There's a lot of bragging in standup comedy and in life but mainly in standup comedy. There's a thing the Edinburgh Fringe you may not have heard of it but it's a month-long comedy festival in Edinburgh where thousands of comedians go and play to an average audience of four people. It's great for some, awful for others, and then at the end of the Fringe those who were successful generally post their thank you's – to no one of course, so they're not thanking anyone, they're just bragging about successful they've been feeding into this narrative that everyone is successful when of course they're not. The average audience of four people, a lot of comedians suffer in Edinburgh and end up bankrupt with additional mental health problems.

But on the flipside when a comedian posts about how awful their Fringe is going we all think – well tell your friends, tell your real friends not Facebook, Facebook is not your friend. People click 'care' but do they really care? Of course they don't really care, because if they really cared they'd pick up the phone and come round and give you a hug. Clicking 'care' on Facebook they may as well replace the 'care' button with a button saying 'bare minimum' – oh how do I feel about this? Bare minimum that sums it up. So braggy posts about standing room only are awful and awful posts about four people only are equally awful - tell your friends not Facebook!

So what is the solution? There is no solution of course because we have all jumped the shark and everything good and bad has to be played out into the ether, the black hole of genuine empathy that is Facebook. Oh I'm great, oh I'm shit, love me, hate me, nothing is genuine and nothing is what it seems. My son said to me the other day that we should have a day without Facebook, and I said to him that day was my childhood and it was glorious. And he said tell me about your childhood. And I said it was amazing, I had 5000 friends, it was maxed out at 5000, and every day was brilliant, and my parties were standing room only. And he said daddy is this true, and I said nothing is true any more, including this conversation. The truth? That went many years ago.

DAILY NOTES VOL I

Sep 3rd 2023
Switch Disco & Ella Henderson – React

I love gameshows, rubbish gameshows, ones where you have to react quickly and make a choice, hit a button, lose your dignity - and the one I love the most is a gameshow here in the UK called Tipping Point, you might not have it where you are in the world but you need to know about this gameshow. Tipping Point presented by Ben Shepherd who I've heard from a friend is a very nice man and he comes across as a nice man presenting on the surface a very nice, quite boring quiz show. General knowledge questions obviously and then the centre piece of the game and where it gets its name from - there's a massive machine in front of them which recreates the penny arcade pushy things machine we've all played in amusement parks where you stick in 250 2p coins and get fuck all out, maybe 50p which you stick straight back in again in the vein hope of winning the fake Rolex watch that no one has ever won in history.

OK so far so good, but what I love about these game shows is when a lovely presenter like Ben Shepherd has been presenting it for too long, you can see him going slightly mad. He uses phrases that aren't phrases – when one counter goes on top of another counter he says oh no 'we have a rider'. No we don't, cause that's not a thing, we just have one counter on top of the other, when someone chooses a drop-zone for their counter to drop into the big penny arcade pushy thing – he proudly pronounces 'Fire up drop-zone three'. Nothing is being fired up, it's just someone from the back-office pressing three on their computer and the light comes on in drop-zone three.

But most worrying of all, he's given the machine a sex – in the age of not presuming gender I think it's slightly problematic for many reasons that Ben Shepherd has assigned the female gender to the machine, constantly bemoaning that she's playing up or she needs 'a bloody good slap'. I've made up the last one. I can only think Ben Shepherd has been there so long he's fallen in love with the machine. I'm only still in comedy so I can one day be on the celebrity version of Tipping Point called Tipping Point Lucky Stars and I will thank my lucky stars as I'm spit roasting that beautiful machine with Ben deep into the morning. Fire up drop-zone cock. Apologies, I'm sorry, we all have a tipping point.

DAILY NOTES VOL I

Sep 4th 2023
Oliver Anthony Music – Rich Men North of Richmond

I was over in west London this weekend in Earls Court where the Rich Men hang out North of Richmond – and this whole strip Richmond, Chiswick – look at a map of London, the size of Richmond Park – ridiculous – it's absolutely enormous. London is rammed, in the east End we're all living forty on top of each other, whereas west London, Richmond, there's a park the size of Australia. There's fucking wild deer in there, it's like the fucking Serengeti. Everyone is crammed into London shoe-boxes and in Richmond there's a park big enough for gazelles, giraffes to wander around, it's Jurassic Park.

Anyway talking about big old wild animals on the point of extinction, we were in Ealing Broadway this weekend visiting the BBC Earth exhibition, which is a celebration of David Attenborough and his BBC series about wildlife, you know the ones I'm sure you've seen them – and this is Asia, and this is Africa, and this is the same old shit. No obviously he's brilliant David Attenborough and this place was great – huge screens showing clips from his programmes, and you lay back on bean bags and took it all in – so relaxing – I mean with one slight caveat… He's so old David Attenborough he could of course die at any time, he himself could become extinct, which would put a dampener on the whole thing. Like my grandma – 99 – could die at any time… 5 minutes before she's 100 which would be awful because you'd still get the card from the King and it would be inappropriate particularly if he's trying to be jokey – in tortoise years you'd be dead… she is dead.

Anyway this is the future of entertainment isn't it – lying down, not even sitting any more – it's the evolution of cinema – seats get more comfortable, then recline, then sofas, then beds in posh cinemas now in North of Richmond – this is the natural evolution of the species isn't it - watching television on 100 foot high screens lying down – I mean it was a good but at the same time fucking depressing, is this what we've come to as a species? Paying £80 to lie down and watch a big telly? That's evolution pretty much completed isn't it?

David Attenborough, all of us, it's time to go, it's time to give up, it's time to flip us over and start again.

223

DAILY NOTES VOL I

Sep 5th 2023
Calvin Harris / Ellie Goulding – Miracle

I'm not religious but I'm ready for my miracle, I'm ready to see a miracle. In *Life of Pi*, Pi makes people believe the unbelievable, so he has made them believe in God. I am ready to believe the unbelievable, I am so ready. But it never happens. And then I was in Iceland, not the country the shop, if you don't know it it's a shop called Iceland and as the name suggests it's a land of ice, fifty massive chest freezers. I'd imagine Iceland the shop is ironically single-handedly causing global warming. Its fifty chest freezers full of some of the worst food imaginable. What's the worst food you can imagine? Is it six frozen sausage breakfast patties? Is it four cheese and onion crisp bakes? Is it Iceland Meal in Bag Bacon Creamy Pasta? Is it Heinz Tomato Ketchup Filled Hash Browns 600g. Yeah you heard me they've pre-filled the hash browns with ketchup. Why??! Is it Heinz Beans Filled Hash Browns? Buy the separate items please God buy the separate items. Is it Fries to Go, Crispy Fried in 2 minutes? IMPOSSIBLE. Is it four Doner Kebab Quarter Pounders? Is it Slimming World 12 Pork Stuffing Balls? If you're slimming why are you eating 12 Pork Stuffing Balls? Is it Slimming World Chorizo-Style Meatball Pasta? What the fuck is Chorizo Style? Is it Frozen Cheesey Sticks? Is it the Cathedral City Cheese and Ham Toastie? Buy the separate ingredients it's cheaper you lazy fuck – is it Cheesy Branston Bites? Yes breadcrumbs, cheese and Branston filling. Is it Mr Brains Faggots? Is it Mr Faggots Brains? Or is it Vimto Cheesecake? Yes, we have a winner, it's Vimto Cheesecake.

Anyway I was in there this morning just minding my own business about to buy the frozen fruit I need to go with my breakfast smoothie to go along with my brown sauce filled hashbrowns and there it was, the miracle I've been waiting for – the £1 pizza. Now I know this goes out to the whole world and you might not immediately recognise this as a miracle, but believe me this is a miracle. Pizzas in this country everywhere else, £4, £3 absolute minimum, so here it was, the miracle, the £1 pizza, this isn't a mini pizza this is a full-size pepperoni pizza – not pepperoni style, pepperoni real pizza. £1. And just like I knew it would be when a miracle occurred, I opened the door, I saw the light, there was dry ice, it was magical. And I'm about to eat it. And therefore, I am about to die. I hope I see God

Sep 6th 2023
Kylie Minogue – Tension

So you're having a lovely day with your partner and then one of you says the wrong thing and then there's a little argument and then tension. Let me rephrase that we're having a lovely day and I say just a normal thing and then my partner all of a sudden hates me and then there's tension. Why is that? Why do people do that? I don't do that, if anyone ever says anything that annoys me, I do get annoyed but internally, it's like my stepdad holds in his sneezes - you still do the thing, but you don't make a big thing of it, and you don't ruin everyone's day.

Suck it up goddammit so I've said something that has slightly annoyed you? Suck it up, have a few minutes, realise how much you love me and then move on. Because I know what you do in that period of tension and it's not good is it – you hate me, you hate me for that little thing I've done, and you think fuck him, fuck him and everything he stands for, I could do better than him, I could just go out now or get on tinder or grindr and find a new fella that doesn't annoy me like that prick, what an annoying little prick – aargh tension, tension. None of that is true, I'm still the great guy and you love me and you're gonna love me again in three hours so just suck up that sneeze, suck up all that tension and go aaaargh I love you Nathan Cassidy is a great guy. It will save everyone so much time.

Seriously, try it, grow up, no not grow up, that's too much, just try it, as I say to my kids - try it you might like it. But I know what you're thinking, what about the make up sex? Not with the kids, with each other. That is good, because you've had half a day, a few days of hating on me and then the make up sex, oh my God, of course Nathan is a great guy, I loved him all along. It's not great for me, because I spent all that time while you were tense knowing I was a great guy, and knowing you'd get over it and have this make up sex, I knew this make up sex was coming and you know what - I resent it, the make up sex I resent it, and when I see you're enjoying it I get annoyed, I hate you, I'm annoyed, but what do I do? I look at you, I suck up all that annoyance I have an orgasm that I don't enjoy and I move on. Because I am Nathan Cassidy, and I am the better man. And more than anything, I hope you never read this, because then there really will be tension.

Sep 7th 2023
Summer Too Hot – Chris Brown

Oh its hot, oh my God its hot, it's so hot in London right now, so hot, erm… yeah it's that slight pause when you're making small talk, that's the bit in life I hate the most. The slight pause, so many people are so fearful of the slight pause that they garble, they waffle on and on about the weather and nothing because they can't bear the slight pause, and I can't bear the slight pause its excruciating isn't it - you're making small talk with someone you don't know very well, on a first date or whatever and then there's the slight pause and it crosses your mind even for a brief second – well what now, what if we both can't think of anything to say to each other, but we're having dinner, do we just look at each other, look away, do we start humming, what the fuck do we do now?

Anyway, that is how I'm feeling doing this book today, I can't think of anything, so I'm just waffling, about the weather and nothing, so much better it would be if I could just pause and agree with you that there's going to be moments of silence in every conversation, our conversations aren't rehearsed – this one certainly isn't – it's not theatre, obviously there are going to be moments of silence but we don't allow them do we so we just have to waffle about the weather – oh it's so hot, lovely but too hot, bad for the plants, bad for the pets, nice weather for ducks, bad weather for fucks, did you see those ducks on the lake gang raping the other day, nice weather for fucking ducks, how are you, how are you, how's the kids, holiday plans, how's work, how's fucking work, tell me all about your boring old work. For Christ's sake lets agree to pause.

That awkward pause isn't awkward at all.

It's beautiful, and if you agree to it, it the basis of any beautiful relationship.

Because if you can agree to do nothing,
say nothing,
and just look into each other's eyes,
that my friends is the genesis of love.

DAILY NOTES VOL I

Sep 8th 2023
I'm Just Ken – Ryan Gosling

I haven't seen the *Barbie* film, I hear its very good, so I've got nothing to go on apart from this song, and you know it's ok, everyone loves Ryan Gosling but he can't sing very well can he, but you know he's like me in a way, incredibly good looking, incredibly likeable, he's not gonna be good at everything is he? I mean I'm great at singing I'm just not very good at tight rope walking, but then again what prick wants to be good at tight rope walking?

You see these cunts don't you, ooh I'm so good at tight rope walking - no one gives a fuck mate, you've just invented that, nobody needed it. And that's how I feel about the *Barbie* film and that's why I've not seen it yet, there's enough art now, there are enough films, enough books, you have to be seriously confident in what you're producing to think well I can add something here, and if you can't add anything then what are you doing, you're just cluttering up the landfill of entertainment aren't you, some would say I'm doing that with this podcast, but those people are stupid and probably spend their lives tight rope walking.

Oh I'm tight rope walking between the twin towers have you seen that, literally the only good thing about 9/11 - that twat can't do that again. Philippe Petit (or Phil Small that's his real name if you speak English) - Phil Small in 1974 walked between the twin towers on a tight rope and there's a film about him called The Walk but the man I respect most from this film is the police officer waiting for him on the south tower who shouts 'stop fucking walking on a tightrope, just stop it'. Because it's nothing is it Philippe Petite, yeah you're nothing, Feel small, I'm not saying his name there I'm saying Phil Small. I'm saying feel small, you're nothing, you're just Ken, you're making up the numbers. Nobody's interested, do something worthwhile, we don't need another film that we will forget within minutes, do something worthwhile. I don't know anything but tight rope walking. Do some like research into the flu – yeah you heard me, do a little bit of research into flu. Try and come up with a cure for the flu, that would be of some benefit. Particularly flu in men. Yeah man flu. Our immune systems are lower yes that's right. So our wages should be higher. I'm just Ken.

DAILY NOTES VOL I

Sep 9th 2023
NewJeans – SuperShy

There's a drink I had all the time as a kid called Vimto, and I didn't really think anything about it at the time obviously I was a kid, it was just a fruit based fizzy drink – why would I think it was anything special? Well I recently find out it is special – first off it was created in Manchester by a chemist – oh yeah now you're interested - a chemist John Nichols in 1908. Now just like KFC, it was created using a secret recipe containing herbs, fruits and spices. Don't be *SuperShy* Vimto, reveal your secret herbs and spices. No they won't. Because Vimto is a multi-billion-dollar business.

Why is Vimto so successful? Well it was originally sold as Vim tonic, a medicinal product made to give people vim and strength. It was exported to British troops in India in the 1920s. But here's the big one – for nearly 100 years it's been huge in Muslim communities and Ramadan – Vimto sells 25 million units during Ramadan, 52 million bottles are sold every year in Saudi Arabia – now why is this? Well the only theory you can find online is that its mixture of berry and sugars give those who have been fasting for long hours a much-needed energy boost. But it must be something more than this.

When I was ill with ME when I was 20 my mom gave me Vimto and I drank it bed bound through a long straw from a heavy bottle on the floor – and I was like mom why are you giving me Vimto, are you mad? Just give me water. But she was clever my mom – she knew that I needed something more than water at that key moment in my life – I need vim – I needed energy – I needed the beautiful mixture of grape, blackcurrant and raspberry along with the natural extracts of herbs, barley, malt and spices. It's something in there, it's secret, it's mystical, its shy.

Vimto begins with a V, Arabic's 28 letter alphabet has no letter V – it's exotic, it's mystical. Vimto's famous advertising strap line – I see Vimto in you. I do, I see it going in you very, very soon. No? Really? Don't you want to live forever? Don't be shy, drink me. That's the way to live forever, by drinking me. That's the secret ingredient you see, it's eternal life. Genuinely. John Nichols is still alive. He's diabetic and bright purple but he's still alive.

DAILY NOTES VOL I

Sep 10th 2023
Taylor Swift – Cruel Summer

So this is the last day of Summer today, not in any official way it's just here in the UK we look at the weather forecast and think this is it, the last warm day before six months of cruel winter sets in. But we're a nation that loves the winter aren't we, because it gives us an opportunity to moan – ah this fucking weather, this miserable fucking weather. Particularly the north of the country, up north as it's known in the UK, up north, you may not know this if you're not from the UK, it rains all the time. That's right, it's like the Amazon rainforest, without anything to look at.

Up north it just pisses down with rain all the time and everyone's miserable. It's where the Beatles are from. That's why they had to stay in and learn the guitar. Down south we don't need to learn the guitar, that's why you've got acts like Taylor Swift – you know what I'm saying because down south in the UK its beautiful hot weather all the time, and there's loads of things to look at, it's all beautiful, we haven't got time to learn anything down south, because what happens is we're all given lots of money by our parents as we grow up and so we realise fairly early on that we don't need to better ourselves. And because our parents have money they also have connections so what little talent we have is magnified and so later on in life we do exactly what want to do and just trample over the people from up north who are tired through years of learning the guitar and getting wet. Stop trampling on us! Na fuck off back to up north you losers with your talent, and they're all wet and under our feet and we kick them back to Yorkshire and you've got to be cruel to be kind but this is our world, this is our sunshine and you can't have it.

And occasionally a band like the Beatles breaks through and we're resentful aren't we and have to say things like but yeah Ringo Starr was shit. And how long did they actually last – 6 years? One Direction lasted longer than them, and had better records. Yesterday or You Don't Know You're Beautiful – there's only one I could dance to that's for sure. Beatles – shite. And we feel better about ourselves again - we're the best, we'll always be the best.

DAILY NOTES VOL I

Sep 11th 2023
Home – Michael Bublé

So there was a prisoner escape in the UK last week, in London, very rarely happens so it's exciting isn't it – Daniel Khalife escaped from Wandsworth prison, he was a prison cook, by tying himself to the underside of a food van and just being driven out. Which was the original ending to *The Shawshank Redemption*. Dig a tunnel for twenty years and then ah I'll just tie myself to the underside of that food van. Anyway he gets out, they search the food van after an hour and of course he's gone. So where is he? A £20,000 reward goes up for this guy, apparently not a dangerous guy, he's a 21-year-old who is on remand for allegedly trying to gather information for Iran. And the police say on the news, 'People of the UK, you're now a nation of 70 million CCTV cameras'. But are we though? Because the first sighting of him comes in. Apparently, someone has seen him 'walking away from the food van'. Bullshit. That's just someone trying to get the 20 grand. He was strapped to the underside of the food van and then wasn't strapped to the underside of the food van. What's your next sighting? I saw him on planet Earth? For three days the police keep saying 'we're definitely gonna get him' whilst also after three days saying 'please hand yourself in that would make it easier'.

They had no idea because after three days they close off Richmond park and we all think they've got him. But when asked was this based on any intelligence the chief of police has to admit 'no, it's just the nearest park to the prison and it was a hot day we thought he might be sunbathing'. I repeat, we are like deffo closing in but it would be loads easier Daniel mate if you just hand yourself in. Confirmed sightings also include him 'in a prison cooks outfit'. Hiding in plain sight there, but again, probably not in the park, and finally the very latest police reports suggested he has changed clothes and was now wearing 'dark clothing on his legs'. I understand that is police speak for 'trousers'. Anyway after all this he was found a few miles away and all of our excitement thinking we could get the twenty grand had to end as he was riding along a canal on a bike just having a fun day out and he was pulled off by a police officer. What a happy ending. And as it turns out – he had been in the park sunbathing all along! The best police in the world, and the best prisoner of all time is now, very sadly, back home.

Sep 12th 2023
Ed Sheeran- Afire Love

I love this song – I love love, when you find someone that looks at you with true love the feeling is incredible, it's the same eyes that you've seen before but it's different, how is it different I cannot explain, it's just afire love. Now be careful of course, the eyes are dangerously close to the crazy eyes, you know the way someone looks at you when they're obsessed with you but unfortunately they're a nutcase. Oh if only you weren't a nut case then this could be on, at least for a bit, we could have both had a good time.

I was in a musical in London's West End twenty years ago called *The Donkey Show* and for this musical, if not for my dignity, I had to perform in little red rubber pants which left nothing to the imagination apart from maybe what it tasted like, which to clear everything up once and for all, is a mixture of strawberries and heaven. That's the dick, the balls taste of sea-salted caramel. Everything has sea-salt in it these days, even this sentence. Imagine in the 80's if there was a bit of sea-salt in your chocolate – you'd have spat it out and shouted 'Marjorie fucking hell, have you stuck fucking sea-salt instead of sugar in my fucking chocolate, are you trying to fucking poison me?!'

Anyway, I had performed in this musical and then a few of the cast were chosen every day to be on the door handing out merchandise and saying goodbye and whatever and this woman approaches me and says I loved the show, and I said thank you, and she looks at me, she gives me those eyes, those eyes of afire crazy love and she says do you want to come out with me later, you can do anything you want to me, and I was like fuck man you've ruined it, you've moved too quickly you've gone too deep too hard, but I tell you what she gave me the eyes and those eyes stay with you, and I've only seen them again recently, and yes these are eyes of true love, but because they are so close to the crazy eyes they are slightly triggering of all the crazies. Well there's only been a few crazies, and don't think I'm thinking about them every time you look at me and tell me you love me and give me those eyes, don't think that, because then you may never look at me in that way again. Please look at me that way, but please please don't go sea-salt crazy.

DAILY NOTES VOL I

Sep 13th 2023
Nina – Ed Sheeran

Who's the most famous Nina? According to google? I guessed Nina Simone, gotta to be Nina Simone, but I type in Nina, and it's Nina Dobrev – the actress, never heard of her. People say 'never heard of them' as if it belittles someone somehow, never heard of them, doesn't mean they're not successful, which Nina Dobrev clearly is – she's a Canadian actress best known for portraying Elan Gilbert and Katherine Pierce on the CW's supernatural drama series *The Vampire Diaries*. Really Google? What the fuck is the CW – never heard of it, higher up the rankings that Nina Simone – yeah I guess that's just a product of who's searching and this Nina Dobrev is more current and whatever, alive, but I think it's up to Google to educate people you know, just because you're alive doesn't mean - Nina Simone that's the person that people should know about if they're looking for the most famous Nina.

Most famous Nathan? It would be arrogant of me to think… but let's have a look anyway – Nathan Fillion, no idea, never heard of him, genuinely never heard of him, anyway so I type in 'Nathan C', Nathan C is an acclaimed music producer and DJ - never heard of him, 'Nathan Ca', Nathan California, no that isn't who I meant google FFS call yourself a search engine, 'Nathan Cas', Nathan Case on Linked In – Head of Reducing Reoffending Statistics – what the fuck Google – you type in Brad you get Brad Pitt, you know what I mean. 'Nathan Cass', senior manager of Asda in Bishop Stortford, ah fuck off. Who the fuck is Googling the senior manager or indeed any manager at the Asda in Bishop Stortford? Complete piss take.

'Nathan Cassi'…no I don't want a girl called Cassi Nathan on Facebook, never heard of her – isn't it obvious who I want by now Google, no you need another letter do you? Jesus. 'Nathan Cassid'? I'm not giving you that – I'm just doing Nat Cassidy – Nat Cassidy is an award-winning actor, playwright, novelist, director and musician, what the actual fuck. Never heard of him, never will hear of him, seriously, Google, Sonia from *Eastenders* - that's Natalie Cassidy. Nina Nina Nina – send for an ambulance I think I'm losing the will to live, yeah I need an ambulance… what's my name? Nathan Cassidy… no I do not work in the Asda Bishop Stortford – fucking hell.

Sep 14th 2023
If I Let You Go – Westlife

Episode 1000 is fast approaching only 13 to go – unlucky for some – you mainly - until I take a pause, and like anything you love you think I can't let you go, but of course you can, it's hard but of course you can. I struggle to stop doing anything because it's not about me, it's about you, but I feel you've had enough, and I'm letting you down gently, we can still be friends, and I mean really good friends we can still hang out but we just won't, you know, make lovely podcasts every day, but we can do other things together like you can come and watch me do standup, and like any relationship it's not completely over is it, it's never over, you know like any relationship.

Come on you know what I mean, all relationships even the worst ones you think, you know under the right circumstances, we could just, you know, I'm not saying we would, but we could because you know, we know how everything fits and it does fit, we fitted, and then we stopped but it doesn't mean we still don't fit in the same way, we do. You know what I'm saying, I mean penises tend to fit vaginas but, you know what I'm saying I don't need to spell it out, it's like, once it's gone in before you know how it fits, is it snug, is it rattling around like a couple of old coins in a jar, you know what I mean, anyway.

Episode 1000 is not the end, I will come again, and you will receive my explosions of creativity as if I've never been away. You know what I mean though, anytime somebody says to me ah mate I've split with so and so it's like you haven't split have you, that suggests you were joined in some way, you weren't joined in any way and you can easily get back to doing the things you used to do with them, Jesus the wasted time I've spent comforting people only for them to get back together, it wasn't getting back together because they were never apart. So there you go, rest easy , don't cry for the next 13 episodes, just laugh, if they're funny, which they probably won't be that funny I've run out of ideas, but know one thing's for sure, this isn't it, it won't be too long , I will come again, I'll be exploding into your ears before you know it. But judging by the quality of this episode, will you want me? Of course you will, no one ever lets anyone truly go.

Sep 15th 2003
Good Good – Usher, Summer Walker & 21 Savage

The interesting thing about evil people, some evil people, is they're not evil are they, because they believe what they're doing is good. Just because you believe what you're doing is good and what someone else is doing is bad doesn't mean its necessarily the case, I mean obviously if they're killing people and you're not killing people then you're probably on the good side and they're not so good. But in issues of morality and religion the dividing lines are less clear.

I knew someone, and there are plenty of people like this, that believed that if you don't have God in your life then you're a bad person. I'm not a bad person because I don't believe in God, as I've always said show me God and I'm ready to believe. And people say what would it take Nathan for you to believe in God. And my bar is really low. Show me ANYTHING, anything that might even slightly hint at the fact that there may in some realm be a God and I'm ready to believe… And people say well you believe in some things that may not be real, and I say like what and they say memories, you believe your memories to be real when often they're not, you believe what you think is true, but it may be false. And I say yes all well and good, but get me back to God, this is what God loving people do, they move you away from the thing that you can't see, which is the miracle. Show me a miracle and I will believe in God, make me believe in a miracle and I will believe in God.

And they said to me – well how do you think the Earth was formed? And I say the Big Bang. And they asked me what was the Big Bang – and I say well it was an explosion in space that created the universe. It came from nothing. So you're saying that God did not create the universe, it was created from an explosion from something no bigger than a grain of sand and that created the universe, isn't that the miracle you've been looking for?

And I thought… you've got a point there. The Big Bang, believing in that isn't so far removed from believing in God. In fact now you say it like that, God is in some ways easier to believe in. I want to believe you see, believe me I want to believe.

DAILY NOTES VOL I

Sep 16th 2023
Hollywood – Lewis Capaldi

The golden age of Hollywood – undoubtedly 1999 and the greatest movie ever released – Double Jeopardy starring Tommy Lee Jones and Ashley Judd. Where do we start? Brief plotline – dodgy looking husband says to wife let's go out on a boat, your best mate will look after our four-year-old kid, they go out, she wakes up covered in blood, where's the husband? He's nowhere, he's in the fucking sea, body never found, she's charged with the murder, and convicted, end of film. But it's not the end of the film because she says to the best mate from prison - you bring up my kid and she says fine and then one time she calls them up and the kid goes daddy! WTF – daddy's alive? And then the plot thickens, or thins depending how you look at it, because she's in prison, no way of checking up whether this geezer is alive – I mean absolutely no way, don't ask. So she has to wait to get out of prison to investigate. She'll have to wait a long time no. Ur, no, because wherever she is in America the sentence for murder is a surprisingly lenient 6 years. I know right, almost worth killing someone, the writer of this film for example.

Well anyway, it gets better because now he is alive if she kills him this time she gets off scott free because double jeopardy right, you can't be tried for the same crime twice – although, you obviously can, you can't just kill someone, ever. Anyway, ignore that because that would ruin the fun, and the fun starts because the baddies name is Nicholas Parsons. Nicholas Parsons! No? If you don't know just how funny that is, just look it up, he was a light entertainer here in the UK, a ludicrous name to choose. Would be like the villain being called Donald Duck. Anyway that's the least of the films problems and joys, its potentially simultaneously the best and worst film ever made, it's got more holes than a thousand sieves, and at the end of the film, she kills Nicholas Parsons and then goes to see her son after eight years. He's at school, shall I phone ahead – na, I'll just turn up and surprise him. And that's what she does – she turns up, walks up to him and says, hi, I'm your mom, you know the one that you thought was dead, I'm alive. Great news right. In less good news, your dad's dead and I killed him. Anyway, let's go home and watch TV. They don't write them like that anymore, thank goodness, because I've killed the writer. The golden age of Hollywood.

DAILY NOTES VOL I

Sep 17th 2023
Tina Turner – Private Dancer

Dance like nobody is watching they say – but that's hard, because genuinely when I'm dancing on my own, I'm a phenomenal dancer. Dance in front of people, I stiffen up, I'm an awful dancer, how do I dance as if no one is watching? But of course they are watching and they are judging, because in any environment where people are dancing, the other people around are talking about you, they're watching you, and you're either a phenomenal or a shit dancer, there ain't nothing in between. I spend my life being judged on stage, but there's a variety of different opinions you can have of me - he's good, he's amazing, he's the greatest living standup or dead standup, I mean he's not dead he's just better than the dead guys too. When they were dead? No when they were alive. He's better than all living and dead standups when they were alive? Yeah.

Is that really what he thinks? It is actually in that moment that he climbs on to the stage and hears those first laughs he has to believe that, a standup has to believe that, because that's what gets you through and that's what makes you great, that belief that you are the greatest. If you believe you're the greatest then you could be the greatest. And there are some nights where someone comes up to you and says that was the greatest standup I've ever seen, and I've seen a lot of standup, so right there in that moment they're saying you are better than all the alive and all the dead standups (when they were alive).

And that's how I wanna feel with dancing, just one time. Maybe ok dancing and singing, and piano playing. I can do all three, and I think I can be the greatest. Imagine, you do a dance, a song, you play the piano, you're Beyoncé but with piano playing abilities and you come off stage and someone says to you that's the greatest live performance I have ever seen. And you say that's amazing, really? And they say yes really. Because I've never seen a live performance and so that was the greatest and at the same time the shittest. Oh, I really thought I was the greatest. And they'd say Nathan, where the hell do you get this over confidence? And I say to them because I do comedy as if no one is watching. And they'd say, yes Nathan and that's because most times, hardly anyone is.

DAILY NOTES VOL I

Sep 18th 2023
Where She Goes – Bad Bunny

Obviously this song I don't understand because it's in Spanish and I'm English and being English I don't talk any other languages because I don't need to. I'm joking obviously but the English speaking countries are very arrogant about their language aren't they? It's like, ooh, really, I've got to learn this one have I? French was the one I learned at school and when you dip into other languages it's often the same thing – ooh, why have I got to do that, why is there masculine and feminine, why is it la table and not le table, because a table is feminine, really? Yeah really, well who decided that – the gender randomizer? Well English is ridiculous too. Maybe, but at least a table doesn't have a sex, why is it feminine? Where is the table's vagina? Childish – table, vagina, it's all just made up words.

Why is English so good? Apparently it's one of the hardest languages to learn. No it isn't because there was a kid in my school year called Danny and he was the thick kid, there's always a thick kid in every class and Danny was the thick kid, but what made that more remarkable is that it was a grammar school, so everyone else was clever, but Danny was really thick, but thinking about it you got into this school on the back of a test that was multiple choice, so one in a thousand times a really thick kid is gonna get in purely because they've lucked out on the multiple choice. So there he was sitting in a French lesson and Danny could speak English perfectly, but he couldn't pick up French at all. And he said le table. And the French teacher, Mr John, John is a first name, why do they make things so differently, said no Danny it's la table. And Danny said le table. And the French teacher said no Danny its la can you say la – and he said le, and Mr John said no Danny la, say la… le. And that's when I knew, English is easy because even the most stupid person in the world has mastered at least that, French impossible.

And I talked to Danny afterwards and said why couldn't you just say la, and he said I could, but why does a table have a sex, I mean tables don't have vaginas do they. And I thought no, but the desk that you always sit at does have a prick. That joke wouldn't work in Spanish or French of course. English is so much better.

DAILY NOTES VOL I

Sep 19th 2023
Harry Styles – Little Freak

So amongst all the terrible things happening in the world, there are theories of course that the media raise one thing up to take our minds off something else, look over here then we'll stop focussing on the truly awful people in the world, and yet again it has happened this weekend as we're all looking in one direction as on Friday in Harrogate in the UK, Gareth Griffin from Guernsey, let's say the name again so you've all got it, so you all know who this man is, Gareth Griffin, exposed his eye-watering vegetables to the world at the Harrogate Autumn Flower Show. And if you want the sordid detail, Gareth had a 9kg onion that he claims, as he would, is the world's largest onion. But this has yet to be corroborated by the authorities, in this case the Guinness Book of World Records.

Yes it's the National English Honor Society (NEHS) Giant Vegetable Competition where they celebrate the freakishly massive onions, colossal cabbages, mega marrows, big beetroots and ten foot round garden peas, I've made the last one up probably – but yes every year we have this from Gareth and his bunch of saddos as they all get their junk out and we have to weigh it or measure it to see whose is the heaviest or longest. Paul Proud (a made up name surely) took home the prize for cabbage, parsnip, carrot, beetroot and cucumber and Chris Parish took home a prize for his giant pumpkin, which weighed 102kg which to put that into perspective is the size of his ego.

Yes they're all men these people and they need to be stopped, what the hell are they doing and how the hell are they doing it? My first question - is there a veg doping programme? How often are Chris Parish's vegetables tested for steroids? Would Paul be so Proud if we took a sample of his giant cucumber and found he'd been injecting it with water? Yeah Paul, not so proud now you little cunt. And finally, we're back to Gareth Griffin and his 9kg onion and you have to ask yourself, what is really going on here, what's really going on in the world, this onion has layers, and you peel back the layers and you'll see something that THEY do not want you to see. Open your eyes vegetables, the real freaks are all getting away with it over there.

Sep 20th 2023
Ed Sheeran – Sandman

The Sandman, a genie who makes children sleepy by sprinkling sand into their eyes. And as this podcast draws to a close and says goodnight with only eight more episodes left, you can't help looking back. Episode two I think it was, I was talking about smoke getting into the eyes of bees, and stopping them fucking until their dicks exploded, and that's the thing it's time to go back to the start, which I often do with my kids in my mind, and all I remember from their first few years was trying to get them to sleep, trying to get those annoying screaming little fuckers to sleep.

Particularly my son, he was like a bee, always in your face, always trying to get a bit of your drink, fucking annoying as a baby - and so to try to get him to sleep I'd go up to him in his cot and I'd put a little bit of sand in his eyes. No sorry, I didn't do that, I'd stroke just between his eyes and that would eventually after fifteen minutes or so send him to sleep, and I'd have to do that every night, and some nights it wouldn't work, but because he'd got used to me being there as he fell asleep he'd want me there otherwise he wouldn't fall asleep, so if I wasn't stroking between his eyes I'd have to sit there at 1 in the morning or whatever in the doorway so he could see me and only then would he fall asleep, and then at 530 in the morning, he'd be crying because he'd be fucking awake and he'd want to go downstairs and do what he did every single morning which is watch the film *Elmo in Grouchland*.

So I'd prop him up in a little rubber chair or whatever, and I'd try to get to sleep next to him on the sofa, and by about the 15th month of this routine, 6am starts, *Elmo in Grouchland*, it was like I was a bee, with smoke in my eyes, being instantly calmed, knowing what was important in life – for the bees they think there's a fire, so they eat as much honey as possible. And for us, we are just like the bees, we know the end is coming, so what do we need – love. We need our family around us, and we need as much love in our eyes. And my son will get all this one day, as he strokes me between the eyes to get me to sleep.

DAILY NOTES VOL I

Sep 21st 2023
Number 1 – Tinchy Stryder (feat N-Dubz)

So as we go into the final week of this podcast, I can only say thank you to everyone that's listened, I am thinking back to the start and to think we now have a million downloads – I remember those first few days, it would be 10, maybe 20 people. It's always those first few steps that are both exciting and terrifying in anything, but I'd say particularly in the arts, because if something doesn't work you look insane. What are you doing? This is ridiculous. And it has been ridiculous. But I repeat, if Freddy Mercury got up at an open mic music night today and no one had heard of him and his songs had never been heard, and he started singing *Bohemian Rhapsody* scaramouch scaramouche can you do the fandango everyone would say as one, 'this guy is shit and insane'.

And here I am today number one podcast all over the world, right now in some places I could never imagined – Madagascar, Papua New Guinea and as always we're in the charts in America too and that really blows my mind, I've broken America, well not really, because I've never been number one in America, we've been in the top 40 and in the UK too. And when I was growing up being in the top 40 was everything, every week on *Top Of The Pops* they would play out the top 40 records. Nowadays imagine being 40th on a list of anything – oh I came 40th, well you're a loser then aren't you, if you're not number one then you're a loser.

But I'm just as proud and thankful of being in the top 40 in America and the UK, than number one around the world, but hey, here's the thing, we have one week left of this, so maybe, just maybe, we can go out on a high, and get it number one in as many places as possible, and we can get it to number one in the UK and my dream the USA. So how can we do that, well what I've learned from standup comedy is this, we don't need to make ourselves better, we just need to bring down everyone else, so please get on line and start slagging off all other podcasts apart from mine, spread shit, call them all paedophiles and watch me rise.

That's right, they go high and we go low, and then they go low, we go high. See you at number one baby.

DAILY NOTES VOL I

Sep 22nd 2023
True – Spandau Ballet

In 2015 Martin Kemp, guitarist for the band Spandau Ballet, said the word 'shag' on morning television. He was there to promote his new role in *Birds of a Feather*, the sitcom all about a woman Dorian who likes to fuck. She wasn't the main character, she lived next door, she became the main character because her character's motivation was to get lots of and I quote the sitcom 'king size cock'. Anyway Martin Kemp, guitarist of Spandau Ballet, was on morning television promoting this role presumably not through desire but through contractual obligation and he said 'I play Dorian's love-interest, but I think the more appropriate term would be shag interest'. And then Martin Kemp said 'wait can I say that at this time of the morning?' and the presenter Kate Garroway said 'no, you can't say that. You have to take it back'. 2015. Martin Kemp was forced by Kate Garroway to say 'I take it back', and according to Kate Garroway's rules it was then fine, according to the court of Kate Garroway you can say the worst possible thing and if you immediately say I take it back then it's fine. Please remember that when you ready the last line of this.

Because cut to eight years later, in 2023, at the King's Coronation someone referred to our Queen Consort Camilla on live television as a bitch. Someone shouted 'Camilla is bitch who shags around' on live television and what did Kate Garroway do, eight years after chastising Spandau Ballet for the very same offence? She skated over it. So what's changed in eight years you're asking, why the change of heart? Well 2015 was before Covid of course, which gave us all perspective… to Kate Garroway more than anyone – because her husband Derek Draper became the UK's worst affected living patient with Covid. Kate now realises along with everyone that swearing is unimportant and anyway arguably Queen Consort is bitch who shags around because true story she based her early life on the character of Dorian from *Birds of a Feather*, she's not the main character she lived next door to the main characters but she became main character through her love of cock, through shunning the concept of morality in preference to getting king size cock inside her, in her case literally King size, and basically being very much the petrol in the engine of the car that killed Diana…
I take it back!!

DAILY NOTES VOL I

Sep 23rd 2023
Harry Styles – Daydreaming

When I was tripping out on diazepam in the middle of the day at the Edinburgh Fringe with my bad back and the animals from *Life of Pi* were floating around the room – the tiger, the hyena, the zebra and orangutan - I imagined myself as the tiger, you always dream big when you're day dreaming don't you, that you're going to be the most powerful, the most beautiful, the most majestic, so of course I was the tiger, beautiful, majestic and, regal and victorious. Dreaming is also the place to have nightmares, there are bad dreams, dreams that your life is shit and all you eat is 12 pork sausage balls and Vimto cheesecake from Iceland. But daydreams are all good, you never have a bad daydream, there is no such thing as a bad daydream. Which must teach us something right, the middle of the night is for our worst thoughts because that's not really us is it, the us in the middle of our night, dreaming while we sleep, the middle of the day when we are awake is for our best thoughts, our best hopes our best dreams.

A daydream happens usually when there is a lack of stimuli, when there is nothing, we fill the gaps with drifting away, and we imagine situations and scenarios that are almost always positive. There's something about being awake isn't there that even on our worst days brings hope. Don't get me wrong some days you don't want to go on, so you go back to bed, you close your eyes, you wish yourself to sleep or worse, because you know that as soon as you're awake you have that annoying little voice inside of you, maybe things will be ok. I mean they probably won't be, but it's inside of you nagging you to keep going. Maybe you'll amount to something better than pointless. You probably won't but you keep going. Maybe it's just me but sometimes I wanna give up everything and just sit there on a mountain, eyes closed, but that doesn't work unless you're sleeping does it, because you start to day dream, and you think maybe Nathan, maybe you shouldn't stop, maybe you should do another 1000 episodes of this podcast, maybe something amazing will happen, keep going, stay in the game, stay in the game.

Fucking hell, when can I ever rest? When you sleep Nathan, rest only when you sleep. And as you sleep, do enjoy those night terrors.

DAILY NOTES VOL I

Sep 24th 2023
End Game – Taylor Swift (feat. Ed Sheeran & Future)

I was chatting to two people last night and they were convinced that the end was coming for humanity, and he said get out of here, go and live in the middle of a desert, no nukes are aimed at deserts - you will be in a desert and the rest of the world will burn. I mean yes, he might have a point, but what's better, to die quickly or have a slow painful death, you know like this podcast. But the thing is, given a choice, most people would choose the slow painful death, because bottom line is most of us don't want the end, most of us fear the end game. And is the end game coming today? Today, an asteroid will come screaming into Utah's West Desert, slowed down by parachutes and we're going to mine so much from its constituents… hang on isn't this the plot of the movie *Don't Look Up*? Should we be terrified, mining an asteroid for fame and fortune and celebrity? No, luckily it's only bits of a mountain sized asteroid being brought back by Nasa's Osiris-Rex capsule, and it promises to tell us where do we come from – it could answer questions like where did the oceans get water, where did the air in our atmosphere come from, what is the source of the organic molecules that make up all life on Earth? Fascinating stuff, in a way.

How did life start, how were the planets formed? Erm, I don't care. Of course you care Nathan, erm not really, I just care about today, tomorrow, I don't even really care about yesterday, it's gone, it's all gone. What can we do today tomorrow? Well we can collect samples from the asteroid today that what we can do. Yeah but why? Well it will tell us maybe how water was formed, I don't care, we have water we need to conserve the planet… Very naive Nathan, research like this leads to innovation. Yes cool, that is about the future but I'm not getting excited if you're telling me something that happened 4 billion years ago, I don't give a fuck. Well maybe you're give a fuck when I tell you the person responsible for choosing the place on the comet where we collected the sample from – Brian May from Queen. You see I was right, this is *Don't Look Up* isn't it? It's fame, its celebrity and it's nonsense, and that's why the end is coming. I'm not worried about yesterday I'm worried about today. What's happening today? I'm going to move to the middle of a desert, I'll be safe there. Erm, sure, just be careful of the asteroid. Dum dum dum, another one bites the dust.

Sep 25th 2023
Rod Wave – Call Your Friends

So how are we celebrating the end of Daily Notes in two days' time? Episode 1000? How are you celebrating, call all your friends. Well, you know most of my friends don't truly care about my podcast to be honest. What do you mean? Well they don't listen really. So… but they're still your friends. Yeah I call them friends but… well what is a friend? Well it's your crew. Crew? I'm not 15. That's what my son calls it - crew. I'm not 15, I'm not in a band. What the fuck is a friend? Someone you know who, you have mutual affection with. Yeah, but friends come and go don't they, they come when you're young and they go when they have kids and move to Rottingdean. Where's that? Not sure, I've never been because my friend moved away and had kids and I hardly see him now - so is he my friend? Of course he's your friend. You'd go and visit your best friend even if they moved out of town – erm, for a bit.

What separates friends from lovers? You don't have sex. And in my eyes nothing else should separate you. I want friends to feel the same as lovers, apart from the sex bit, you would do anything for them, and they would do anything for you, you would die for your friend. There are friends like that, I know - well they need another name then, don't group these people with your friends who don't really care about you truly, you should care about someone so much that you feel all those feelings than towards a partner you just don't have sex with them. Like a brother a sister? No most brothers and sisters hate their siblings, they only see each other at funerals. A best friend? Don't give me that best friend divisive bullshit – oh they're my best friend – what are you seven? I'm talking about couple of people, you're never gonna have more than five, those friends that love you, would do anything for you, would die for you or as a minimum listen to more than about six episodes of the podcast and ask are you still doing that podcast thing, *Psycomedy* isn't it? No I'm doing another one. What? I thought you were my friend, I've nearly done 1000 episodes, oh that's why I never see you. No you never see me because we are not – what's the word… I know… crew. You're my crew – we are on the same vessel, navigating through life, looking up to the stars together and dreaming. You're my crew, we are literally all in the same boat. Just like *Life of Pi* – we get rid of the cunts, and then I have my crew. But in *Life of Pi* there was no one left, no one but Pi. And so it goes with God.

DAILY NOTES VOL I

Sep 26th 2023
End of the Road – Boyz II Men

So this really is the end of the road. Only one episode to go. So what's the big reveal Nathan? How do you mean? Well with your stuff there's always a hidden agenda, a hidden thing. Well not really, although remember of course if you go back and you look at the first letter of every episode it spells out a different Beatles song, this time it's been *Eleanor Rigby*. Why did you choose *Eleanor Rigby*? Look at all the lonely people. You're not lonely Nathan you have friends - read yesterday's man I don't want friends I want crew. Are you 15? Read yesterday's, I'm not reading yesterday's – go back and read, go back and listen to all the episodes, only then will you know me. There is no twist. There's always a twist. You always make people look one way and they don't see the real thing you're saying. OK you want a twist…

I was at University, I was playing *End of the Road* really loud and had my window open, and someone banged on the window and I thought it was gonna be someone complaining - and he said 'ah man nice to meet you, I love that track and love the fact you're playing it loud'. And I said thanks and he went away and I never saw him again. And what he saw was a happy, confident person that loved life. And he went away, and he didn't realise what was really going on…

That's how much most people know me, audiences, friends whatever - they come along, they see the happy me, the confident me. Maybe just two weeks before that guy knocked on my door I was so full of anxiety that I couldn't leave my room, so I ended up shitting in a Tupperware box. Hating myself, hating the way I was, the way I looked. And that's how I was the day after he knocked too. And it all goes back to those years of my life, when I was a kid, those years I don't remember. But the thing is I do remember them, I just don't want to tell you what happened. All this, everything I do is so you don't look back there, to when I was a kid.

I've done these 1000 episodes so no one looks back there - so I don't look back there, and so I need the love of a million people, because I didn't have the love of one. Because again I ask you, what story do you prefer? What story would you rather me have told? The one with comedy and heartbreak and piano and crap singing and occasionally good singing, or the truth? What story would you rather I tell? And that's why I keep spinning this lie, playing this music loud with the window open, hoping that someone comes and says its good. But now I'm ready to let that person in and show them the real me, but only if you want to be in my boat and come on this journey with me.

Hope you enjoyed this journey. And now it's time to say goodbye.

Sep 27th 2023
Say Goodbye – Katherine McPhee

Episode 1000. There's… nobody there. I'm tuning in to Daily Notes and there's nobody there. What does he care? Well I do care. All the lonely people, where do they all belong? Look at all the lonely people. But we're not lonely, we are in the same boat aren't we, it's a massive boat but here we all in the same boat, spinning through an ocean of space. I'm actually at my uncle's funeral later today. I didn't know my uncle really, only met him a few times. My dad had two brothers, and this is the last brother to go, and I will have gone to both funerals. Funerals of two uncles I couldn't really remember that well. And I don't remember this uncle at all, but he's family and so you go to the funeral. Well not always. Because the funeral is in Merthyr Tydfil, which is a hassle to get to, it's in Wales, which is deceptively far from everywhere, even Wales. And I was in two mind whether I should go but other people dropped out, saying it was too far to go. But for me, I'll always be there, because an end is always a beginning.

Often people get sad because something is ending. The ending is the best bit, you always get the most dramatic moment at the end. What about the ending of *Lost*, that was shit? I didn't see it, I don't watch much television. You don't watch television? What do you do? I do this, things like this podcast and this book. And when it's finished like it is now, I just start the next thing. The end is always the beginning. And if you've read every page of this book and you're sad, don't be, you can just go back to the start and realise how clever it was. Because the first letter of every episode is the lyrics from *Eleanor Rigby*. Why did you do that? Well…

Here I am again, writing the words of a sermon that no one will hear.

But that's not true. If there's a distant family member that dies, go to the funeral. Because you'll meet other distant family members while they're still alive. The ending is also the beginning. There is only one true ending in your life, and that ending is shit, because it really is the end. So enjoy all the endings before that, they are all just beginnings.

There we go, this is the end. Now, start.

DAILY NOTES VOL I

DAILY NOTES VOL I

FROM THE AUTHOR

Nathan Cassidy is an award-winning stand-up comedian and writer. See his clips, live dates and more at www.nathancassidy.com

Also by Nathan Cassidy:

BOOKS

Resurrection by Boris Johnson (Available on Amazon)
Believing in God (Available on Amazon)
If… I Caused the Financial Crash of 2008 (Coming Soon)
The Cure for the Common Cold (Coming Soon)

PLAYS

Double Murder
F-List Celebrity (Available at the British Library)
The Cure for the Common Cold
Watch this. Love me. It's deep.
I Have A Dream (Coming Soon)

FILMS and TV

Fifty (Amazon Prime)
Bumblebee (Amazon Prime)
Observational (Amazon Prime)
I am Orig (YouTube)
My London Party

MUSICALS

DIY-The Musical

PODCASTS

Psycomedy
Daily Notes

Twitter: @nathancassidy
Instagram and TikTok: @thenathancassidy
Facebook: Nathan Cassidy Comedian

Printed in Great Britain
by Amazon